Book 1

THE HISTORY
OF THE
IDEA OF EUROPE

Contributors

Pim den Boer • Peter Bugge • Ole Wæver

Edited by Jan van der Dussen and Kevin Wilson

  JOU

The Open University, Open universiteit, Jutland Open University, European
Association of Distance Teaching Universities

A note for the general reader

The History of the Idea of Europe forms part of a second level course in the humanities and social sciences. The course AD280 *What is Europe?* is produced by the Open University in association with the European Association of Distance Teaching Universities. Open University students are provided with supplementary material, including a *Course Guide*, which gives a complete list of all printed and audio-visual components.

AD280 What is Europe?

Book 1   The History of the Idea of Europe

Book 2   Aspects of European Cultural Diversity

Book 3   European Democratic Culture

Book 4   Europe and the Wider World

First published in 1993 by

The Open University, Walton Hall, Milton Keynes, MK7 6AA

Editorial and pedagogic material copyright © 1993 The Open University; Essay 1 copyright © 1993 Open University of The Netherlands; Essay 2 copyright © 1993 Peter Bugge; Essay 3 copyright © 1993 Ole Wæver

Edited, designed and typeset by the Open University

Printed in the United Kingdom by M & A Thomson Litho Ltd

ISBN 0 7492 1104 0

If you would like a copy of *Studying with the Open University*, please write to the Central Enquiry Service, PO Box 200, The Open University, Walton Hall, Milton Keynes, MK7 6YZ.

The other institutions which participated in the creation of *What is Europe?* were:

Open universiteit,
Valkenburgweg 167,
PO Box 2960,
6401 DL Heerlen,
The Netherlands

Deutsches Institut für Fernstudien
an der Universität Tübingen,
Post Fach 1569,
7400 Tübingen,
Germany

Jutland Open University,
Niels Juelsgade 84,
8200 Aarhus,
Denmark

Fédération Interuniversitaire
de l'Enseignement à Distance,
l'Université Paris X
200 Avenue de la République,
92001 Nanterre,
France

Contents

NOTE: Where there is no English-language published version, the quo-
tations from foreign authors that appear in these essays have been translated
by the author or editor.

General preface to 'What is Europe?'

Prepared for the Course Team by Kevin Wilson, Chair of the EADTU Humanities Programme Committee

The four books in the *What is Europe?* series are the product of a collaborative enterprise under the direction of the Humanities Programme Committee of the European Association of Distance Teaching Universities (EADTU). The universities involved in the project are:

- The Open universiteit, Netherlands

- The Jutland Open University

- The Deutsches Institut für Fernstudien an der Universität Tübingen

- The Centre d'Analyse des Savoirs Contemporains at the Université des Sciences Humaines de Strasbourg on behalf of the Fédération Interuniversitaire de l'Enseignement à Distance

- The UK Open University

The Humanities Programme Committee of the EADTU was established in 1989 with a brief to promote joint course development. The four books in this series form the academic core of its first course. The materials will be offered in English, French and German in 1993.

Starting to plan a course on Europe in the heady year of 1989 was both a challenge and an opportunity. With Europe in a state of flux, we quickly rejected as too narrow the idea of a course focused only on the European Community. We dismissed just as quickly the idea of a European history course, not on grounds of irrelevance, but because numerous such courses were already available. Instead we agreed to write a course on European identity in its various historical, cultural, social, political and economic aspects. This topic is at the centre of current debate on Europe, it calls for a wide-ranging approach across academic boundaries and it stands to benefit from the different national perspectives that may be harnessed to the project.

The course has four objectives:

1   To provide a context for the understanding of contemporary European developments through a consideration of the history of the idea of Europe.

2   To consider aspects of European cultural diversity through investigations into language, education, mass-media and everyday culture.

3   To examine the theory, function and practice of democracy as fundamental components of European culture.

4   To locate Europe as a political and economic entity in a context of global change.

These objectives – and the European nature of the course – are reflected in the titles and provenance of the respective books:

1   *The History of the Idea of Europe* is a Dutch–Danish collaboration.

2   *Aspects of European Cultural Diversity* emanates from Germany, though one of the authors is British.

3   *European Democratic Culture* is a French product, though there are Italian, German and British, as well as French, contributors to the book.

4   *Europe and the Wider World* comes from the UK.

Each institution presenting the course will generate its own teaching materials around the four books. For example, students of the UK Open University will have a book of Sources and Commentaries, an audio-cassette and a Study Guide to accompany each of the books; there will also be a collection of maps, a revision audio-cassette and, to accompany Book 4, a TV programme.

We have framed the title of the series (and the course) as a question – *What is Europe?* – yet we are under no illusion that there is a simple, straightforward answer, or even a series of agreed definitions that satisfy. Nor are we making the assumption that Europe is stamped with a unique identity, or that it has a manifest destiny, or that a singular meaning is revealed in its history.

We follow in the footsteps of Hugh Seton-Watson, who tells us that 'the word "Europe" has been used and misused, interpreted and misinterpreted in as many different meanings as almost any word in any language. There have been and are many Europes…'[1] The question, then, is a provocative device to set you thinking, to prompt further questions. Instead of rushing into definitions we have approached the topic from a number of points of view and from the standpoint of various methodologies, raising questions about how 'Europe' has been conceptualized, organized, structured and utilized, both in the past and in the present. The contributors to this series do not have any particular axes to grind. The essays are not propaganda pieces for a 'European spirit', cultural unity, a single market, political union, or any other European project. On the contrary, they are scholarly explorations designed to enhance our understanding of the many facets of European identity.

So, the essays cover a wide canvas. They deal with various ideas of Europe in the past and present; with different aspects of everyday life and associated tensions making for cultural uniformity or accentuating cultural difference; with a political culture founded on public opinion, law and democracy; and with Europe's relationship with the United States, Russia and the developing countries and with its place in the world economy.

The series as a whole presents Europe as a work in progress rather than a finished object, a construction yard rather than a museum. As a project Europe can never be completed. It will always need to be re-made, emancipated from the past, re-invented.

Acknowledgement: The work of the Humanities Programme Committee of the EADTU has been carried out with the support of the Commission of the European Community within the framework of the ERASMUS Programme.

---

[1]   SETON-WATSON, H. (1985) 'What is Europe, where is Europe?: from mystique to politique', *Encounter*, July/August, vol. LX, No. 2, p. 9.

Introduction to Book 1

The Europe of the 1990s has become a major focus of public discourse. The end of the Cold War and the collapse of the Soviet Union has opened up the possibilities of re-connecting western and eastern Europe; and the quickening of integration processes within the European Community has raised the prospects of economic, monetary and political union. What kind of Europe are we building and why? How does this new Europe relate to the patterns and experiences of European history? Are there distinctive European values? Is there a coherent, recognisable European identity? What do Europe and being European mean? These issues are not new but, since they are now being variously addressed by politicians, journalists and academics – both inside and outside Europe – they have a sharp contemporary relevance.

Accordingly, there is a strong inclination to re-examine the history of Europe and to search for a European idea in history. The quest is not an easy one. Borders have fluctuated, institutions have waxed and waned, nations have formed, disappeared, re-formed. There is even a temptation to presume that the purpose of history has been for East and West to come together in an EC-like Greater Europe where self-satisfaction, democracy and progress rule, although, as you will see, such presumptions are not espoused by the authors of Book 1.

Investigations into the meaning of Europe, into European values, into European identity inevitably have raised – and continue to pose – a number of conflicting questions. Does the European 'project', as represented by the European Community, ultimately rest on a sufficiency of shared values, culture and history? Does this commonality explain why we have come so far; is it a precondition for the stability of a European union that it is rooted in a cultural unity, in a strong sense of 'European-ness'? Or is the European project destined to come to grief on the rocks of the nation-states? Is the mainspring of Europeanness the very diversity of national and regional cultures and, if so, is not the pursuit of *one* European identity *per se* a chimera? Are shared values mainly to be found at the level of political principles – the state under the rule of law, democracy, human rights – and not in political and social practices? Does the making of Europe depend on finding solutions to certain inherited problems – the problem of nationalism for example? Or can the European Community, as the latest manifestation of a European project, be driven by a desire to build a new Europe, the legitimacy of which is geared to the future and not to the past? Such questions point to sharply contrasting notions of what Europe represents but, irrespective of the answers, they rest on the assumption that the idea of Europe is embedded in a mix of three related concepts:

- There *is* something called 'Europe' (some kind of European 'specification').

- Europeans *hold* a perception of themselves as being European (they have something of a European 'self-identity').

- History *reveals* schemes for European unity (politics *for* and *in the name of* 'Europe').

The essays in this book recognize but do not draw their inspiration from such positive assumptions. Instead the authors set out to explore the history of the idea of Europe within a welter of political, social and cultural processes and, in so doing, inevitably raise questions that cross the boundaries of history, culture and politics.

In the first essay Pim den Boer argues that a distinct, self-reflective idea of a Europe with a history and meaning of its own only emerges with the French Revolution. Before the French Revolution the term Europe had been utilized as a geographical concept and had been associated with the concept of liberty in the time of the ancient Greeks, with Christendom in the fifteenth century, with balance-of-power politics from the sixteenth century and with civilization in the eighteenth century. But these notions are not perceived as constants. Rather they are fragments that enter and then leave the dominant discourse on Europe at various historical stages. After the French Revolution and its associated turbulence and change it became normal to look historically at phenomena and concepts as the products of historical development. An historical vision was used both to defend traditional European values and the *status quo* and to encourage new prospects for Europe and hence promote change. Pim den Boer contends, therefore, that the emergence of a strong concept of Europe in the late eighteenth century and early nineteenth century is linked to changes in the concept of history and in the ideas of culture and civilization. He also indicates that these ideas became increasingly active within the context of various nationalisms.

The culture and civilization issue is pursued by Peter Bugge in his consideration of the idea of Europe between 1914 and 1945. In the immediate aftermath of the revolution in Russia and the First World War, Europe appeared to be a culture in crisis; old values disintegrated and politics and society seemed to rest on shifting foundations. In this climate intellectuals projected different visions of a new Europe though the nationalism of old Europe still dominated political thinking. Bugge organizes his essay around the notions of *perceptions* of Europe and *projects* for Europe – between how Europe was seen, described and analysed on the one hand and how, even in a period when the nation-state stood supreme, there were a number of plans and schemes for the organization of the continent prior to Hitler's attempt to hijack Europe in the name of Fascist Germany.

In the years immediately following the Second World War, with nationalism generally discredited and with the USA and USSR dominating the political and ideological scene, moves were made in the direction of economic and political co-operation in Western Europe. In considering the idea of Europe since 1945 Ole Wæver builds his argument on the *fusion* between perceptions of Europe and projects for Europe. The fundamental difference from the inter-war period is that, post-1945, there is now a process of European integration and the term 'project' means participating in this process rather than just proclaiming idealistic schemes for Europe. Wæver approaches the idea of Europe from the perspective of international politics and international relations. This is not to say that he ignores history but essentially he is concerned with political action and his approach imparts a strategic dimension to the concept of Europe. Wæver examines various political constellations – EC, nation-states, regions – in contemporary Europe, explores the issue of European identity and assesses the contemporary relevance of the European idea.

Taken together the three essays in the book range over the idea of Europe from the politics of ancient Greece to contemporary plans for economic and political union. Over time the concept of Europe has evolved at two levels and around two broad themes: on the one hand Europe and its *others* with Asians, Turks, Russians and Americans variously functioning as an antithesis (external discriminators); and on the other Europe as a *commonwealth of nations*, a Europe of shared political, social and religious values, of an affinity in diversity constituting a synthesis (internal characteristics). As we move towards the twenty-first century the past identifications of Europe – the geographical definition, the equation with political freedom, the association with Christendom, the connection with culture and civilization, all still have a contemporary relevance.

In general discussion, the description of Europe perhaps most in vogue is that of 'unity in diversity'. Europe is presented as the continent that never bowed to a single ruler, that never made culture uniform, that never settled for final truths, that kept questioning, debating, remaining self-critical thereby generating a unique dynamism. The paradox of the underlying reality of Europe containing no singular European essence is not lost on the authors of this book. The exploration into the history of the idea of Europe is both a fascinating and frustrating enterprise. The present book reveals that there is a rich reservoir of ideas linked to Europe but it also illustrates that there is no stable core, no fixed identity, no final answer.

Essay 1
Europe to 1914:
the making of an idea

Prepared for the Course Team by Pim den Boer
Professor of Cultural History, Universiteit van
Amsterdam

Introduction

The term 'Europe' has a long history, but the idea of Europe is a recent phenomenon. It was not until the beginning of the nineteenth century that this idea, as a result of a new outlook on the nature and origins of Europe, came to have clear outlines. It is in particular the French Revolution that marks the watershed in thinking about Europe.

The name Europe had existed for thousands of years and for centuries it had been something more than a neutral geographical expression. Nevertheless, until the end of the eighteenth century, Europe was a notion covering certain implicit and explicit assumptions rather than a concept with a clearly defined meaning. Searching for the idea of Europe over the centuries turns the historian into something of an archaeologist peeling away the layers of meaning that have accumulated around the concept in different historical periods. Linguistic usages in various historical contexts suggest a certain European self-awareness, that is to say, an awareness of being part of Europe and of Europe being the discriminating element, but the term itself has covered a variety of meanings, which have changed with the changing historical circumstances.

In this essay I have indicated three main elements in the history of the idea of Europe: the identification of Europe with liberty, with Christendom and with civilization. Each of these had its own origin disappearing for a considerable length of time before re-surfacing again. The association of Europe with political freedom was first made in ancient Greece, in the fifth century BC, while it was not until the fifteenth century that Europe came to be identified with Christendom. Then, during the Enlightenment of the eighteenth century, Europe was for the first time identified with civilization. However, it was in the nineteenth century that these various identifications of Europe were not only rediscovered, but also reassessed and given unprecedented prominence.

Until that time the history of the idea of Europe should largely be seen as a history of separate concepts. At the beginning of the nineteenth century, however, after the revolutionary changes, there originated the notion of the *history* of European culture as an idea in itself. Within this context the idea of Europe became the subject of political debate and took on an ideological dimension, the three identifications of Europe mentioned before playing a crucial role. During the first half of the nineteenth century, various strands of political and religious opinion – reactionaries and conservatives, Catholics and Protestants, liberals and democrats – thus formed their own views on the historical development of Europe, with clear links to expectations and ideals for the future. In this way the ideals of freedom and Christianity were projected into the distant past and subjected to thorough examination, while civilization came to be more or less synonymous with the idea of progress.

This essay begins by going back in time to consider different identifications of Europe as developed in the past, putting them, in turn, into a proper historical context. Then, it will explore the various ideas of Europe as they took shape in the period between the French Revolution of 1789 and the revolutionary year of 1848. By way of conclusion the final chapter covers the years from 1848 to 1914 – a time of boundless belief in the supremacy of European civilization but also a time of aggressive nationalism which undermined the notion of belonging to a European society with a common destiny.

The outbreak of war in 1914 put a temporary block on the notion that Europe is much more than a geographical expression and the idea that the inhabitants of Europe are part of a single shared culture. When, as we shall see in Peter Bugge's essay, discussion of the idea of Europe is resumed after the war, it takes quite a different course emphasizing new possibilities for the future of Europe rather than dwelling on particular visions of its past.

Finally, it should be stated that the approach adopted in this essay is not so much an historical treatment of a self-contained idea but more an archaeological excavation of the concept of Europe as used in the past. From this standpoint it will be shown how a certain European self-awareness is sometimes present – implicitly or explicitly – and sometimes absent throughout the long history of the European continent. It goes without saying that this can only be done by providing a relevant context for the ideas themselves. Additionally, the historical outline is intertwined with a short discussion of cartographical and iconographical evidence in order to show how certain implicit ideas about Europe may be brought to the surface.

Europe and Antiquity

The origin of Europe as the name of a continent is shrouded in mystery. As early as the fifth century BC, the Greek historian Herodotus wrote that he did not know why the world was considered to consist of three parts, or why the three continents, Asia, Africa and Europe, bore the names of women:

> …no one has ever determined whether or not there is sea either to the east or to the north of Europe. All we know is that it is equal to Asia and Libya [Africa] combined. Another thing that puzzles me is why

three distinct women's names should have been given to what is really a single landmass, and why too the Nile and the Phasis – or according to some, the Maeotic Tanais and the Cimmerian Strait[1] – should have been fixed upon for the boundaries. Nor have I been able to learn who it was that first marked the boundaries or where they got the names from.

(Herodotus, The Histories, p.285; footnote added)

The division of the world into separate continents is thus very ancient, as are the names of those continents. This tripartite view of the world seems even to have existed among the ancient Egyptians, although without the names and the boundaries indicated by Herodotus.

Mythology and etymology

Europa, in Greek mythology, is the daughter of a Phoenician king. Zeus, the supreme god of the ancient Greeks, falls in love with her and transforms himself into a bull while she and her friends are playing on the beach. Europa strokes the bull and sits on its back. The animal then swiftly rises to its feet, gallops into the sea, and swims to Crete taking Europa with it. Once in Crete, Zeus assumes human form and begets three sons by Europa. The abduction of Europa was a popular theme in literature and the visual arts during the classical period. Christian authors later dwelt on the same myth in order to illustrate the unedifying behaviour of the supreme god of the pagan Greeks.

Is there a connection between the abducted princess and the name of the continent? Some scholars used to think that the Greek word Europa was derived from the Phoenician, in which it might mean 'evening land' – the land of the setting sun. Some have claimed a Greek origin for the word – Europa meaning 'the dark-looking one'. Neither explanation seems likely and the derivation remains obscure.

The boundaries

Since geographical knowledge at the time was far from perfect, the way in which Europe's boundaries were defined was also vague and subject to variation. According to Herodotus, the king of Egypt had sent out Phoenicians, who sailed round the whole of Libya (Africa), and Darius, the Persian king, had dispatched an expedition to find out where the Indus flowed into the sea. The expedition had sailed eastward down the Indus and when it reached the mouth of the river it returned westward along the coast. To Europe, however, no expeditions had ever been sent. Herodotus wrote that it was not known whether there was sea to the North and to the East. The Mediterranean separated Europe from Africa, that much was clear. In the East, the Sea of Azov and the River Don were often considered to mark the boundary between Europe and Asia. In the West, the Pillars of Hercules (the rocks of Gibraltar and Ceuta, on the European and the African side respectively) indicated the start of the ocean which was assumed to surround the entire world.

---

[1] See Figure 1; Tanais is the River Don, and the Cimmerian Strait is now the Bosporus.

Greeks and Persians

The neutral, geographical expression 'Europe' obtained a special connotation as a result of the confrontation between the Greeks and the Persians.

Greek colonists settled on the west coast of Asia Minor, the Ionian coast. The Aegean Sea had for centuries been a connecting route which made possible intensive commercial contact. Colonization increased the awareness of the differences between Hellenes and non-Hellenes. The language spoken by the latter sounded very strange to the Greeks, and to characterize this gibberish they called the non-Greeks 'barbarians' – people who could make only an unintelligible 'bar-bar' noise. The designation 'barbarians' did not at first have a negative meaning; the pejorative connotation developed only later.

The expansion of the Persian empire gave rise to the revolt of the Ionian city-states, which sought help from their Greek homeland. Thus began the wars between the Greeks and the Persians.

It is in this historical context that Greek authors from the fifth century BC began to connect the geographical concepts of Europe and Asia not only with differences in language, customs and characteristics but also with distinct systems of government. The city-state of Athens became the symbol of Greek freedom, while Persia was seen as the immense empire of an absolute ruler who respected neither god nor law. The opposition between Greece and Persia was viewed by the Greeks as representing that between Europe and Asia, and stood for freedom as opposed to despotism.

Hippocrates around 400 BC, the well-known physician of classical antiquity, posited a connection between climate and behaviour:

> We have now discussed the organic and structural differences between the populations of Asia and Europe but we have still to consider the problem why the Asiatics are of a less warlike and a more tame disposition than the Europeans. The deficiency of spirit and courage observable in the human inhabitants of Asia has for its principal cause the low margin of seasonal variability in the temperature of that continent, which is approximately stable throughout the year. Such a climate does not produce those mental shocks and violent bodily dislocations which would naturally render the temperament ferocious and introduce a stronger current of irrationality and passion than would be the case under stable conditions. It is invariably changes that stimulate the human mind and that prevent it from remaining passive.
>
> *(Hippocrates, Influences of atmosphere, water and situation, p. 165)*

To this climatic explanation, Hippocrates went on to add a further political one. The major part of Asia is subject to a despotic form of government, he argued, and is therefore not free. When the inhabitants of Asia fight, they do so to glorify their ruler rather than themselves. They therefore take care not to be considered good soldiers, which has a very pacifying effect on their temperament. A good argument in support of his theory, Hippocrates claimed, was the fact that the Hellenes and non-Hellenes alike who lived in Asia, but were not groaning under despotism, were just as bellicose as any other people in the world.

The comparison of the climates and political systems of Europe on the one hand and Asia on the other, continued to play a role even when the historical situation changed drastically in the fourth century BC, after the subjection of Greece by Philip of Macedon. Hippocrates' argumentation evidently influenced the *Politics*, the political dissertation by the philosopher Aristotle (384–322 BC), but it was modified and adapted to the contemporary situation.

According to Aristotle, the peoples of Europe, products of a cold climate, are courageous but not particularly skilled or wise. This is why they are usually independent, there is little cohesion between them, and they are unable to rule others. Inhabitants of Asia, on the other hand, have the brains and the skills, but lack the courage and strength of will. That is why they remain servile and subject peoples.

Thus far, Aristotle follows Hippocrates' train of thought, but then comes an important difference. In Aristotle's view, the Greeks have an intermediate geographical position between the Europeans and the Asians. That is why they combine in themselves the positive characteristics of the peoples of both continents. The Greeks, according to Aristotle, are free, they have the best political institutions and they are capable of ruling all other people.

The Greeks had admittedly been conquered by the Macedonians from the cold North, but they soon became instructors of the latter in all intellectual matters. Aristotle himself became tutor to Alexander, son of Philip of Macedon – the Alexander who conquered enormous stretches of Asia laying them open to Hellenic influence. In a way, the Greeks could feel that by means of Alexander's conquests they were avenging themselves on Persia for the damage done to them in the past.

Under these circumstances a feeling of superiority unconnected with Europe may have developed, since it was the Greeks who had proved to be the best 'political animals', in an ideal intermediate position between the ferocious and warlike Macedonians (Europeans) on one side and the skilled but servile Asians on the other.

The contrast begins to become blurred

Even after the death of Alexander the Great in 323 BC, when his short-lived empire began to collapse, there was increasing Hellenization in the East, as well as influences from the Eastern cultures on the West. The notion that the various continents are inhabited by peoples of different character loses its emphasis, but the geographical denotations do continue to be used. The names of the continents remain the same, and find general introduction in the sense that, as a result of the propagation of Hellenic ideas, the Greek names are generally accepted, as are so many other Greek terms. After all, our intellectual framework is one of the most manifest inheritances of ancient Greek civilization. From then on, the geographical names are rarely so closely associated with possible differences in temperament.

Extension of geographical knowledge

Since as early as the seventh century there were numerous Greek settlements along the whole coast of the Black Sea, but also in the West. Greek mariners sailed to Sicily and to the French and Spanish Mediterranean coasts and Greek colonists settled there. Marseilles, then called Massalia, was an important town. Greeks also sailed past the Pillars of Hercules and along the Atlantic Coast. At the Guadalquivir estuary was Gades (now Cádiz), an important town which according to tradition was founded by the Phoenicians as early as 1100 BC. The Phoenicians and the Carthaginians were the first to discover the areas where tin occurred (such as Cornwall), and they succeeded in keeping their tin routes secret until they were made generally known by the Romans in the first century BC.

A Greek from Marseilles, Pytheas (310? BC), is supposed to have been the first mariner to sail round the British Isles and to describe the people and climate. He is said even to have visited Norway or Iceland, and an island abounding with amber. It is said to have been Pytheas' calculations which formed the basis for the lines of latitude across northern France and England on the map of the world – unfortunately lost – made by the learned librarian of Alexandria, Eratosthenes, at the end of the third century BC.

At that time, Alexandria, at the boundary between Asia and Africa, was a centre of learning where a great mass of geographical knowledge had been collected. It was generally assumed that the earth was a sphere, and Eratosthenes succeeded in producing a remarkably accurate calculation of its circumference. The expeditions by Alexander the Great into Asia and those launched by the Ptolemies, the rulers of Egypt, in Africa had increased geographical knowledge considerably. The description of the known world as provided by Eratosthenes in his *Geographica* was reasonably accurate. His knowledge of Europe and of the northern regions in particular was however sparse. His work was subjected to fierce criticism on this point by later geographers such as Strabo, the Greek of partly Asian origin, born in the north of Asia Minor in the first century BC.

Strabo, who studied in Athens and Alexandria, also collected a great deal of data in Rome. He praised the Romans for their military prowess and for their political acumen. They had subjected almost all of Europe, with the exception of the regions north of the Danube and between the Rhine and the Don, said Strabo. Thanks to their conquests, many regions had been explored. Eratosthenes could not yet know much about the north and west of Europe: he had no more than the stories of Pytheas, who claimed to have explored the entire north of Europe as far as the boundaries of the world. And that claim, said Strabo, was one that nobody could believe, because even Hermes, the god of travel, had not done so.

For Strabo, Europe was the most varied continent, and that most bountifully provided for by nature. Only the north is made uninhabitable by the cold. Europe has the ideal combination of fertile and peace-loving countries on the one hand and inhospitable regions inhabited by warlike and courageous people on the other. But the peaceful element prevails, Strabo hastily adds. Hegemony over Europe used to belong to the Greeks, later being exercised by the Macedonians and now the

Romans. As far as war and peace are concerned, Europe is the most independent continent, free of foreign rule, says Strabo.

He also mentions that Europe yields the best fruit, as well as all the useful metals, while it imports spices and precious stones from elsewhere. It has an abundance of cattle, but few wild animals.

In the *Natural History*, the extensive, encyclopedic and popular, but not very critical, compilation by Pliny the Elder, written in the first century AD, Europe is called the most charming of the continents and is said to comprise not a third, but half of the world. His work is a step backwards in comparison to the knowledge acquired by Hellenic geographers. He praises Europe for having nourished the people that had conquered all others.

Pliny praised and overestimated the size of Europe, but he no longer sharply contrasted Europe and Asia, nor did he recognize the differences in temperament and political system that Hippocrates described. The phenomenal expansion of the city of Rome and the foundation of the Roman Empire were never considered as *European* expansion.

A fundamental distinction did however exist between those who had Roman citizenship in some form and those who did not. But in the Roman Empire there was no question of a notion of a European identity, a feeling of oneness shared by all Europeans.

Europe in biblical commentary

Introduction

The term 'Europe' is not to be found in the Bible, and for the patriarchs, prophets and apostles a concept of Europe did not exist. Nevertheless, Europe became a Christian notion, or at least a part of the Christian way of thinking. The Greeks' tripartite division of the world, together with the Greek names, is also to be found in the bible and biblical exegesis. In the first book of Genesis we are told of Noah's three sons, Shem, Ham and Japheth, and how, after the Flood, 'of them was the whole earth overspread' (*Authorised Version*). The Bible gives a long list of their children, grandchildren and further descendants, who are said to have populated the earth, which was otherwise empty of people. It also contains a number of vague indications of where they settled, but precise geographical information is lacking.

The view of Flavius Josephus

In the first century AD, Palestine was conquered by the Romans. Jerusalem fell in 70 AD. The Roman Emperor's retinue included a Jewish scholar, Flavius Josephus (37–?100), who was also a soldier and statesman. He had been taken prisoner, and had subsequently gone over to the Romans. Josephus undertook the task of writing the *History of the Jewish War* (from 170 BC to his own day) and also the first history of the Jewish people, usually referred to as *Jewish Antiquities*. The latter major work is an attempt to prove the antiquity and greatness of the Jewish people in a world dominated militarily by the Romans and intellectually by the Greeks.

Josephus faithfully follows the Biblical narrative, but by referring to Greek and non-Greek writers attempts to make it plausible and to fit it into the Graeco-Roman view of the world and of history. He describes how Noah's progeny spread out to populate the whole earth, the interior parts, the coasts and the islands. According to Josephus, some people still bear the name their fore-fathers gave them, while other names have changed. It was the Greeks who brought about this in nomenclature. When, long after the Jews, the Greeks became powerful, they also appropriated to themselves the glory of the past and assigned Greek names to the various peoples. Josephus then gives the old Biblical names, together with what he considers to be the contemporary Greek equivalents.

It is Josephus who was the first to localize the way in which Noah's progeny spread out over the world, using the Greek geographical terms. The seven sons of Japheth settled in the mountains of Asia Minor and spread north as far as the River Don. They also settled in Europe, right across as far as Cádiz. Josephus points out how the Greek names with which his readers were familiar have displaced the Biblical names. The children and grandchildren of Shem and Ham are also localized by Josephus, and he also gives their later Greek names. Africa was inhabited by the descendants of Ham, and Asia, from the Euphrates to the Indian Ocean, by those of Shem.

According to Josephus, therefore, Europe was populated exclusively by the descendants of Japheth, and Africa exclusively by those of Ham. Parts of Asia were also taken by Japheth and Ham, but the greater part, to the east, fell to Shem and his tribe. Josephus also, of course, tells the story of the curse placed on Ham's progeny as a result of his ridiculing his father when the latter had fallen asleep drunk and naked. However, nowhere does Josephus speak more highly of any one continent than another. In fact, he does no more and no less than combine Jewish genealogical history with Greek geography.

Europe and the Church Fathers

In his exegesis, the most erudite of the Church Fathers, Saint Jerome (348–420), whose authority was unquestioned for centuries, takes over Josephus' text almost literally and translates it into Latin. Jerome adds that the name Japheth signifies 'enlargement' or 'spreading out' and that the text in Genesis: 9, 27 that Japheth 'shall dwell in the tents of Shem' contains the prophecy that the Jews, who are descended from Shem, will be ousted in erudition and knowledge of the Bible by us Christians, the descendants of Japheth.

Another extremely influential Church Father, Saint Augustine (354–430), expands yet further on the prophetic implications of the names of the sons of Noah. Augustine was of Berber descent, and was born in Tagaste, in Numidia, in the Romanized part of Africa. He spent a long period in Italy and then became the bishop of Hippo Regius, an important port on the north-east coast of what is now

Algeria. After the sack of Rome by the Goths in 410, a stream of refugees made their way to Africa and there were many who blamed Christianity for the lack of fighting spirit shown by the once so powerful Roman Empire. Against this background Augustine set out to write a vindication of the Christian church and to disprove the classical (pagan) world view. The work he produced, in 22 books, we know as *De Civitate Dei contra paganos* or *The City of God against the pagans* (413–426).

Augustine examines in detail (Book XVI: 1–2) the hidden significance of the biblical story of the sons of Noah. Noah was gifted with prophecy and cursed the descendants of his son Ham, whose name means 'hot' and indicates future heresies. The name of Noah's eldest son, Shem, means 'the named' and contains the prophecy that from the descendants of Shem, from the Jews, Jesus Christ will be born. In the tents of Shem, that is, in the churches, the peoples descending from Japheth will spread out, and the name of the youngest son, Japheth, thus indicates 'enlargement' or 'spreading out'.

Augustine is engrossed by the allegorical interpretation of the Bible. The drunkenness and nakedness of Noah are taken to prefigure the sufferings of Christ. Hence the curse placed on Ham, the middle son who takes his place between the first fruits of the circumcised Israelites (Shem) and the full harvest of the uncircumcised Christians (Japheth). The text in Genesis about the sons of Noah is therefore interpreted and explicated as a prophecy. The Christians are seen as the progeny of Japheth, but understandably enough, Augustine, writing on the coast of north Africa under threat of attack by sea from the north, does not see a connection between this assumption and the continents.

In a different context, however, Augustine does make a passing reference to the tripartite division of the world, stating that Asia occupies one half of it, with Europe and Africa, divided from each other by 'our Great Sea', making up the other half.

Not only was Italy pillaged by the Goths, but the Iberian Peninsula was also ravaged by barbarian invasions. The stream of refugees who fled to north Africa included a young priest from Braga, an extremely important bishopric in the north of present-day Portugal, by the name of Orosius. Augustine made a profound impression on the young man, and suggested to him that he write an historical summary which, like his own work, would defend the truth of Christian belief against the heathen. So successful was Orosius that his *Historiae adversus paganos* became the indispensable Christian history of the world, an essential volume in the few libraries there were at the time.

At the beginning of his work, which is dedicated to Augustine, Orosius stated that his reading of the classical historians had led him to the discovery that earlier times were not only just as dire as his own, but were even more unfortunate in that man was further from the comforts of the true religion (*Historiae* I, p. 9). He wished to describe the vicissitudes of the human race from the Creation to the foundation of Rome, from there to the rule of Julius Caesar and the birth of Christ, right up to his own times (p. 12). So as to enable the reader to understand better where the various wars and disasters have taken place, Orosius provided not only 'knowledge of events and dates, but also of places'. He began by describing the whole world, which was 'divided into three by the Ancients, and later subdivided into areas and provinces'. This description is in fact completely separate from the historical summary. Orosius makes no connection with the spread of Christianity and with the sons of Noah. His description is based on other, heathen, geographers.

Orosius gives the Mediterranean, across which he had fled to Africa, its usual Roman name of 'mare nostrum' or 'our sea' (p. 14). Although a refugee from Europe, where he was probably born, he shows no trace of any identification with that continent. This fierce defender of the Christian Church thus talks of our sea, but not of *our* Europe.

Orosius began his extensive description of the continents with Asia, followed by Europe and Africa. As was usual, he considered the River Tanais (the Don) as indicating the boundary between Europe and Asia. He speaks of the altars and borders of Alexander the Great, which were supposed to lie along the Don, but which in fact were to be found along the river Jaxartes (the Syr Darya, which flows in to the Aral Sea). The boundary of Europe continues via the Sea of Azov and the Black Sea (where he mentions the town of Theodosia, now Feodosiya, in the Crimea), to Constantinople on the strait connecting the Black Sea with 'our sea'. To the west, Europe is bounded by the Ocean at Gades (Cádiz) in Spain and by the Pillars of Hercules (Orosius I, pp. 13–14).

In accordance with the Roman tradition, Orosius considers the Danube and the Rhine as constituting the boundary line north of which live the barbarians. To the west is Alania, in the centre Dacia and Gothia, and then Germania, 'of which the greater part belongs to the Suevi'. Orosius' description is a compilation of a whole range of classical authors. A few of the remarks he makes suggest a more specific knowledge of northern Europe, but nevertheless he broadly follows the old division into Roman provinces.

When describing Africa, Orosius notes that it is smaller than Europe, has a smaller population and that less is known about it, since the heat of the African sun is more harmful for living things than is the severe cold in Europe (Orosius I, p. 33). He clearly considers Africa to be the continent least well provided for by nature. He does not, however, compare Europe and Asia. The barbarian invasions from the north shook the familiar world of the Roman Empire to its foundations. In Europe, the future of the young Christian Church was anything but certain.

Europe, and the sons of Noah, on the map

The oldest known maps of the world are to be found in medieval manuscripts. No maps produced in classical antiquity have survived, although we do have maps of the world which were reconstructed at a much later date, during the Renaissance, on the basis of classical texts. It was not until the fifteenth century that Ptolemy's work on geography, dating from the second century AD, was rediscovered and that attempts were made to reconstruct his lost map of the world.

The oldest, and by far the most complete, medieval map of the world is to be found in manuscripts of works by Isidore, Bishop of Seville from 602 to 632.

Isidore has been called the last scholar of classical antiquity, but he was also the author of the first Christian encyclopedic handbook, which enjoyed great popularity for more than five centuries.

The description of the world given by Isidore in his *Etymologiarum sive Originum Libri XX* is the same as that given by Augustine 200 years before. The world is divided into three parts. Moving from the south via the east to the north, Asia takes up half of it; continuing towards the west, we cross Europe, and returning from there to our starting-point, we find Africa. The western part of the world is divided in two by the *mare magnum*. Isidore begins his description of the world, as did Orosius, with Asia. He mentions that it is here that Paradise was situated. Elsewhere in the work, he provides a survey of the descendants of Noah, and on the basis of this explains the names of the peoples, as was done five centuries earlier by Josephus.

Isidore, however, found himself confronted with a very different problem from that of Josephus. Writing history was no longer a question of finding connections between Jewish antiquity and the intellectual heritage of the classical world. Rome had lost its position; the Germanic peoples had become a major power factor. Where their kings had converted to Christianity, the bishops and priests were not merely religious and intellectual leaders but also represented the most important form of administration in those turbulent times.

Isidore considers an explanation of the origin of words to be of capital importance (hence the title *Etymologies* or *Origins*) and he devotes a great deal of attention to the origins of the names of peoples. The information provided by Josephus (whether or not via Saint Jerome) is, however, insufficient. Some new Germanic peoples, most certainly those who belonged to the Christian Church, such as the Visigoths, should also be included in the biblical genealogy. In Isidore's words: 'the Goths, whose name is assumed to be derived from Magog, son of Japheth, are a mighty and brave people, tall and strong of frame, inducing terror by the nature of their weapons' (*Etymologies* IX: 2, 89). Isidore also explains the names of other new peoples, but he admits that linguistic corruption had rendered their origin uncertain. The Lombards or Langobards, he claims, are called thus because of their long beards, which they never cut, and the Vandals are called after a river on whose banks they used to live. 'The barbarism of these people, expressed in their names, is repellent to us', writes Isidore (*Et.* IX:2, 97). Most of the names, therefore, he does not trace back to the descendants of Noah but to geographical denotations and to legendary (non-biblical) figures.

As mentioned before, Isidore narrates the manner in which the sons of Noah spread across the earth at a different point in his work from when he is describing the world itself. He also reproduces, at yet another point, the prophetic explanation of the names of the three sons of Noah already provided by Augustine. He adds to it that the name Ham, which means heat, and which Augustine connected only with heresy, contains the prophesy that the descendants of Ham would live in warmer regions, closer to the sun (*Et.* VII: 6, 17; see Hay, 1957; 1968 edn, p. 14).

Isidore's text does not lead immediately to the conclusion that Shem, Ham and Japheth were assigned one continent each, but the maps added to the text later do in fact indicate such a neat division. The original, early-seventh century manuscript has not survived, and so we cannot be entirely certain whether Isidore actually produced this map of the world himself. It is most probably a later addition, however. The map is entirely in accordance with the description provided by Augustine.

In its simplest form, the world is like a pancake, the top half of which is taken up by Asia and the bottom half of which is divided in two, with Europe on the left and Africa on the right. In this representation, Asia is the same size as Europe and Africa together. This means that the size of Europe is not overestimated as much as by Pliny, who considered it to take up half the world.

The boundary between Europe and Africa is constituted by the Mediterranean, that between Africa and Asia by the Nile, and that between Europe and Asia by the River Tanais and the Meotides Paludes, now known as the Don and Sea of Azov. The whole world is surrounded by the Ocean (see Figure 1).

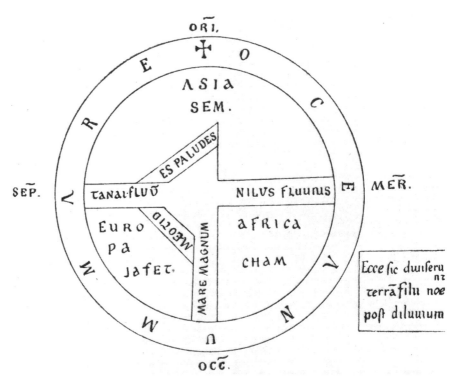

Figure 1   The so-called Noachide map, Isidor-Codex 236, Saint Gall Monastic Library, Switzerland (tenth century). From: K. Miller, Mappae Mundi, *Volume VI (Stuttgart, 1898). (Photo: British Library Board, London.)*
Legend:
Ecce... = Lo: thus did the sons of Noah divide the world after the Flood.
Tanai. Fluv. = the River Don
Nilus Fluv. = the River Nile
Meotides Paludes = the Sea of Azov

What is probably the oldest surviving map, from the late seventh century, does not indicate the Ocean, but does show an uninhabited part of the world. The existence of antipodes was already disputed by Augustine, as was the spherical shape of the world (see Figure 2).

The maps are (in the most literal sense of the word) 'oriented', in other words aligned towards the east, where the sun rises and where Paradise is supposed to have been situated.

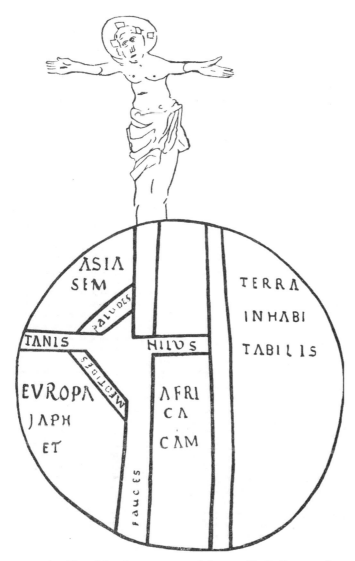

Figure 2   The oldest known map of the world. Palimpsest in Isidor-Codex 237, Saint Gall Monastic Library, Switzerland (late seventh century). From: K. Miller, Mappae Mundi. Volume VI *(Stuttgart, 1898). (Photo: British Library Board, London.)*

The idea that each of the sons of Noah populated one of the three continents is a simplification reflected not only in the map but also in religious instruction. In the time of Charlemagne, Alcuin's commentary on Genesis already taught that the answer to the question of how the world was distributed among the sons and grandsons of Noah was: Shem received Asia, Ham Africa and Japheth Europe (Alcuin, *Interrogations et responsiones in Genesim*, see Hay, 1957; 1968 edn, pp. 38–39). If prophetic significance were now to be attached to the names of the sons of Noah and the biblical texts, the foundation would be laid for identifying Europe with Christianity. But that stage was yet to come.

We will return to the subject of maps and Europe's place in pictorial representations of the world, in later sections.

Europe and the Middle Ages

Charlemagne: king and father of Europe?

In the seventh century, the unity of the Mediterranean area was broken up. The decisive factor was the enormous Arab expansion which commenced in that century. Syria, Palestine and Persia were conquered. Damascus became the centre of power from which the eastern Roman Empire was attacked. Egypt and the whole north coast of Africa were conquered. In 711, Tariq ibn Ziyard and his forces crossed into Spain at what then came to be known as Jebel-al-Tariq (the mountain of Tariq), which is the source of the name Gibraltar. The Moors advanced across the Pyrenees, but in 732 were decisively defeated near Poitiers by a coalition army led by Charles Martel, the 'mayor of the palace' (chief minister) of Austrasia, the eastern Frankish domains of Champagne and the Meuse and Moselle area with Rheims as capital. A contemporary chronicler, originating from Cordoba, referred to Charles Martel as the consul of Austrasia and used the term *europeenses* to describe the coalition army (Fischer, 1957, pp. 50–51). It is perhaps noteworthy that this collective name was used in relation to an external threat, but too much value cannot be attached to it in view of the fact that the expression does not occur again until very much later.

With the rise of the Carolingians the centre of power shifted to the north. The Merovingian figurehead monarch was deposed, and Pepin became the ruler of the whole of the Frankish kingdom. The Pope, in conflict with the Lombards, placed Rome under his protection. Charlemagne subdued the Saxons and in Italy conquered the kingdom of the Lombards. After a Saracen attack on Narbonne, Frankish forces founded the Spanish Province south of the Pyrenees. In Rome, on Christmas Night in the year 800, the Pope's protector Charlemagne, was crowned Holy Roman Emperor. The Frankish king was seen as the successor to the Roman Emperors in the West and as having restored the *imperium romanum*. Poems refer to Charlemagne as *rex, pater Europae* (king, father of Europe) and he is praised as

Europae veneranda apex (the revered crown of Europe; Gollwitzer, 1951, p. 165). Such expressions had previously referred to Gaul, but the court poets now replace Gaul by Europe. Even so, Europe seems to be little more than a term indicating territory, with no emotional connotations, suitable for ceremonial occasions but nevertheless an example of literary artifice.

With the disintegration of the Carolingian Empire and the end of its short-lived absolute monarchy, the term Europe ceases to be used to indicate a sphere of power. But, with the Saxon Emperors, when, in the tenth century Otto the Great defeated the nomadic Magyars at the Battle of Lechveld (955), he was called the liberator of Europe (Widukind, *cf.* M. Bloch, *La société féodale*, p. 15). Once again it required an external threat for the term Europe to be used rather than merely providing a scholarly, geographical reference.

The rise of Latin Christendom

In our search for a concept of Europe it is worth looking in some detail at the Crusades. In order to do this it is necessary to provide some historical background.

Even after the defeat of the Magyars the dangers facing the Latin Christian world had by no means disappeared. Most of the western Mediterranean was in the hands of the Moors. Not only was the greater part of Spain and North Africa theirs, but also the islands of Majorca, Corsica, Sardinia, Malta and Sicily. Their power also extended to a considerable part of southern Italy.

In the struggle against Islam, the Byzantine Empire, inheritor of Roman imperial power in the East, was indeed an ally, but in other respects a rival. In the East, Constantinople was under pressure from the Moslems, while in the West the Serbs and Bulgarians, and later the Russians of Kiev, came within the sphere of influence of the Greek Christians. The power of the Emperor in Constantinople extended along the Dalmatian coast, and beyond to the other side of the Adriatic, where claim was laid to Venice and southern Italy.

In the tenth century the Byzantine emperors had driven the Moslems back in the East as far as the river Tigris. In the following century, the rise of the Turkish Seljuks had changed the situation radically. Led by Alp-Arslan, who had been crowned caliph in Baghdad, they wrested Syria and Jerusalem from the caliph of Egypt and Armenia, and Asia Minor from the Byzantine Emperor. The situation in Constantinople became desperate. Only the coasts were still in Greek hands and their fleet had been destroyed. In 1095 the Byzantine Emperor sent a diplomatic mission to the Pope, the head of Latin Christendom, to request military assistance. This request led to Pope Urban II's famous call, promulgated in Clermont-Ferrand in November 1095, for a Crusade to 'liberate the Holy Sepulchre in Jerusalem'. The Church instigated an extensive propaganda campaign and military operations were carefully prepared. Filled with religious ardour and worldly greed, warriors from Flanders, Lorraine, Normandy, southern France and Italy assembled in Constantinople. Asia Minor was conquered, with Antioch falling after a siege lasting seven months. Finally, on 15 July 1099, Jerusalem was taken and a number of small Christian princedoms were founded on the French model.

There are no eye-witness accounts of the literal wording of Urban II's appeal, but we do have an account of it written many years later by the English historian William of Malmesbury (*c.* 1090–1143). This is remarkable for the way in which the perilous situation of Christendom is connected with the classical tripartite division of the world. The Pope is said to have first stated that the 'enemies of God' had taken possession of Syria, Armenia and the whole of Asia Minor. 'They abuse the Holy Sepulchre and make our pilgrims pay to enter Jerusalem. That is bad enough, but these enemies, furthermore, have a much greater part of the world in their possession. They inhabit the whole of Asia, which our forefathers rightfully considered to be half the world.' 'It was in Asia,' the Pope continued, 'that Christendom first blossomed. It was in Asia, with two exceptions, that each of the Apostles met his death. The Christians who now live in Asia live in poverty and are compelled to pay taxes to the enemies. They long for the freedom which they have lost.'

'Africa too,' the Pope went on, 'has been held by force of arms by the enemies for more than two hundred years.' He pointed out that, in earlier times, Africa had brought forth renowned defenders of the Christian faith. Here he was undoubtedly referring to Saint Augustine. Europe remained to be mentioned.

> But even that part of the world belongs in only a small portion to Christianity, for who would dream of calling the barbarians in the north Christians, who live on distant islands and seek their food in the Arctic Seas like whales? But even that small part of Europe which is ours is threatened by the Saracens and Turks. Three hundred years ago, they conquered Spain and the Balearic Islands, and they hope to conquer the rest of Europe too.

The Pope then went on to make a number of encouraging remarks about the cowardice of the enemy who, like every people living in the great heat of the sun, have more brains than blood. 'Let those who go there set a cross upon their garments as an outward sign of inner faith... They shall receive absolution for all their crimes' (William of Malmesbury's *Chronicle of the Kings of England*: see Giles (ed.) (1847), Stubbs (ed.) (1889) and Hay, 1957; 1968 edn).

Despite all the internal differences between the churches of the East and the West, Christians, bearers of the Cross, had some interests in common. Unity was often hard to find, but there were nevertheless communal symbols, gestures, spiritual ideals and earthly motives. It is of interest that the Pope, the leader of Latin Christendom, states that the geographical location for this form of communal identity was to be found in Europe, if only in part of it. Within Europe, the northern barbarians were considered as being excluded. Outside Europe, the Christian Church's loss of Africa was regretted, and a call was made for the conquest of the distant Jerusalem. But at this stage, despite some association between Europe and

Christianity, there was no question of a precise identification between Europe and Christendom.

In the course of the twelfth century, the threat to Christendom from the North and East became less. A ring of Latin Christian principalities came into existence: Norway, Sweden and Denmark in the North, Poland, Bohemia and Hungary in the East. The Normans, who in the ninth and tenth centuries had confined themselves to destructive raids, played a leading role in the eleventh and twelfth centuries in strengthening the position of Latin Christendom (Southern, 1953, pp. 25–6).

In the course of the twelfth century, western military successes in the East found expression in theological writings and secular poetry. Otto, Bishop of Freising, (1113–1158), writes in his great *Chronicle of the World* that 'all human wisdom and power begins in the East and ends in the West' (Otto of Freising, Chronica V prol. MGH, Script 20, 213, *cf.* van Laarhoven, 32). Otto of Freising was well-connected. His mother was a daughter of the German Emperor and his brother had married into the family of the Greek Emperor in Byzantium. His Chronicle is greatly inspired by Augustine, but in Augustine's thinking there is nothing similar to Otto's idea of the superiority of the West. Chrétien de Troyes, the poet of courtly romance, sang the praises of Paris as successor to Athens and Rome. Even mystical writings indicate the shift from East to West and attempt to explain it allegorically. If we are to believe Hugh of St Victor from Paris, the bows of Noah's Ark faced East and its stern West, expressing where Paradise lay at the beginning of time, namely in the East, and where the Day of Judgement would take place at the end of time, namely in the West (Brincken, 1973, p. 304).

It is perhaps going too far to posit a connection between such theological speculation and a growing self-*confidence* in the West. It is probably more justifiable to speak of a growing self-*awareness*. Be that as it may, these twelfth century ideas are stated in terms of an East–West dichotomy reaching far back in history. A connection between the growing self-awareness and the geographical concept of Europe is still infrequent; however, there are straws in the wind.

The oldest map of Europe

A splendidly illustrated autograph manuscript from the early years of the twelfth century includes, on a page of its own, the oldest known separate map of Europe. The map was probably drawn by Lambert, a canon of Saint-Omer, and is to be found in his *Liber Floridus*, a sort of encyclopaedia bringing together all kinds of bits of information in an order which is not always clear, and which may well be the result of later merging and selection.

Europe is described in the text as constituting a quarter of the world. In this connection, mention is made of the fact that Theodotus, in the time of Julius Caesar, stated that it constituted a third, but that the true extent is only a quarter. Elsewhere there is a splendid illumination showing Augustus with a globe in his

Figure 3 Liber Floridus, *A. Derolez (ed.) Ghent, 1968, p. 280, Fol. 138v. (Photo: British Library Board, London.)*

hand, divided in the customary manner with Asia in the upper half, Africa to the right and below and Europe to the left (see Figure 3).

According to the text accompanying the map, Europe contains 11 seas, 40 islands, 20 provinces (the Roman territorial division), 21 mountain ranges, 120 towns and cities, 21 rivers and 33 different peoples. The description is based on earlier writers, in part classical ones. The division of the world by the sons of Noah is not mentioned.

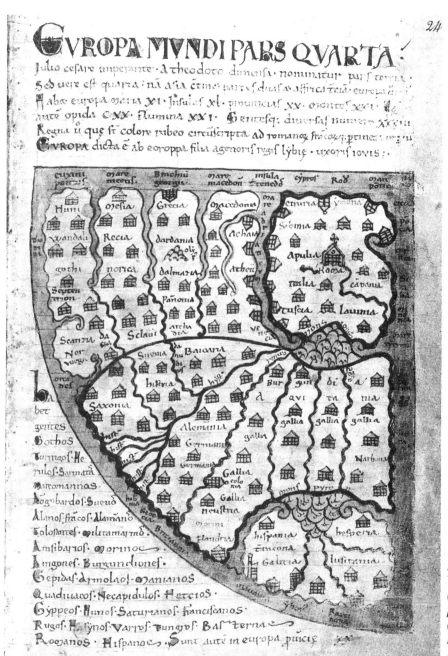

Figure 4 Liber Floridus, *A. Derolez (ed.), Ghent, 1986, p. 481, Fol. 241. (Photo: British Library Board, London.)*

It is noticeable not only that there is a separate map of Europe, but also that it is one within which a distinction is made between the continent of Europe itself and the Roman-Frankish Empire, the borders of which are marked in red. This distinct area includes Italia, Gallia, Flandria, Alemania, and Saxonia: in other words, roughly the Carolingian Empire of Charlemagne. Spain is excluded, as are Britain, Scandinavia, and the whole area to the east of the Adriatic from Venice down to Greece and Macedonia (see Figure 4).

However imperfect the geographical knowledge and cartographic skill demonstrated by this first map of Europe, it is nevertheless the earliest illustration reflecting the conception of Europe as a separate geographical unit, and one which is divided politically.

The map represents a longtime past historical situation, not the one actually existing in the early twelfth century. Canon Lambert makes no connection between Europe and Christendom. He still sees Europe as a continent containing many heathen peoples. The impression is given that the Christianization of Europe was not seen as a priority. Protecting the Holy Sepulchre in Asia was considered more important. The First Crusade had led to the conquest of the Holy Land. In Canon Lambert's survey of world history from the Creation onwards, this was the climax so far: Anno Domini, 1099, Godefridus Dux (Godfrey of Bouillon) conquers Jerusalem... (*Liber Floridus*, p. 42, Fol. 20v).

Europe and Christendom

Christendom and the map of the world

In the fourteenth century the geographical writings of Ptolemy, dating from the second century AD were rediscovered. This led to attempts to reconstruct the maps which had been lost. One of the results of this was that the extent of Europe on the map of the world became much smaller. Maps of Europe itself were now also drawn according to Ptolemy's indications. The first of these seems to have been designed in Byzantium as early as the mid-fourteenth century by the chronicler Nikephoros Gregoras (v. den Brincken Archiv 296). It was only in the fifteenth century that Ptolemy became widely known in the West. His influence was also noticeable in maps which were otherwise still based entirely on the traditional medieval conception of the world.

A fine example of a map of the world which is traditional in its basic conception, but which also uses Ptolemy as a source, is that produced by Andreas Walsperger in 1448 (K. Kretschmer, Zeitschrift Erdkunde 26, 1891). Walsperger, a Benedictine monk from Salzburg, drew a traditional round map of the world in the form of a pictorial account illustrating a wide range of legends and myths. It is a large, beautifully coloured map, illustrated with little drawings. Paradise is represented as a medieval walled city with many towers, and situated at the furthermost eastern point of the map. The map is aligned towards the north. Europe has become smaller than the traditional one quarter of the world. What is particularly interesting is the way in which the distribution of Christendom is shown. This is probably the first example of the cartographic localization of the small Christian community surrounded by the unbelievers who inhabit the major part of the world. Walsperger colours the Christian cities red and those of the unbelievers black. Europe is perhaps no longer as extensive as it used to be, but he is nevertheless able to colour all its cities red, in other words Christian. Outside Europe, he has also indicated a few legendary places in red, such as 'Portana or Nyessa, the capital city of the Indians, where Prester John resides'. It must have been some consolation for a hard-pressed Christendom that, according to travellers, there were in fact other Christians somewhere far off in other parts of the world. In the early fourteenth century, Ethiopian seamen in the harbour of Genoa had recounted how their country was ruled by the priest-king Prester John (Brincken, 1965, p. 29). More than a century later, Walsperger places this legendary 'other' Christian kingdom in Asia (see Figure 5).

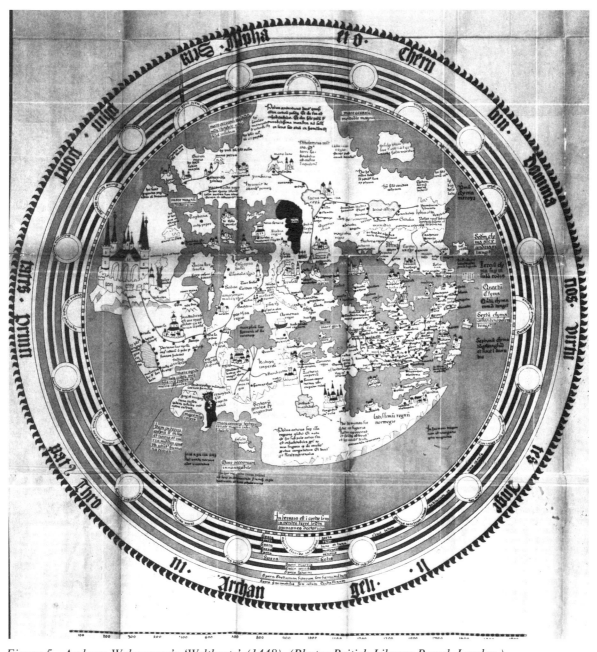

Figure 5   Andreas Walsperger's 'Weltkarte' (1448). (Photo: British Library Board, London.)

Apart from maps of this type, which were of no practical use but which could be studied, amended and marvelled at in monastic libraries, there were of course also the navigation charts used by mariners. These so-called *portolani* record coastal routes with remarkable accuracy and precision, marking the political identity of the various towns and regions with little flags and coats of arms (Hay, 1957; 1968 edn, p. 93). Such information, which was of literally vital importance to mariners, in earlier periods presumably had been passed on by word of mouth. Drawing the boundaries of the Christian world on a map made it possible to visualize them and to express them in concrete form. The surviving *portolani* are naturally not the ones actually used on board ship, but are particularly fine copies intended to be consulted back home in port. They are, however, maps drawn for practical and not for ideological purposes. Nevertheless, they too are a means of reinforcing visually the identification of Europe with Christendom.

The identification of Europe with Christendom

It was only in the course of the fifteenth century that the word Europe came to be used frequently by a large number of authors. From then on the identification of Europe with Christendom also became usual, but this was preceded by the enormous depression, social unrest, vast mortality and political and religious crisis, which Europe endured from the mid-fourteenth century to the end of the fifteenth century.

The urbanization that had been taking place during the preceding centuries was rudely halted; there were revolts among both peasants and town-dwellers; in some areas the plague decimated the population; France and England became embroiled in the Hundred Years' War; the German Empire virtually disintegrated and became the arena for conflicts between numerous princelings; and Italy was more fragmented than ever. In the course of the fourteenth century, the Osman Turks conquered not only Asia Minor but also the Balkans. Pressure from the Mongols had caused these nomads from Turkestan to settle in Asia Minor in the thirteenth century. By about 1400 their empire stretched from the Danube to the Euphrates. The fall of Constantinople seemed imminent, but new incursions and victories by the revived Mongol empire delayed it for another fifty years.

Besides the Holy Roman Empire, the second great medieval power with universal pretensions, the Papacy, also experienced difficulties. The heresies of Wycliffe in England and Jan Hus among the Czechs in Bohemia shook the Church to its very foundations. The universal claims of Rome were greatly restricted by the increasing power of separate states, with these restrictions being laid down in national concordats. The monastic orders, which had been such a significant unifying factor in the Latin Church in previous centuries, came to be organized on a much more regional basis (Hay, 1957; 1968 edn, p. 70). At the beginning of the fourteenth century, Pope Clement V, previously Archbishop of Bordeaux, transferred the Papal residence to Avignon, and there was a succession of Popes of French origin. In 1378, the simultaneous election of two Popes, one in Rome and one in Avignon, brought about the Great Schism, which only came to an end forty years later at the Council of Constance (1414–18).

It was not only Italians, but also many other Christians who considered it scandalous that the Pope had chosen to reside in Avignon in preference to Rome, the Eternal City, where Peter had been crucified and buried. A dispute arose in which the French defended themselves with great inventiveness on the basis of geographical arguments. One of the French polemicists argued in favour of Avignon on the grounds that it was located equidistant from the current boundaries of the Catholic Church, and that the Pope could therefore provide the faithful with spiritual consolation more easily if he resided there (Hay, 1957; 1968 edn, p. 74). He added that Avignon lay closer to the scholars of Paris than did Rome. Another French advocate of Avignon began by stating that Europe, the inheritance of Japheth, was one of the three parts making up the world, and that Christians currently lived in Europe, there being virtually no Christian rulers outside that continent. If one calculated the dimensions of the Christian area (excepting Greece), one found that Marseilles was the centre. The Vicar of Christ on Earth ought to reside at the centre of the Christian world. Christ himself had lived and died at the centre of the whole world. Rome had been chosen as the seat of the Papacy because at that time it was central. Currently, Marseilles was the central point, meaning that Avignon was a suitable residence. And in any case, as the familiar expression 'ubi papa ibi Roma' indicated, Rome was to be found wherever the Pope was (Hay, 1957; 1968 edn, p. 75).

These polemics, despite the fact that we may find them curious, do serve to make clear that Europe was considered to be the Christian continent, and that the eastern boundary of this Europe had been shifted a considerable distance west. After the crisis of Papal authority and the Great Schism had been resolved, all attention became focused on the threat posed by the Turks, but there was no question of any real common defensive organization. On 29 May 1453, Constantinople fell to Mohammed II, known as the Conqueror. This marked the definitive end of the Eastern Roman Empire. The famous Hagia Sophia church was turned into a mosque. The Christian world, which had a Latin and a Greek hemisphere, felt seriously threatened. The authority of the Pope in Rome increased, because he was now, in a sense, the sole defender Christendom had left. It was only later that the Patriarch of the third Rome, Moscow, would take over the role of Constantinople to some extent.

Pope Pius II (1458–64) did the best he could to organize a joint defence of the 'Respublica christiana' against the Turkish threat, but without effect. In 1460, Morea, the last Christian bastion in Greece, fell into Turkish hands. Pius II, a man of great international diplomatic experience, a renowned writer and influential humanist, decided to suit his actions to his words and placed himself at the head of a crusading army, which assembled in the harbour at Ancona. Before the fleet could sail, however, he died of illness.

In a large number of works, Pius II had called for the Christian world to be defended. It was no longer a question of crusades to conquer Jerusalem, but rather of the defence of Europe. The Pope used the terms 'Respublica christiana' and Europe as interchangeable synonyms, also speaking of 'our Europe, our Christian Europe'. He was also one of the first to use the adjective *europeus*, derived from the Latin noun *Europa*. Equivalent adjectives rapidly found their way into the various national languages. It was also he who was the first to use the word *europeus* indicating an inhabitant of Europe (*cf.* Hay, 1957; 1968 edn, pp. 86–7).

The influence of humanism on the concept of Europe

Humanism contributed in a variety of ways to forming a concept of the solidarity of Europe. Like many terms ending in '-ism', 'humanism' is of nineteenth-century origin. Previously, 'humanitas' and 'studia humanitatis' had been used to mean an educational programme based on the study of the works of Greek and Latin authors. The aim of such a programme was to educate a new type of individual by study of 'the classics', since these works were considered to represent the highest form of human achievement. Humanism had a deep and lasting influence on scholarship and education, of the greatest importance in every country in Europe. The predominant role of the classical languages in secondary and higher education was reinforced in numerous countries by their common roots in the classical tradition. Children in the different countries read the same authors in the course of their classical education. Alongside Christianity, humanism became one of the factors linking the élites of the various countries. A classical education was available to the whole educated population of Europe even though this constituted a tiny section of the total population.

A feeling of solidarity was created through the fact that scholars and intellectuals drank in knowledge at the same classical spring. The concept of a '*Respublica litteraria*' developed, parallel to the older idea of a '*Respublica christiana*', which continued to exist and was by no means always in contradiction.

The classical word Europe became more and more usual. Petrarch, the ardent propagandist of mainly Latin authors (in particular his idol Cicero), uses the term repeatedly. Even so, for the very Prince of Humanists, Desiderius Erasmus of Rotterdam (1466–1536), the term Europe in itself had not yet any particular significance. He used it as a matter of course and then only infrequently. For Erasmus, the *Respublica litteraria* was also a network of humanistic rulers and scholars, which visits and correspondence could serve to maintain. The humanism of Erasmus, however, unlike that of Italy, is primarily a Christian and not a European phenomenon. As early as in his *Enchiridion Militis Christiani* (1504), a little manual for the warrior of Christ, in which he attempted to present the art of piety, he greatly lamented the hatred that kept Christians divided. He mentions a whole series of antitheses, such as those between peasants and burgesses, rich and poor, powerful and weak, but also national rivalries: the Italian hates the German, the Frenchman the Englishman, and the Englishman the Scot (Festugière, 1971, p. 178). He seems to find these clashes deplorable because all concerned are Christians. What is clear is that for him Europe is the Christian continent. The *Enchiridion* became widely known through translations of the original Latin into English, Czech, German, Dutch, Spanish and French.

In 1517, in the midst of rumours of war, he published an impressive pacifist manifesto: *Querela pacis*. The work is a 'Lament of Peace, which everywhere has been banished or destroyed', written at the instigation of the governor and chamberlain of Charles V, and dedicated to the Bishop of Utrecht, a bastard son of the Duke of Burgundy. Erasmus strongly emphasized the need for peace between Burgundy and France. The feelings of hatred between the various nations are mentioned once again:

> How very wrong this is! A geographical name of no importance divides them... In earlier times the Rhine divided the French and the Germans, but it does not separate one Christian from another. The Pyrenees separate Spaniards and Frenchmen, but they do not undo the communality of the church. The sea flows between the English and the French but can in no way split the unity of faith.
>
> *(Erasmus in Geurts, 1989, p. 116)*

For Erasmus, it is the unity of Christendom which is primary, and nowhere does he speak of the unity of Europe.

It is specifically within the context of the Turkish threat in the East that Europe becomes a synonym for the Christian world. This is also true in the works of Erasmus. Belgrade fell in 1521 and in 1522 Rhodes was conquered (an event of great significance for trade); the Turkish victory at Mohacs (1526) put an end to Hungarian independence and opened up the way to Vienna, which the Turks besieged for the first time in 1529. All these events made Erasmus and his contemporaries fear the worst for Austria, Poland and the neighbouring countries, perhaps even for Italy. In one of his letters to an English patron in September 1529, Erasmus wrote that 'it is fortunate that peace [the treaty of Kamerijk] had been concluded between the most powerful princes from all of Europe' (Gerlo, 1979, p. 359). The home of Christendom, as a matter of course, had come to be Europe.

Another major humanist, Juan Luis Vives (1492–1540), drew a parallel between the advance of the Turks and the distinction made by the classical Greeks between Europe and Asia, long before the Christian period. In his dialogue about the disputes in Europe and the war against the Turks, *De Europae dissidiis et bello turcico dialogus* (1526), he relates how every Asiatic invasion of Europe has always ended in the complete defeat of the invading forces. He gives as examples Miltiades at the Battle of Marathon, Themistocles at the Battle of Salamin, and the Roman consul Sulla who, at Chaeronea in 86 BC, defeated Mithradates, supposedly a descendant of the kings of Persia. In all these battles no more than a few thousand Europeans had succeeded in defeating Asiatic forces numbering many thousands, even hundreds of thousands (Vives, *Obras Completas II*, Madrid 1948, pp. 56–7).

Vives, of Spanish Jewish extraction was a Christian believer, but saw the struggle against the Turks in the context of the classical distinction between Europe and Asia, which naturally had nothing to do with Christendom. A few years earlier, however, in 1522, he had written to Pope Adrian VI about the turmoil in Europe, saying that 'Christ demanded of us that this extensive and sorrowful

Europe, internally torn and divided as it now is, should remain one single body' (ibid., p. 18). On the other hand, citation of the classics in other later writings implies that the concept of Europe is gaining an independence of its own which will eventually weaken the identification of Europe and Christendom.

Reformation and Counter-Reformation

For Latin Christendom, afflicted as it had already been for centuries by schisms and heresies, the sixteenth century saw the disappearance of even the illusion of unity. This was the result not only of the Protestant Reformation but of other religious groupings and minorities. A thorough in-depth Christianization of Europe took place and the Protestant and Catholic Reformations can certainly be seen as processes leading to an intensification of the actual practice of the Faith.

In the course of the sixteenth century, irreconcilable religious oppositions were created. There was division not only between Catholics and Protestants, but particularly within Protestantism itself, where far-reaching fragmentation came about due to the secession of a large number of religious groupings.

Furthermore, there were sizable minorities, for example the Jews and many other dissenters, but they were tolerated only to a very limited extent and in particular locations. The internal cohesion of religious groupings became much greater. There was little or no peaceful coexistence between the various religions. It was this division, fragmentation and disunity which began to make a simplistic identification of Europe with Christendom increasingly difficult to sustain.

European rulers and the balance of power

Machiavelli

The idea that a different political regime applies in Europe from that in Asia, as formulated in antiquity at the time of the Persian Wars, is met with once more in the political theory of the Renaissance.

The complete secularization of political thought is to be found in the writings of Machiavelli (1469–1527), an official in the Florentine chancellery. His most famous work, *Il Principe* (The Prince), was published posthumously in 1532. His name became, and remains, synonymous with the lesson he taught, that of Machiavellianism. The state is a goal in itself, and the ruler must if necessary be prepared to make use of reprehensible methods to maintain his power. The interests of the state take precedence over all other considerations. For Machiavelli, kings did not receive their power by divine providence, as they had in the medieval Christian conception of the world. Political ends justified the means.

According to Machiavelli, a prince can rule in one of two manners. He can do so either by exercising absolute power, with all other persons in the state being subject to him, or he can surround himself with relatively independent lords whose power is not derived from his favour but from their birth (*The Prince*, Chapter 4). In the first case, therefore, one has a prince with a number of slaves as ministers, whom he is gracious enough to allow to assist him in administering the state. In the second case, the lords control territory of their own and rule subjects of their own who have a natural affection for them. Machiavelli cites Turkey and France as examples of these two forms of government. In France, the sovereign has many nobles around him, whereas in Turkey he is an absolute ruler surrounded by mere slaves. A prince who chooses to invade an Asian state will find himself confronted by the whole of that state. This means that an Asian empire is difficult to defeat, but when it falls to an invader, it falls as a whole. This could be seen in the case of Alexander the Great. Machiavelli is able in this way to explain the fact that after the death of Alexander the Persian Empire did not revolt against Alexander's successors.

The situation in the West is, in contrast, quite different. Here too, Machiavelli, as became a thinker with a humanist background, takes his examples from classical antiquity, namely King Pyrrhus and the Romans, who found themselves confronted with far greater difficulties in the West than in the East. The Romans repeatedly had to deal with uprisings in Spain, Gaul and Greece as a result of the large number of small princedoms there (*The Prince*, Chapter 4).

Honesty compels one to admit that, although Machiavelli uses the term Asia in *The Prince*, he does not refer to Europe. His argumentation is, however, directed entirely towards the situation in the latter continent. For this reason, he has been seen as the first writer to provide a purely political and entirely a-religious specification of what Europe means (Chabod, 1963, p. 32).

For Machiavelli, the Roman Empire had had its day, and the idea of the restoration of a universal Christian empire, which is constantly at the forefront of medieval political theory, plays no role whatsoever in his thinking. He proceeds from the assumption that there are several sovereign states in Europe. In the course of the sixteenth century, the relations between the various European states came to be compared to a set of scales, with the ideal situation being one in which there is a balance of power. This was necessary for stability in foreign relations, and stability meant peace. The theory of the balance of power would come to play an extremely important role in the creation of the political, non-Christian, concept of Europe.

The theory of the balance of power had already been used in the second half of the fifteenth century to characterize political relations within Italy. At that moment there were four powerful states there. In order to contain Venetian expansion, and to preserve their freedom, Florence, Milan and Naples formed an alliance (E. Kaeber, 1907, pp. 12ff). In particular, it was Guicciardini (1483–1540), a leading official of the Papal States and organizer of the Papal armies who, in his history of Italy, focused on the concept of the balance of power as the driving force in external relations. The Medici family, the rulers of Florence, played a key role in this, and Lorenzo the Magnificent (1449–92) is later portrayed as keeping a huge pair of scales in balance (Kaeber, 1907, p. 13).

The balance of power in the sixteenth century

The invasion of Italy by foreign armies had disastrous results. In 1500, the King of France occupied Milan, and Naples lost its independence, being transferred to the King of Spain. This was the start of the Spanish–Habsburg domination of Italy. In 1525, the King of France was decisively defeated at Pavia and taken prisoner, thus putting an end to the great influence of France in Italy. In 1527, the Pope was taken prisoner and Rome was plundered by the mercenary armies of the Habsburgs. The enormous power which the House of Habsburg succeeded in achieving in Italy, its possession of the throne of Spain and that of the German Empire, and the fact that it also ruled Burgundy and the Low Countries, resulted in the other princes of Europe, primarily the Habsburg's arch-rival, the King of France, striving towards the creation of alliances in order to counterbalance the power of the Habsburgs.

In the mid-sixteenth century Venetian diplomats also explicitly described the ongoing struggle between the Spanish Habsburgs and the French Bourbons in terms of a balance which, in the interests of peace in Europe, had to be kept in a state of equilibrium (Kaeber, pp. 15ff). The concept of the balance of power, which in the fifteenth century had still been used only for the situation in Italy, came to be applied in the second half of the sixteenth century to the situation in Europe as a whole.

Queen Mary of Hungary, a sister of Charles V and governess of the Low Countries, wrote in 1553 that she was aware of the extent to which the various states of Italy, in particular Venice, feared the dominance of one of the two most powerful princes (Charles V and Francis I) and that the Italians were concerned to ensure that a state of equilibrium was maintained between these two powers (Kaeber, p. 20). The successes of Charles V were watched with concern. It was feared that the restoration of a universal monarchy would mean the end of the freedom of many states. Nevertheless, Charles V denied that he was attempting to establish a universal monarchy. The driving force behind his actions was dynastic interest, as was the case with the other princely houses at the time. Associated with this motive was his passionate wish to restore and spread the Catholic faith. For Charles, it should be said that the concept 'Europe' played hardly any role in his thinking. In his instructions to his son Philip in 1543 and 1548, for example, the word Europe is not used, there being mention only of the Empire, the Christian faith and the dynasty (Alvarez, 1975, pp. 90–118, 569–92). The hard-pressed Francis I sought allies against the Habsburgs, looking both to the Protestant princes of Germany and to the Sultan. In 1535, France entered into an alliance with Suleiman the Magnificent, with whom, after the siege of Vienna, an armistice had just been agreed, together with the partition of Hungary. Christian Europe was more divided than ever.

After the abdication and death of Charles V in 1558, his brother Ferdinand became German Emperor and his son Philip II received the Spanish Throne, together with the Italian dominions and the Netherlands. At the naval Battle of Lepanto (1571), Turkish domination of the Mediterranean was broken. France was weakened by civil war and Philip strove to create a universal, Catholic empire.

This was the context of an address directed to the King of France in 1584, which clearly states that whether there is war or peace in the Christian world depends on the balance of power between the two most powerful princely houses, those of France and Spain. The text still speaks of the balance of power in 'the Christian world'. The English historian William Camden (1551–1623) was praised in heroic terms as the arbitrator between Spain, France, and the Netherlands, which were in a state of revolt:

> …and true it is, which one hath written, that France and Spain are as it were the scales in the balance of Europe and England the tongue or the holder of the balance.
>
> *(Quoted in Kaeber, p. 28, note 2)*

In all likelihood, the destruction of the Spanish Armada (1588) was the reason for the Queen of England being credited with the position in Europe which Lorenzo the Magnificent had fulfilled in the microcosm of Italy a century earlier.

The balance of power in the seventeenth century

The destruction of the Armada was a serious setback for the House of Habsburg, but at the beginning of the seventeenth century its power was still considered to be the main threat to peace in Europe.

In 1619 Ferdinand II became Emperor, but Bohemia, dominated by the Protestant Czechs, refused to recognize him and proclaimed the Protestant Elector Palatine their king. In the ensuing war, Bohemia was defeated and became an hereditary possession of the Habsburgs, while Bavaria assumed the electoral function of the Palatinate. The internal balance of power in the German Empire was thus disturbed. Only Prussia and Saxony remained as Protestant powers offering a counterweight to the Austrian Habsburgs.

Cardinal Richelieu, the effective ruler of France, was much preoccupied with the Huguenot rebels, but succeeded nevertheless in persuading the Kings of first Denmark and then Sweden to intervene within the German Empire against the Emperor. In 1631, the Catholic French cardinal concluded a subsidy treaty with the great Lutheran King of Sweden, Gustavus Adolphus, who won victory after victory over the Imperial troops, but was himself slain at the siege of Lützen in 1632. After a number of victories in the next few years, Emperor Ferdinand II was once more all-powerful and Richelieu, in his own view, was forced to declare open war on the Habsburgs.

Political writings of the time repeatedly refer to the role of France as arbitrator in the German question. State interest clearly prevailed above the mutual ties between the Catholic princes. It was even pointed out that it was in the interests of the Pope himself that there should be a balance of power in which Protestant rulers also formed part of the Catholic Habsburgs (Kaeber, p. 32).

French policy, and in particular that of Richelieu, was even justified by the Huguenot rebels. In his political work *De l'interest des Princes et Estats de la Chretienté* (1638), one of their leaders, the Duke of Rohan, expresses the general opinion that France and Spain are the two poles of international politics and that the balance between these two great powers must serve as the guide-line for the policies of the other states.

In the second half of the seventeenth century, the international political situation was determined by the expansionist aims of Louis XIV. The power of the House of Habsburg became much less dominant and gradually France came to be seen as the most significant threat to the balance of power in Europe. The first person to point the finger of guilt at France was the Austrian statesman Franz Paul Baron Lisola, in a publication which appeared in 1667 in French, German and English, and which was intended to convince England to ally itself with Austria and to warn Protestant rulers of the French King's plans (Schmidt, 1966, p. 173). Lisola adopts in its entirety the theory of the balance of power as formulated thirty years before by the Duke of Rohan, but uses it against France. In his view, the King of France wished to establish a universal monarchy and had therefore become a threat to the freedom of Europe, to religion and to trade. Lisola couples the idea of the balance of power in Europe not only with peace but also with freedom of religion and the growth of trade (Schmidt, p. 173).

Louis XIV's attack on the United Provinces (the Dutch Republic) in 1672 resulted in a stream of pamphlets in which Louis' opponents frequently use the term Europe, whereas the French propaganda machine constantly represents the Sun King as the most powerful of the Christian princes and the great defender of the *respublica christiana*. A pamphlet published in 1677 is entitled *Europe a slave unless England break her chains*. The ruler of the Dutch Republic, William of Orange, was able to fend off the French attack and attempted to disrupt the links between England and France. William of Orange referred to himself as the 'preserver of the liberty of Europe' ('handhaver der Europese vrijheid') and a small but influential group of English anti-establishment politicians known as Whigs supported him. Henry Sidney wrote to William in 1680 that everyone was thinking of him and considered him to be the only person who could save England and ensure 'the liberty of Europe'. The Whig opposition attempted to have the phrase 'the safety of Europe and the Protestant religion' added to an address by the King, but Charles II, who had been educated at the court of Louis XIV during the English Civil War, refused, choosing instead 'for the safety of England and the repose of Christendom' (Schmidt, p. 174).

William of Orange's landing in England and the Glorious Revolution (1688) had as their slogan the freedom of Europe and the Protestant religion. The grand alliance against Louis XIV went under the banner of 'the freedoms of Europe'. At one of the many rounds of diplomacy between all the interested parties, the French showed a preference for the term 'Chretienté', whereas the English, led by William of Orange, spoke of 'Europe'. The collection of documents relating to the Peace of Ryswick (1698), which was published in England, states in its introduction that the European states are now in a happy balance and that England and its illustrious confederates have broken the chains by which the liberty of Europe was entangled.

By around 1700, Europe had become the standard framework for political think-ing. The theory of the balance of power had found broad acceptance and had be-come closely associated with the ideal of freedom (or freedoms) for Europe. 'Europe', which in the sixteenth century had still been a somewhat unusual syn-onym for Christendom, had by the end of the seventeenth century come to be the preferred term at least in Anglo-Dutch and Protestant circles.

The balance of power in the eighteenth century

In the course of the eighteenth century the conceptual link between 'Europe' and the idea of a balance of power was further developed. It was operative at the level of both political thought and political practice. The universities, for in-stance, taught the system of the balance of power to their students, and learned treatises were published on the subject. In England, the phrase 'Liberty, religion and trade' was associated with the theory. Freedom for a number of states, each with equal rights, the free practice of the Protestant religion and the unhindered development of English trade were all encompassed by the notion of the balance of power.

In the sphere of political practice, the old system in which England's role was to keep the balance between the Bourbons and the Habsburgs, was in the mid-eighteenth century disturbed by the rapid rise of the power of Prussia and by the growing influence of Russia. Frederick the Great's conquest of Silesia was the start of a long conflict with Austria. In 1756, the so-called 'Diplomatic Revolution' took place, with the arch-enemies Bourbon and Habsburg forming a coalition against Prussia which was supported by England. The result was ulti-mately a new and far more complex system, which even at the time was felt to be confusing. What later came to be known as a 'pentarchy', rule by five powers, came into being in Europe, and was able to maintain itself until well into the nine-teenth century, despite the tempest unleashed by the French Revolution and Napoleon. The five main players were England, France, Austria, Prussia and Russia.

Among those propagating the theory of the balance of power one notices the growing influence of theorists of natural law and international law. Christian pacifism already had a long history. From Erasmus' *Querela pacis* in the early sixteenth century to the *Essay towards the present and future peace of Europe* by the Quaker William Penn, the founder of Pennsylvania, at the end of the seventeenth, there were a number of idealists who produced plans for peace (Kurt von Raumer, *Ewiger Friede. Friedensrufe und Friedenspläne seit der Renaissance* ('eternal peace: hopes and plans for peace since the Renaissance'), Freiburg-München, 1953). In the early years of the eighteenth century, one finds the very worldly Abbé de Saint Pierre, whose inspiration seems to be no longer religious in any real sense at all, drawing up a plan to ensure peace in Europe at all times. His *Projet pour rendre la paix perpétuelle en Europe* (1713) was the instigation for a number of publications in mid-century by Rousseau, in which the philosopher argues for the setting up of an organization of European nations based on the fundamental principles of international law. In our own century, these Utopian idealists have come to be seen as prophesying the two great international organizations set up after each of the World Wars, the League of Nations and the United Nations.

It was not only pacifist idealists who attempted to subject the relations between states to rules but also pragmatic jurists. Grotius (1583–1645) was in no way a pacifist by principle but wished to humanize warfare and make it conform to agreements. His great work on the law of war and peace, *De jura belli et pacis*, published in Paris in 1625 and dedicated to the King of France, is based on the concept of natural law. It is one of the foundation stones of international law.

In the eighteenth century, the Abbé de Mably described the 'public law of Europe'. He considered that this new form of European law should take as its starting point the existing international treaties, which were the result of the balance of power. Mably, who had served for a long period at the ministry of foreign affairs in Paris and was thus extremely well informed, brought out a series of constantly updated editions of *Le droit public de L'Europe fondé sur les traités* (Amsterdam/Leipzig, 1773) in which he published the most significant international treaties. He considered them as the archives of the nations of Europe, containing 'what all nations are entitled to, the reciprocal commitments which bind them, the law to which they have submitted themselves, the rights which they have acquired or lost' (*Le droit public*, 1773, tome I, p. X). He considered all the treaties agreed before 1648 as being documents of interest only to historians. His intention was to provide an up-to-date survey of the way in which the states of Europe had put a definitive end to their quarrels and formed their alliances. In Mably's view, the treaties between the nations had come to be endowed with the same authority as the civil legislation of individual states. This was an optimism based on stability in the relations between the states of Europe, a stability which was of course lacking, as had been the case in the past and would be in the future also. A lasting state of equilibrium in the balance of power is something Europe has never enjoyed.

In any case, the term 'Europe' had come to be taken for granted in political circles. It was not only the standard framework for political thinking but was also inseparably associated with the idea of the balance of power. These political concepts were basically completely non-religious. Pacifist ideals and theories of international organization were, it is true, often religiously inspired, but were, nonetheless, not primarily religious in essence. The liberties of Europe were central. The balance was the guarantee for the freedom of princes and of nations.

Representations of Europe

The expansion of Europe

Parallel to the formation of political concepts, determined to a very considerable extent by the problems within Europe itself – and which, as we have seen, implied in various forms a certain concept of Europe – an image of Europe developed around 1500 which was the result of the discovery of other continents and of the conquest of areas outside Europe.

Europe turned from the Mediterranean to the Atlantic, at least in the sense that its economic centre of gravity shifted from the coasts of the former to the ports of the latter. Venice and Genoa lost their pre-eminence and were overtaken by other cities, first of all Lisbon, then Seville and Antwerp and later Amsterdam, Hamburg and London. These were followed on a more restricted scale by Nantes, Bordeaux, Cádiz and many others, each with its own Golden Age.

Trade with distant destinations – the Americas, Asia, Africa – provided an impulse for the economy and was the catalyst of a global monetary system in which barter, cash, and (in particular) credit were interwoven with one another. As a result, concentrations of financial power were created upon which European rulers were to a great extent dependent, and which determined the progress of European expansion.

Europe as represented in modern cartography

We have already seen how the rediscovered work of Ptolomy influenced European map-making from the mid-fourteenth century.

Overseas exploration greatly encouraged the further development of cartography. During the course of the fifteenth century the Portuguese were the first to sail along the coast of west Africa and the voyages of Colombus to America (1492), Vasco da Gama to India via the Cape of Good Hope (1498) and Magellan, the first to circumnavigate the world (1519–21) drastically transformed geographical knowledge. Additionally the invention of printing increased the distribution of maps.

The Low Countries gained a pre-eminent position in modern cartography. Gerardus Mercator (1512–94) produced fine globes for Charles V, who delighted in examining them, and in doing so perhaps came to realize that the sun never in fact set on his empire. Mercator, who brought out a standard edition of Ptolemy, also produced the first modern map of Europe, in fifteen parts and dedicated to Granvelle, the trusted adviser of Charles V and Philip II (Mercator Europa (Duisburg, 1554), Facsimile Lichtdruk Reichsdruckerei nach dem Original in der Stadsbibliothek zu Breslau herausgegeben von der Gesellschaft für Erdkunde zu Berlin (1891)). It was in particular Mercator's world map of 1569, intended for mariners, which became famous, using as it did his ingenious cylinder projection. The map contains instructions for setting a course and reckoning distances. The famous atlas, in book form, appeared in 1595, shortly after Mercator's death. His heirs sold the folio-sized copper plates engraved with the maps of Jodocus Hondius, and these were republished either as they were or in revised form. In the course of the seventeenth century, the Mercator-Hondius atlas became very popular and was republished and translated many times. Hondius also published smaller atlases under the name Mercator, but containing new maps. Many others also published maps and atlases. Slowly the modern cartographic image of the world became usual, with Europe taking up only a small part. It became clear, it is true, that Europe was the smallest of the continents, but the accompanying texts described it in no uncertain terms as the best.

The *Atlas Minor* published by Hondius in Amsterdam in 1607 regards Europe as the first of the continents on the grounds of its fertility, population and the illustrious deeds of its inhabitants. Europe is also called the most noble continent, inherited by Japheth, the eldest son of Noah. Pliny too is cited in praise of Europe. The texts of the atlas take Europe and Christendom to be synonyms. Similarly, when the word 'christiani' appears in the *Thesaurus geographicus* (1578) of Abraham Ortelius, it referred to 'Europaei'; this is clearly identified in the index, where the instruction '*vide* Europaei' is given under 'christiani' (Hay, 1957; 1968 edn, pp. 109–10).

The expansion of Europe is thus seen as equivalent to the expansion of Christendom. Hondius' *Atlas Minor*, mentioned above, contains an intriguing map of the world on which the spread of Christendom is indicated by symbols. This is done not only for Europe, Africa (Abyssinia, Congo) Asia (Muscovy, Tartary) but also America, 'where the original inhabitants do not know Christ, worshipping rather the Devil, except in some places where the Spaniards have established colonies'. In the French edition, this map is not entitled '*Designatio orbis christiani*' ('delineation of the Christian world') but '*de la diversité des religions par tout le monde*'. The French title is in fact more accurate, because Mohammedanism, Judaism and idolatry are also indicated with special symbols. This is the first map that attempts to visualize the distribution of the world's religions by means of symbols (see Figure 6).

Although the position of the Christian Church and Europe on maps of the world is represented in more modest proportions, the accompanying texts reflect a growing pride and arrogance, based on European expansion. Europe and Christendom are frequently considered to be entirely synonymous. Samuel Purchas, a Protestant English author of the early seventeenth century, even goes as far as to consider Jesus Christ himself an out-and-out European!

> Europe is taught the way to scale Heaven ... Jesus Christ is their way,
> their truth, their life; [Jesus Christ] hath long since given a Bill of
> Divorce to ingrateful Asia where he was borne and Africa the place of
> his flight and refuge and [Jesus Christ] is become almost wholly and
> only European...
>
> *(Hay, 1957; 1968 edn, p. 110)*

The author, in whose work Hondius' map of the distribution of Christendom is printed, then goes on to sing the praises of Europe, which despite being the smallest continent in size is still the best in quality. Is not the whole world subject to Europe? Asia and Africa were first conquered by Alexander and later by the Romans. America was discovered and subjected by the Spanish and Portuguese, the northern part by the English and the Dutch. 'Asia yearly sends us her Spices, silks and gems; Africa her gold and Ivory; America receiveth severer customers and tax-masters, almost everywhere admitting European colonies' (Quoted in Hay, 1957; 1968 edn, pp. 120–21).

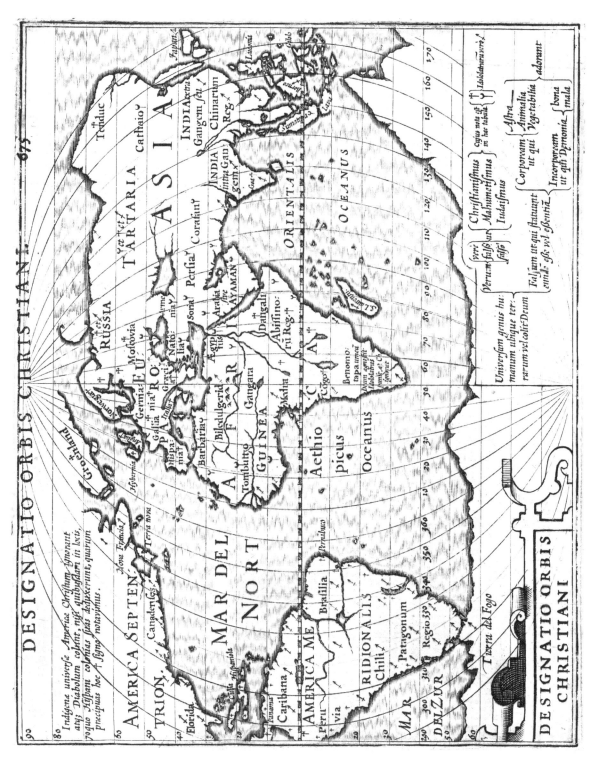

Figure 6   From Hondius' Atlas Minor*: 'Designatio orbis christiani' or 'de la diversité des religions par tout le monde', 1607. (Photo: British Library Board, London.)*

Clearly the Europeans are able to call the shots. Christianity, trade and colonization are the elements in European expansion which formed the basis for unequivocal feelings of superiority.

Europe crowned

The iconological tradition, as well as cartography, can yield information about the way Europe has been represented. In particular there are certain allegorical illustrations that offer some insights into the way Europe was portrayed but, in truth, little has survived from before the sixteenth century. We do not know of any iconological form that can be considered as depicting the great struggle between Greece and Persia, which according to various Greek authors could be considered as representing the antithesis between Europe and Asia. A marble relief from the Roman Imperial period has, however, come down to us on which Europe and Asia are shown as female figures on either side of a large shield upon which the battle of Arbela is depicted (see Figure 7, *Lexicon Iconographicum Mythologiae Classicae* (LIMC) Vol IV (1988) Europe, p. 92). (In 331 BC, Alexander the Great inflicted a decisive defeat on the Persian King Darius on the plains between Arbela and Gaugamela in Mesopotamia. Almost four and a half centuries later, in the spring of AD 116, the Roman Emperor Trajan followed in Alexander's footsteps, marching through Gaugamela and Arbela in the course of a campaign to annex Assyria and Babylon. The wars between the Romans and the Parthians revived memories of the exploits of Alexander and were undoubtedly the inspiration for the commemoration in stone in the second century AD of a battle that took place in the fourth century BC.) This is the only undisputed portrayal of Europe as a continent. Four other such portrayals exist but are open to a different interpretation. Similarly, there are only a few portrayals of Asia from the classical period. Various series of coins exist from the second century AD which depict the provinces of the Roman Empire. These do in fact show 'Asia', but are not personifications of the continent, representing rather the Roman province of the same name. The same is true of the numerous portrayals of Africa that have come down to us, depicting the Roman province rather than the continent.

There was of course a rich tradition of portrayals of the myth of the Rape of Europa, not only in antiquity but also in the Middle Ages: Europa and the Bull – it is naturally a moving tale and an inexhaustible motive for artistic representation, but it is not the allegorical portrayal of a continent.

We know of no more than a single object from the whole medieval period on which the three continents are portrayed as persons, namely a twelfth-century candelabra made in Liège, on the foot of which the three continents are depicted (see Figure 8). Europe is shown armed, carrying a shield inscribed 'bellum' (war) and a sword. Such warlike symbolic portrayals of Europe also occur in much later periods but this early association of Europe and war is somewhat puzzling.

The first allegorical portrayal of America would appear to date from around 1500 but it is only in the second half of the sixteenth century that allegorical representations of continents (a total of four at that time) with standard attributes and symbols became popular (Knipping, 1974, p. 361). Europe is portrayed as a woman

Figure 7   The commemoration in stone of the wars between the Romans and the Parthians in the second century AD. From Lexicon Iconographicum Mythologiae Classicae. *(Photo: Ashmolean Museum, Oxford.)*

wearing a crown. She alone is thus crowned, while the other continents are not. By around 1580 'Europe crowned' had become a normal motif in prints (see, for example, Figure 9).

Even earlier, in 1537, an extremely curious map of Europe, in the form of a woman, was produced by the Innsbruck humanist Johannes Archduke of Austria, Holy Roman Emperor, King of Hungary and Bohemia (only copy now in Museum

Figure 8   Twelfth-century candelabra from Liège. The three continents are depicted on the foot. (Photo: Zentral Institut für Kunstgeschichte, München.)

Figure 9 'Europe crowned', Philips Galle after Marcus Gheeraerts, Europe circa 1580, Rijksprentenkabinet, Rijksmuseum Amsterdam. (Photo: Rijksmuseum-Stichting, Amsterdam.)

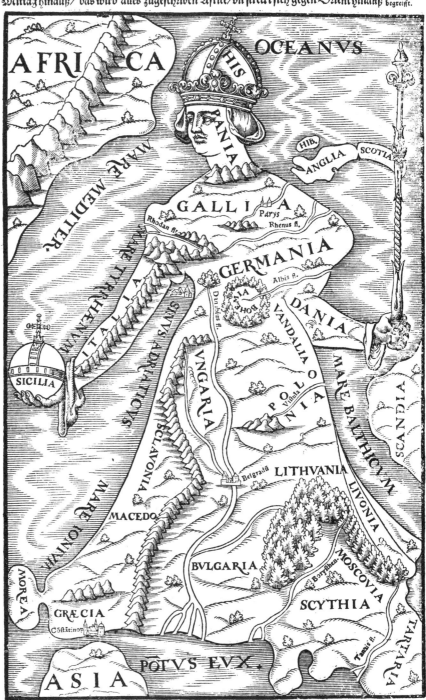

Figure 10   Europe as queen, from Sebastien Münster, Cosmographia Universalis *(1588). (Photo: Basel University Library.)*

Ferdinandeum in Innsbruck, *cf.* Bagrow (ed.), 1930, pp. 46–7). This inventive combination of map and queen can be found again in one of the later impressions of the cosmography of Sebastian Münster, a traditional work that was popular in the second half of the sixteenth century (see Figure 10). It is a portrayal of Europe such as to please the Habsburgs. Spain is the crowned head and Bohemia the heart; Italy forms one of her arms, and she holds Sicily as an orb. In her other hand she has a sceptre which touches Scotland and England.

The same portrayal is to be found on a richly decorated silver bowl made in Nuremburg in 1589 for the intended marriage of the Emperor Rudolf II and the Infanta Isabella, which was to strengthen the ties binding the Austrian and Spanish Habsburgs. The marriage did not take place, but the bowl has been preserved. It shows the Battle of Lepanto (1571) in which the Turkish fleet was crushed by the combined forces of Spain, Venice and the papacy off the coast of Greece. Nuremburg is depicted as the heart of Europe (see Figure 11).

At the end of the sixteenth century Cesare Ripa in his *Iconologia* (1st ed. Rome, 1593; many later reprints and translations), brought together various strands of iconographical scholarship (see Figure 12). In the original Italian edition, Europe is portrayed as the only crowned continent, being the most important: the 'Chief and Queen of the Whole World'. On either side of her are shown Horns of Plenty, one filled with fruit and grain, the other with white and blue grapes, as symbols of fertility. She carries a temple in one hand as a sign of perfect religion. With her other hand she points to crowns and sceptres as proof of the fact that it is in Europe that the most powerful of potentates and princes reside, the Emperor and the Pope. Ripa does not forget to mention that, by the Grace of God, the Christian Faith has also penetrated the New World. The charger and weapons stand for war-like valour, the book and the owl for scholarship, the musical instruments for the liberal arts. The carpenter's square, brushes and chisels indicate the excellence of the Greeks and Romans and other peoples (all European) in painting, sculpture and architecture. A later Dutch edition (1644) adds navigation and printing to the series of images associated with Europe (Ripa, *Iconologia*, Dutch translation, Amsterdam 1644, pp. 602–03).

Ripa's influence was considerable but with respect to the portrayal of the continents, in particular, one finds a great deal of variety – no doubt the aims and ambitions of the different commissioning agents. We have already seen how such symbolic portrayals could serve the purposes of Habsburg, imperial, propaganda (*cf.* overview *Attributen, Reallexicon zur deutschen Kunstgeschichte (RDK)* 1967, pp. 1166–68). A well-known example is the allegory painted in 1636 by Franz Francken showing the abdication of Charles V in 1555, in which the continents are depicted as paying homage to the Emperor (see Figure 13).

Apart from this 'imperial' iconology, clerical and bourgeois emblems developed during the seventeenth century. An example of the latter is the monumental frieze sculpted by Artus Quellinus on the façade of the Town Hall in Amsterdam (1656–58), which was viewed by many in the seventeenth century as the eighth wonder of the world. The peace treaties ending eighty years of war in 1648 were considered to be a victory over the Habsburgs. In the symbolic frieze, Amsterdam takes the place of Charles V in, as it were, a comic parody in marble rather than

Figure 11   The Battle of Lepanto (1571) depicted on a silver bowl, made in 1589 for the intended marriage of Emperor Rudolf II and the Infanta Isabella. From the Kunstgewerbemuseum, Berlin. (Photo: Kunstgewerbemuseum, Staatliche Museen Preussischer Kulturbesitz, Berlin.)

on canvas. The four continents bring their tribute and merchandise to the city of Amsterdam, symbolized as a woman seated on a ship (see Figure 14).

In the course of the eighteenth century one finds the superiority of Europe expressed more and more directly. When the continents are depicted together, their posture clearly indicates their subordination to Europe. Europe is enthroned, whereas the other continents stand or kneel before her, honouring her with gifts (*RDK* V, p. 1161). If the continents are depicted separately, the superiority of Europe is expressed by means of comparison.

This can be seen, for example, in the splendid neo-classical adaptation of Ripa in the second half of the eighteenth century by the architect George Richardson. In the introduction of his *Iconology* (London, 1779), Richardson clearly states that, by classifying and contrasting the allegorical portrayals, he wishes to 'give to the explanations and prints a more striking opposition and variety'. The familiar symbolic attributes are naturally illustrated. The charger and weapons stand for undaunted valour, the owl and the book for scholarship, instruments of all sorts for the liberal arts (see Figure 15). The Horn of Plenty indicates fertility, her luxurious garments mark her superior riches, and her crown makes her the Queen of the World.

Not only is Richardson's style different from Ripa's but the tone is as well. For Richardson, it is the superiority of Europe in the arts and sciences which is primary.

> For learning and arts, the Europeans have been most renowned; all the scholastic sciences they have brought to great perfection and the invention and improvement of many useful and ingenious arts,

Figure 12   'Europa': Cesare Ripa, Iconologia (1644). (Photo: Rijksmuseum-Stichting, Amsterdam.)

Figure 13   Frans Francken, Allegory on the abdication of Emperor Charles V in Brussels (1555). (Photo: Rijksmuseum-Stichting, Amsterdam.)

Figure 14   Amsterdam as a ship receiving the goods of the nations. (Photo: Rijksmuseum-Stichting, Amsterdam.)

Figure 15   George Richardson, Iconography *(1776). (Photo: British Library Board, London.)*

particularly navigation, are wholly owing to the genius and industry of the inhabitants in this principal part of the world.

(Richardson, 1779, pp. 30–31)

Europe now stands next to an elegant temple rather than holding one in her hand. This, according to the eighteenth-century explication, indicates not only 'the sanctity of their religion' but also 'the wisdom and ingenuity of the inhabitants and the excellency of their government' (Richardson, p. 31). Ripa mentions here only that Europe was the continent with the most powerful potentates, the Emperor and the Pope. The explanatory text of this emblematic book is therefore amended by Richardson according to the ideas of the Enlightenment. The image of Europe wearing a crown was polished and refined into an ideal of civilization. It is to this topic that we now turn.

The civilization of Europe

Christianity continued to play a role in the self-image of Europeans during the eighteenth century but it was no longer the dominant force that it had been in previous centuries. By the end of the eighteenth century Europe and Christendom were no longer synonyms. European feelings of superiority were based on a conglomeration of ideas proceeding from the Enlightenment which, in turn, came to be associated with the notion of civilization. In charting the progress we need to consider the ideas of several philosophers and political theorists.

Montesquieu

Montesquieu in 1748 in *De l'esprit des lois* ('The Spirit of Laws') provides a commentary on the political significance of Europe and at the same time extends and gives greater depth to it. Montesquieu is very much in the tradition of those who, from Machiavelli onwards, regard Europe as a secular concept unconnected with the notion of Christendom and who identify Europe with the idea of freedom.

In this book an attempt is made to explain the peculiar nature of Europe, especially by comparison with Asia. It is striking to note that in doing this Montesquieu is following in the footsteps of Hippocrates more than two thousand years before (see above), in dealing with the question of 'how noticeably peoples differ from one another according to the climate in which they live'.

In his own aphoristic manner, Montesquieu deduces political enslavement from climatic conditions. Asia is without a temperate climate: great heat and intense cold adjoin one another, he says. In Europe, however, the temperate zone is very extensive, even though the climates of Spain and Scandinavia differ greatly. In Asia, powerful nations in cold conditions and weak nations in the heat live immediately adjacent to one another, with the result that the former can easily conquer the latter. In Europe, on the other hand, strong nations adjoin one another within the same temperate climate. This, according to Montesquieu, is the major reason for the weakness of Asia and the strength of Europe, of Europe's freedom and Asia's enslavement. It is for this reason that in Asia the extent of freedom never increases, whereas in Europe, depending on circumstances, it waxes or wanes (Livre 17, Ch. 3). The above ideas concern the freedom of Europe in the context of international relations. However, he also formulates the principle of the separation of powers as the precondition for freedom in internal politics. He considers that most European monarchies have a moderate system of government, since the ruler possesses the legislative and executive powers but leaves the administration of justice to his subjects. The Ottoman Empire, where the Sultan unites all three of these powers in himself, suffers under the most appalling despotism (Livre 11, Ch. 6).

So far, we have been dealing with the definition of Europe from a primarily political point of view. Nevertheless, one also finds in the works of Montesquieu the first signs of a culturally-oriented definition, for example in the *Lettres Persanes*, which he published anonymously in 1721. This much-reprinted political satire is in the form of letters supposedly written by Persian visitors to Paris. From the moment they arrive, the Persians are confronted by one surprise after another. Paris is the same size as Isfahan, but the houses are so tall that they would seem to be inhabited by astronomers. The city is built right up into the air, with five or six houses one on top of the other, and the streets are full of an enormous bustle of activity (*Lettres Persanes*, no. 24). The pace of life and work is utterly astonishing for the orientals:

> I have been here a month and have yet to see anyone walking…they run
> and they rush. The slow wagons of Asia, the measured tread of our
> camels – it would frighten them to death…

one of the visitors writes home to Smyrna, and he speaks in this connection of 'European manners and customs' ('des moeurs et des coutumes européennes'). Another letter (*Lettres Persanes*, no. 106) speaks of the urge to work and the passion to enrich oneself ('cette ardeur pour le travail, cette passion de s'enrichir'); one sees nothing but work and industriousness ('on n'y voit que travail et qu'industrie').

Such remarks have been viewed as constituting the first impetus for theories of an opposition between the dynamism, work ethic, and even capitalism of Europe and the inertia, placidity and eternal immobility of Asia (Chabod, pp. 73–4). What is in any case true is that this early work of Montesquieu expresses a belief in the disparate mentalities attributable to Asians and Europeans.

The main theme, however, of *De l'esprit des lois*, published more than twenty-five years later, is political organization. Europe is the continent which is free of despotism. The spirit of the laws in Europe is in opposition to such a system. For Montesquieu, Europe is certainly not the continent of civilized customs and good manners to the exclusion of all other continents. Even so, he does sometimes suggest that European 'moeurs et coutumes' differ form those prevalent in Asia and in Russia. Montesquieu mentions the example of Peter the Great, the Tsar who in the early eighteenth century imposed European customs and manners on Russia (in a non-European way, namely despotically) by forcing the nobility to shave off their beards and by prohibiting the wearing of long robes (*De l'esprit des lois*, Livre 19, Ch. 14). He refers to Russia in this connection, incidentally, as a European nation ('une nation de l'Europe').

Voltaire

The clear idea of communal European customs and manners is also to be found in the works of a far more popular contemporary of Montesquieu, namely Voltaire. In *Le siècle de Louis XIV* (1751), he writes that 'Christian Europe' can be viewed as a large commonwealth of different states, some of them monarchies and others having a mixed system of government, but all of them interconnected. All European states have the same religious background, despite this being divided into a variety of sects, and all have the same principles of civil law and politics, which are unknown elsewhere in the world. It is because of these principles that European nations do not turn prisoners of war into slaves, that they respect the ambassadors of hostile nations and that they sensibly attempt to maintain a communal balance of power (Voltaire in Adam (ed.), 1966, p. 40).

In a section dealing with the arts and sciences a cultural interpretation of the term Europe comes to the fore. Voltaire's thesis is that despite the wars and religious discord which have afflicted it, Europe has seen the rise of a 'république littéraire' (Adam, p. 70; *cf.* Chabod, p. 30). The arts and sciences reinforce one another and provide mutual support. The academies in the various states together form a European republic of artists and scholars:

> The English, the Germans and the French go to Leyden to study. The famous doctor Boerhaave was consulted by both the Pope and the Tsar. His pupils attracted foreigners who became doctors elsewhere.

The true scholars in each discipline have strengthened the ties uniting this great scientific and artistic community of Europe. This, says Voltaire, is a great comfort in a world in which ambition and politics cause so much ill.

We have already seen that, alongside Christendom, humanism was one of the factors uniting the élites of the various countries of Europe. In the sixteenth century, a feeling of community had grown up between all those who enjoyed the same sort of classical education. Voltaire's ideas quite clearly spring from this humanistic conception of the *Respublica litteraria*, but contain a new dimension in that the natural sciences are in his view so very important.

Five years after the *Le siècle de Louis XIV*, Voltaire published his much more extensive *Essai sur les moeurs et l'esprit des nations* (*Essay on the Customs and Spirit of the Nations*, 1756, ed. Pomeau 1963), the first attempt to provide a general overview of the whole of human history up to the century of Louis XIV, as seen from the perspective of the history of civilization. It is a major attempt to write a new sort of world history according to the ideals of the Enlightenment, with the writer distancing himself from the Bible, which until then had formed the standard frame of reference. Voltaire makes plain that the histories of Egypt and China are more ancient and important than those presented in the Bible. He states that Europe, 'our Europe', has become incomparably more populous, rich, and civilized since the days of Charlemagne, even in comparison with the Roman Empire (*Essai*, Résumé 811). Europe has become the continent of the Enlightenment, although some parts are still shrouded in darkness. However, civilization and the development of science and scholarship had originated in the East – Voltaire especially admires China – and in 'our Europe' are of only recent date.

Anarchy and darkness dominated Europe for centuries, Voltaire maintains, but at the end of the Middle Ages its peoples demanded such a measure of freedom and rights that eventually the barbaric system based on slavery was overturned. The nations of Europe gained their freedom, and from then on their inhabitants were considered to be people rather than slaves. Nevertheless, Voltaire is of the opinion that this was not yet sufficient to make them civilized and enlightened (Voltaire in Pomeau, 1963, pp. 776–79). That process would take centuries.

Voltaire considers the Europe of his own time to be the most civilized continent, but he often uses the example of non-European countries as a means of exposing European abuses and evils. He assumes that human nature is basically the same all over the world, and that the differences between peoples result from the differing extent to which reason has been 'cultivated'. By nature they are all equal; the differences between them are the result of their level of cultivation. How splendidly Europe would flourish, were it not for incessant unnecessary wars! And how widespread would be the arts and sciences, were it not that such a great number of men and women are buried alive as monks and nuns! Thus Voltaire, who cannot resist comparing the damage done to Europe by warfare with the nefarious effects he attributes to the monastic life.

The concept of Europe propagated by Voltaire is an anticlerical one. He sees the dominant position Europe has gained in the world as being based on the development of the arts and sciences. Indeed, that is ultimately the consolation he offers in the face of dispiriting events, including those of his own day. The nations of Europe have always managed to rise from the ashes of various disasters and civil wars, due to their knowledge of the arts and sciences (Pomeau, pp. 810–12).

Adam Smith

The growing awareness of a European civilization was based on a tangible increase in the wealth of nations, which could afford to finance costly standing armies and expensive artillery. The theorist and propagandist of a new liberal economic order, in which material self-interest was coolly and soberly made the basic principle of economics, was Adam Smith (1723–90).

In his *Inquiry into the Nature and Causes of the Wealth of Nations* (1776), the Glasgow professor even goes so far as to consider firearms advantageous to civilization, since they are expensive and complicated to manufacture and therefore stimulate economic activity more than the bow and arrow and the catapult (Seligmann (ed.), 1947, p. 198). Montesquieu, by contrast, had pointed out the disastrous economic effects of maintaining large armies of mercenaries. In the same line of thought, Voltaire had lamented the growth of standing armies, although he added the positive note that warfare between armies of mercenaries might spare the civilian population to a greater extent. As he remarks lightheartedly in the *Essai*,

> The citizens of besieged cities are sometimes transferred from one ruler to another without it costing the life of a single one of them. They are merely the winner's prize, gained by whoever has the most soldiers, cannon and money.
>
> *(Pomeau, 1963, p. 812)*

Adam Smith is therefore taking a great step by considering the arms industry a stimulus to the economy, and thus to 'the extension of civilisation'. His spelling of 'civilisation' (with an 's') suggests that the word is taken from the French. 'Civilisation' is a key concept. For an insight into the intellectual climate of the eighteenth century we need to tease out its meaning. But first of all we need to have a look at the related concept of culture.

The concept of culture

The term 'culture' has both individual and social applications. The roots of the concept as regards individuals go back to classical antiquity. For the Greeks, and for Plato (428–347 BC) in particular, *paideia* (literally 'upbringing') was a central concept in personal development and a goal in itself. It was the privilege of only a small section of the population, and was directed towards intellectual development and not everyday activities and trades. The nature of *paideia* was therefore élitist, idealistic and anti-utilitarian.

Educating children was often compared with the cultivation of crops. In Latin, the term *cultura agri* (taking care of the land) finds its analogy in Cicero's (106–43 BC) use of *cultura animi* (forming of the mind). Likewise, in sixteenth-century French, one has Montaigne's comparison between educating children and cultivating plants. 'Culture', originally an agricultural term, is thus used by Montaigne in a metaphorical sense (*Essais*, Livre I, Ch. XXV, 'De l'institution des enfants'). He speaks of 'culture de l'esprit' (*Essais*, Livre I, Ch. XXV), and several of his contemporaries use the word 'culture' in the same sense but without a genitive form following it.

In English, too, the term 'culture' is found in the metaphorical sense. The seventeenth-century philosopher Thomas Hobbes (1588–1679) writes in his *Leviathan* that 'the labour bestowed on the earth is called culture, and the education of children a culture of their minds' (Lindsay, 1947, p. 192).

Alongside this expression for personal intellectual development there was also politeness (French 'civilité'), and in higher levels of society courtliness ('politesse'). A distinction was made early on between bourgeois good manners and the affectation of courtiers. Outward behaviour thus implied a social dimension. Similarly this was the case with customs and manners, which were associated with towns and the courts of princes. Good manners as such had never been definitely associated with Europe. Throughout the Middle Ages, the Imperial court in Byzantium, and not in Rome, had been the great examplar of courtly manners and customs.

After the period of the great discoveries, much attention was paid to non-European peoples, but in the sixteenth and seventeenth centuries this did not lead directly to the identification of Europe with certain superior manners and customs. Indeed, non-European peoples were not infrequently held up as being exemplary. Even cannibalism, a practice which for many was a decisive means of distinguishing between human and animal, and which was the subject of a large number of sensational reports, was considered by Montaigne in the sixteenth century to be less barbaric than the revolting torture meted out by Christians to one another in the name of the true faith (*Essais*, Livre I, Ch. 30).

Nor does Montesquieu associate good manners in general with Europe in particular. 'Politesse' is seen by him as a characteristic of the court. Despotism, an essentially non-European system of government, 'produces idleness, and idleness in its turn gives birth to courtly politeness' ('Le gouvernement absolu produit l'oisivité et l'oisivité fait naître la politesse') (*De l'esprit des lois*, Livre 19, Ch. 27).

'Culture' in the metaphorical sense of intellectual exercise and the development of the faculty of reason has not only the Greek 'paideia' as a synonym, but also the Latin 'eruditio' and the German 'Bildung'. All of these, however, had always been related to individuals. It is not until the late eighteenth century that the social dimension – previously described as 'civilité' or 'politesse' – comes to be associated with 'culture'; in other words, it is only then that the word begins to be used to refer to something collective.

The concept of 'civilization'

The social dimension which the concept of culture gained in the course of the eighteenth century, is a product of the Enlightenment and it was the French word 'civilisation' which came into being to describe it. The word was coined in the 1750s, more or less in passing, by the popular 'Friend of Man' ('ami des hommes') the Marquis de Mirabeau (father of the more famous Mirabeau who played such a significant role in the French Revolution), a great admirer of Montesquieu, popularizer of the enlightened ideas of the Physiocrats and a lively if not profound writer (Moras, 1930, p. 47; Riquetti, 1758–1759, p. 326).

It is noticeable that neither Montesquieu nor Voltaire use the noun 'civilisation', but they do use the adjective 'civilisé'. It has been suggested that Voltaire, whose *Essai sur les moeurs et l'esprit des nations* is the first attempt to produce a general history of civilization, avoided the new word 'civilisation' because he considered it offended against good taste. Even so, the word soon became current, both in French and in other European languages. It can in certain respects be considered as a secularized form of the concept of Christendom (Rauhut, 1953, p. 83), but it is also clearly associated with the belief in progress that became popular during the course of the Enlightenment. In this way the idea of levels or phases of 'civilisation' rapidly became a familiar one.

The new word entered the English language as 'civilization', although some users objected to it, preferring the older form 'civility' (French 'civilité'). A familiar passage from Boswell's life of Dr Johnson, the editor of the *Dictionary of the English Language*, illustrates this:

> On Monday, March 23 [1772] I found him [Johnson] busy preparing a fourth edition of his folio Dictionary… He would not admit *civilization*, but only *civility*. With great deference to him, I thought civilization from *to civilise*, better in the sense opposed to *barbarity*, than *civility*…
> *(Chapman (ed.), 1953, p. 155)*

Johnson's opposition was in vain, and 'civilization' became accepted into the English language.

In German, the term 'Cultur' (originally written with a C) became in the course of the eighteenth century the synonym for 'civilisation'. The word therefore came to be used in German to refer not only to the original concept of the culture of individual persons, synonymous with *Bildung*, but also to refer to the social concept. One finds a parallel to the French usage 'histoire de civilisation' in Johann Christoph Adelung's *Versuch einer Geschichte der Cultur des menschlichen Geschlechts* (1782). The philosopher Herder speaks of *Cultur* as synonymous with *Aufklärung* (enlightenment). He concludes that the distinction between the two terms is merely a difference in metaphors, one from agriculture and the other from light, but with no difference in meaning (quoted in Rauhut, p. 86). However, as the philosopher Moses Mendelssohn noted in 1784, the words *Aufklärung*, *Cultur*, and *Bildung* were new words belonging to a literary style of language which was not comprehensible to the German general public (quoted in Rauhut, p. 87). The word *Zivilisation* was indeed adopted from the French, but was considered to be a rather unfortunate loan word. (See the following essay by Peter Bugge as regards the contradistinction between Kultur – now written spelled with a K – and Zivilisation).

European civilization

Twenty years separate the 'spiritual' sketch of the manners and mentalities of nations by the French *philosophe* Voltaire and the 'materialistic' study of the wealth of nations by the Scottish economist Adam Smith. During those two decades, roughly the third quarter of the eighteenth century, it became usual to associate Europe and civilization with one another. The expression 'La civilisation européenne' was first used in 1766 (see J. Moras *Ursprung*) in a work on the French colonies in North America probably written by the French Physiocrat, the Abbé Baudeau. He recommends not only converting the American Indians to Christianity but also to European civilization in order to make real Frenchmen of them! ('...convertir ces naturels non seulement à la foi chrétienne, mais encore à la civilisation européenne, en faire à peu près de vrais français par adoption...') (quoted in Moras, 1930, p. 47). It is notable that for him European civilization and Christianity are not one and the same thing. It would seem, however, that he, as a Frenchman, considered that civilization and France were indeed one and the same. France had a universal vocation to fulfil, not only to Christianize but also to civilize. In this context, the expression 'European civilization' presupposes a confrontation with non-Europeans after a process of conquest and colonization. Christianity can form part of this, but European civilization is nevertheless more than Christendom alone. This is a remarkable change, for we have seen how the concepts of Europe and Christianity were previously more or less associated. Civilization, then a relatively new word, becomes a synonym for Europe (and for the French, therefore, for France itself).

It should especially be noted that the concept civilization had a clear and positive connotation, coinciding with a growing feeling of European superiority. However, this feeling did not stand in the way of an increasing interest in areas outside Europe.

This seeming contradiction is made understandable if one realizes that the concept of civilization should not be conceived as fixed, but rather as a process directed towards an ideal state. It was the growing popularity of the idea of progress, mentioned before, that was the kernel of this meaning. It implied that within the *process* of civilization a distinction was made between various levels or phases. It was taken as a matter of course in this connection, that Europe should be seen as the embodiment of the highest level of civilization. As we have seen this view is illustrated unambiguously by the way Europe was depicted allegorically, for instance, by the architect George Richardson: the image of Europe wearing a crown reflects such an ideal of civilization.

In the course of the nineteenth century, an enormous expansion in the use and meaning of the term civilization took place. The nineteenth is indeed the century of the total identification of civilization with Europe.

1789–1848: different ideas of Europe

Revolutionary ideas and reflections on the old Europe

The French Revolution was a watershed in social and political thinking and its impact was felt all over Europe. Until the Revolution, the peasants, who continued to constitute the largest single category in the population of Western Europe until well into the nineteenth century, still lived in the shadow of feudalism. Their situation was not as bad as that of their fellows in Central and Eastern Europe, but a great many of them continued to serve and work the land for feudal masters. The seeds of revolution were already present in many of the countries of Western Europe. In the words of Tocqueville, in what is still a fundamental analysis of the Ancien Régime and the Revolution, France was not the god which created the seed but rather the ray of sunshine which caused it to sprout (A. de Tocqueville, *L'Ancien Régime et la Révolution* (1856, in OC 2 (1952) 34).

Peasant revolts were endemic in the old Europe. The great Revolution in France was in a sense the most successful of a whole series of revolts signalling the end of the Ancien Régime and transforming the hated feudal system.

A certain continuity remained, however. For example, the Revolution meant a continuation rather than a break with the traditional centralized internal structure of the country, and the monarchy and Church survived in a modified form. Nevertheless, the feudal legal structure had gone for ever. It is true that, in certain remote backwaters, remnants of the feudal system stubbornly remained right into the twentieth century, but they were feudal atavisms, experienced all the more bitterly by the peasantry because of the fact that the principles of the Revolution were familiar to them and were enshrined in legislation.

'Men are born free and with equal rights, and remain so', according to the famous declaration of 26 August 1789. In the legal structure and the mental atmosphere of feudal society, this new freedom and equality of *all* citizens was non-existent (J. Godechot, *Les constitutions de la France depuis 1789* (Paris, 1979) *Déclaration des droits de l'homme*).

The French declaration of the rights of man (1789) enshrines various ideas and phrases which were first set down during the American Revolution, but had a far wider range of application and was much more a document of principle. Its influence was also much greater, France being the most powerful country in Europe. France was not the New World but an ancient monarchy in which the church and the aristocracy had gained enormous privileges and riches for themselves.

Article 2 of the Declaration states that liberty, property, security and resistance to oppression are the natural and inalienable rights of all. The following article states that full sovereignty rests with the nation and that there is no other source of authority. In the name of this national sovereignty, all 'intermediary bodies or institutions' such as 'estates' and guilds, with all their privileges, are abolished. It is not Montesquieu's ideas of the balance of powers and the laws (in the plural) which are dominant during the turmoil of the Revolution. National sovereignty should rather follow the 'volonté générale' (general will), coined by Rousseau, which finds its expression in the Law (singular). The king's attempt to flee the country in 1791, which ended in his capture at Varennes, and the war with Austria (1792) led to the escalation of the Revolution. The fatherland was in danger and the king was considered a traitor. A turning-point came in 1792, when the Prussians and the emigré forces which had taken Verdun and were marching on Paris were defeated at Valmy. The republic was officially confirmed, the monarchy abolished and the Revolution grew more widespread. The king was executed. The Revolution degenerated into the Terror, with thousands condemned to the guillotine. The Revolution became a monster which devoured its own children. To idealize the Revolution is to falsify history: the principle of equal rights for all was baptized with the blood of the victims, and that blood was by no means always blue.

The ideals of the French Revolution had a great impact throughout Europe, and though in some places at first greeted with much enthusiasm were in others violently opposed. Liberty, equality and fraternity were trumpeted everywhere. The whole of the old Europe was shaken, to the horror of many with established interests. Revolutionary propaganda naturally led to a counter-revolutionary reaction. What is remarkable in this connection is the fact that the idea of Europe and the realization of belonging to a European community were much more clear among those who attempted to resist the revolution than among its supporters. It is almost as if, in the revolutionary mentality, there was hardly any place for Europe in between citizenship of the world and of one's own nation. In contrast to this the counter-revolutionary writers do indeed display a realization of Europe, often mixed with a desire for the restoration of the old situation.

A good example of this is to be found in Edmund Burke, whose *Reflections on the French Revolution*, published in 1790, was immediately translated into French and shortly after into German. Some years later, in 1795, after the end of the Terror and with France under the rule of the moderate Directory, Burke describes Europe as follows:

> At bottom [religion, laws and manners throughout Europe] are all the same. The writers on public law have often called this aggregate of nations a commonwealth. They had reason. It is virtually one great state having the same basis of general law, with some diversity of provincial

customs and local establishments. The nations of Europe have had the very same Christian religion, agreeing in the fundamental parts, varying a little in the ceremonies and in the subordinate doctrines. The whole of the polity and economy of every country in Europe derived from the same sources. It was drawn from the old Germanick or Gothick customary, from the feudal institutions which must be considered as an emanation from that customary; and the whole has been improved and digested into system and discipline by the Roman law. From hence arose the several orders, with or without a monarch...in every European country... From all those sources arose a system of manners and of education which was nearly similar in all this quarter of the globe; and which softened, blended and harmonized the colours of the whole. There was little difference in the form of the universities for the education of their youth, whether with regard to faculties, to sciences, or to the more liberal and elegant kinds of erudition.

And Burke ends with the remark that:

From this resemblance in the modes of intercourse, and in the whole form and fashion of life, no citizens of Europe could be altogether an exile in any part of it... When a man travelled or resided for health, pleasure, business or necessity from his own country, he never felt himself quite abroad.

(Burke, Three letters on the proposals for peace with the Regicide Directory of France, 1796; in Rogers (ed.) 1850, p. 299)

Burke writes about this Europe in the past tense. The French Revolution has broken with the state based on the system of 'estates', with the Christian church and with the ancient universities. France is the centre of Jacobinism, there are militant factions in every country in Europe. There is a state of civil war throughout Europe, a war between those who support 'the ancient, civil, moral and political order of Europe, against a sect of fanatical and ambitious atheists...It is not France extending a foreign empire over other nations: it is a sect aiming at universal empire and beginning with the conquest of France'. The Jacobin leaders had been successful. They had conquered France, the centre of Europe, and were now attempting to gain control of the rest of Europe. (Burke, ibid., letter 2, *Genius and character of the French Revolution as it regards other nations*, 1796, in Rogers (ed.), p. 306).

Napoleon and the new Europe

The Revolutionary storm subsided, only to be followed by a tempest in the form of Napoleon. From the point of view of this study, there are two significant points to be made. In the first place, the expansion of France under Napoleon meant that the ideas and institutions of the Revolution were spread, leading to a measure of uniformity and coherence in large parts of the European continent. Furthermore, domination by Napoleonic and French tyranny formed an excellent breeding ground for nationalist movements.

His aristocratic opponents referred to Napoleon as a 'Robespierre on horseback'. His *Code Napoléon*, rescinded the first attempts at social legislation which the

Revolution had introduced and replaced them by the protection of private property; nevertheless, all became equal before the law and feudalism was abolished. Likewise all privileges and *corps intermédiaires* (intermediary bodies or institutions) were abolished.

Napoleonic expansion was the result of French national fervour, and after the initial enthusiastic reception of the liberation armies in Belgium, the Netherlands, Germany and Italy, it unleashed nationalist movements everywhere. At the pinnacle of his power, Napoleon announced the Continental System, aimed at the arch-enemy England, which had begun a naval blockade. Russia joined the system. One could therefore truly speak of a 'Fortress Europe'. The Austrian Emperor gave Napoleon his daughter's hand in marriage (1810), thus uniting the Corsican Buonaparte clan with the imperial Habsburg dynasty.

Never before had there been such a concentration of power in Europe. Besides the *Grand Empire*, there was a circle of subservient states ruled by members of Napoleon's family. On the continent itself, only Sweden, Denmark, Norway, Austria, Russia and the Ottoman empire were not directly within the Napoleonic sphere of influence. The Russian campaign of 1812 was a turning point which led to the collapse of the Grand Empire, but it was only in 1815 that Napoleon was finally defeated at the Battle of Waterloo. The unity, under French domination, which he had wished to impose on Europe was replaced by the old idea of the balance of power (see above).

In August 1816, when Napoleon had finally been defeated and was an exile on Saint Helena, he looked back on his life and referred to himself (naturally making everything finer than it had actually been) as the 'médiateur natural entre l'ancien et le nouvel ordre' ('the natural intermediary between the old and the new order': *Mémorial* I, in Walter (ed.), 1963, p. 1075). He had wished to bring about an 'association européene' which would have brought prosperity and happiness to the continent. There would have been the same system throughout Europe, with the same principles: 'un code européen, une cour de cassation européenne, redressant pour tous les erreurs...' ('one European code, one European court of appeal redressing all errors'). There would have been a single European currency, a uniform system of weights and measures, the same laws. Napoleon also proposed a European Academy and European prizes to stimulate scientific research. Europe was to become one family and one people, and travellers would have found themselves in a common fatherland wherever they went (see also *Mémorial* II, p. 345, 6 November 1816).

This is a vision of a future Europe which is diametrically opposed to Burke's view of the European past. For a long time, following on from the ideas of Burke, Europe's past would play a more important role than its future.

Europe's historical foundations

The most important result of the Revolutionary turmoil for the concept of Europe was that it received an historical credence, which had previously been lacking. The tremendous break with tradition as such was incomprehensible. After some time the turbulent events, the chaotic succession of regimes were seen as historical necessities. All these upheavals were the catalysts of change in the intellectual climate, which made it normal to see a whole range of phenomena as the result of historical development. In this post-revolutionary period quite a number of notions, which had been theoretical and abstract, became historical concepts. This historical way of thinking enriched and deepened the concept of Europe. The term 'Europe' came to be used in a much more conscious manner. It had a familiar ring for centuries but now came to be endowed with historical interpretations and political ideas. The idea of Europe became more significant, but there was no question of a version that commanded general agreement. Various groupings had their own idea of what Europe had been and ought to be.

Europa Christiana

'Es waren schöne glänzende Zeiten, wo Europa ein christliches Land war' ('they were splendid times when Europe was a Christian Land') is the first line of the famous essay *Die Christenheit oder Europa* which Novalis[2] wrote in 1799 (Novalis, in Kluckhohn and Samuel (eds), 1983, p. 501). The work is a poetical exhortation to religious revival and is full of nostalgia. According to Novalis, medieval Europe had been one large Christian community with a single spiritual leader: the Pope. The Papacy had now been destroyed (the Pope having being imprisoned, and the Papal States turned into a republic in 1798). The Middle Ages should serve as a source of inspiration for the revival of the Christian faith and the visible Church, without national borders being considered.

In France too, the country where the sharpest criticism of the church had been expressed and where a mercilessly anticlerical policy had been pursued, there was a radical change in the value attributed to Christendom and the Middle Ages. Chateaubriand[3] had an enormous effect with his *Génie du christianisme* (1802), in which he sang the praises of the influence of Christendom on poetry, literature, music, architecture, theology and forms of worship. Christianity had a formative, salutary effect in all areas of life. Compared to classical Antiquity, the Christian Middle Ages had an unmistakable moral superiority. Were not infanticide and divorce common in Antiquity, and was it not the case that before the rise of Christianity there had been no political cohesion? 'Les sociétés flottaient éternellement entre l'anarchie populaire et le despotisme' ('Societies continually fluctuated between popular anarchy and despotism'; Reboul (ed.), 1966, p. 250).

The reassessment of the Christian Middle Ages gave the concept of Europe a historical foundation. The idea of Europe was thus given a clearly defined and developed historical perspective, which had been lacking even as late as the eighteenth century. The concept of European culture has indeed arisen in the eighteenth century, but the *history* of European culture as an idea in itself originated only in the

---

[2]   Novalis was the pen-name of Friedrich von Hardenberg (1772–1801), a German romantic poet who was called the 'Prophet of Romanticism'.

[3]   François René, Vicomte de Chateaubriand (1768–1848), French writer and politician. His *Génie du christianisme*, a vindication of the Church of Rome, elevated him to pre-eminence among French writers of his day.

nineteenth. The concept of Europe became a dynamic one. This historical vision of Europe was closely connected with contemporary political, social and religious ideals and ideas of what the future should bring. The concept of Europe was therefore not only historicized, but also politicized; in other words, it was seen more and more in historical terms, with contemporary political debate forming the frame of reference. Roughly speaking, the division was one between the supporters and the opponents of the ideals of the Revolution, but within both parties there were considerable differences of emphasis with regard to the vision of Europe.

Europe according to the Holy Alliance

In 1815, the Tsar of Russia, the Emperor of Austria and the King of Prussia formed an alliance intended to promote brotherhood between the peoples of Europe on a Christian basis and under the leadership of the old legitimate rulers. It was an ecumenical alliance of Greek Orthodox Russia, Catholic Austria and Protestant Prussia, a supranational organization which tolerated no interference with the alliance of throne and altar and whose members undertook to intervene in the case of national and liberal agitation which formed a threat to the restoration of the old order.

It is remarkable that within the concept of Europe, ascribed to by the supporters of the Holy Alliance, Russia is not only given equal footing as a member of the Concert of Europe but that, according to some writers, the Slavic–Greek Orthodox element could ensure the regeneration of the old Latin–Catholic and German–Protestant Europe (Gollwitzer, pp. 235–6*ff*). Within this vision, Russia is therefore not placed in a sort of waiting-room where, in accordance with the eighteenth century ideas of the Enlightenment, it must first receive the benefits of more civilization before being admitted to the world of European culture, but is viewed as the saviour of European Christian civilization, which in the West has fallen into decay.

Idealized visions of the religion and politics of the Middle Ages were very popular in the post-revolutionary period. These ideals were grafted onto the concept of Europe. The desire for peace and the recovery of authority by the grace of God was in a sense projected back into the Middle Ages and then used as an historical argument in contemporary political debate.

As we saw above, it was only in the fifteenth century that it became usual to identify Europe with Christendom. At the beginning of the nineteenth century, however, the idea of Europe was projected back much further in history. A search was instigated for the roots of European civilization. Europe, which in the Middle Ages had in fact hardly existed other than as a geographical expression, became an accepted historical category. The historical writings of the nineteenth-century romantics made it appear that in the Middle Ages there had been a conscious idea of Europe. The notion gained ground that out of the ruins of the Roman Empire (the Latin element), the Barbarian peoples (the Germanic element), led by the Christian Church, had been amalgamated to form the true European civilization. This ideal Europe, which was seen as being situated in the Middle Ages, had, in present times, fallen into decay under the influence of atheism and Revolution and needed to be restored to its old glory.

Such ideals could sometimes take on mystical form. But there were also defenders of the Holy Alliance whose motives and visions of Europe were of a more mundane nature. An example of this attitude towards Europe is to be found in none other than Metternich (1773–1859), the Chancellor of Austria. As he himself said, Europe was one single fatherland (Chabod, p. 109). After the Napoleonic period, he had become more conscious than ever of the mutual interdependence of the states of Europe. In Metternich, and in other proponents of *Realpolitik* in the Restoration period, one finds not a romantic–religious enthusiasm but rather the idea of Europe as a commonwealth of states, which must see to it that a balance of power is preserved, along the lines that had existed between the sixteenth and the eighteenth century. Metternich, who attempted to pull the strings of the pentarchy, the five ruling states England, France, Austria, Prussia and Russia, was mocked as the 'Baron de balance'.

The Restoration thus saw a gigantic alliance to counter the revolution. The opponents of the revolution could be motivated by entirely different considerations. It is therefore possible to trace two completely divergent visions of Europe – that of Christian unity among the romantics and that of the balance of power among the conservative realists – among the defenders of the Holy Alliance.

Europe according to the liberals

The opponents of the Holy Alliance were numerous, and their progressive and revolutionary ideals were based on completely different ideas of Europe. Yet among progressives the idea of Europe was also bound up with a vision of the continent's historical development. In many respects this vision was opposed to that of the reactionary romantics. It corresponded, however, with the latter, when the interpretation of the *history* of Europe became the topic of a debate in which historical arguments were used to reinforce current political ideas and ideals.

It is notable that liberal authors were already making a distinction between West and East European powers (Gollwitzer, p. 220). One of them even speaks of a division of Europe into 'deux zônes de sociabilité', a western one which is liberal and an eastern one which is conservative. The distinction can be seen as one between constitutional and absolutist forms of government. This division of Europe which extended westward beyond the Atlantic to take in the Republic of the United States and eastward to include the empire of the despotic Tsar of Russia, was considered a new and fundamental characteristic of modern times (Gollwitzer, pp. 222–3). The contrast between East and West would continue to be very popular when circumstances gave occasion for it to be utilized (see, in the following essay by Peter Bugge, the discussion of the Second World War).

Among the liberals the author with the greatest influence on the formation of the historical foundations of the idea of Europe was François Guizot (1787–1874). During the period of the restoration of the Bourbon monarchy, he was one of the leaders of the liberal opposition. As Professor of Modern History at the Sorbonne, he gave notable lectures on the origin and development of the system of representative government which were vehemently rejected by the supporters of divine monarchy. In 1828, after his suspension had been lifted by the university authorities, Guizot was able to recommence his lectures and began an analysis of the history of Europe from the fall of the Roman Empire to the French Revolution.

For Guizot, European civilization (which he also refers to as modern civilization) begins with the fall of the Roman Empire and the rise of Christendom, in his opinion. What makes Europe superior to all other civilizations is its diversity. Whereas other civilizations are always dominated by a single principle and a single form, a construction which leads to tyranny, the characteristic feature of European civilization is precisely that different principles and forms cannot exclude one another. The variety of elements in European (modern) civilization, Guizot argues, is the basis for the freedom which it currently enjoys (Guizot, *Histoire de la civilisation en Europe*; Rosanvallon (ed.), 1985, p. 77). With the fall of the Roman Empire, the establishment of the Christian church led to a divorce between worldly and spiritual authority, which other civilizations had never known. This divorce between the world of deeds and the world of thought is, in Guizot's view, the fundamental source of the freedom of conscience for which so many struggles and so much suffering had taken place in Europe and which had only been victorious at a late stage, often against the wishes of the clergy.

Despite his respect for the Church, the protestant Guizot does not idealize the Middle Ages. He sees the Reformation of the sixteenth century as the rebellion of the human spirit against absolute authority in the spiritual field. Guizot considers the Reformation as an '*élan de liberté*' ('outburst of liberty'; p. 262) and as an enormous step forward towards freedom of thought and the emancipation of the human spirit (p. 264).

Guizot also views the Glorious Revolution of 1688 in England as an extremely positive factor in the development of liberal Europe. William of Orange, the leader of the protestant (Dutch) republic, was a chief opponent of the absolute monarchy of Louis XIV, and set himself up as the head of a European league for religious and civil freedom (Rosanvallon, pp. 284–5).

The ideas of the Enlightenment in the eighteenth century are also seen by Guizot as progress, as a stage in the liberation of the human spirit. Nevertheless, he also points out how, during the French Revolution, the absolute rule of radical ideas, without account being taken of other rights, made it possible for tyranny to arise (Rosanvallon, pp. 300–3).

In his opinion every human power, even that of democracy, needs to be kept within bounds. Freedom, which forms the essence of European civilization, is the result of its pluriformity, which must be guaranteed.

Guizot's vision of the development of Europe became the standard view in liberal circles, not only in France but also elsewhere, in particular in England. It was not only a lucid analysis of the history of Europe, but also one that could be used to reinforce the political demands of the liberals in the struggle against the alliance of throne and altar.

The revolution of 1830 in Paris meant the end of the ultra-royalist regime of the Bourbons and established the constitutional Orléanist monarchy, in which Guizot played a key role as chief minister. Events seemed to justify the liberal vision of the development of Europe, but in the late 1840s powerful democratic movements, to the left of the liberals, grew up in many countries.

The increasing demand for democracy and for social reforms to favour the broad lower classes of the population were also reinforced by calling on history. Alongside the liberal vision of the historical development of Europe, a democratic vision of history came into existence which, as in the case of the reactionaries and the liberals, was also closely associated with current political and social ideas and ideals. In 1848 the year of revolutions, visionaries turned activists.

Europe according to the democrats

It was in the 1840s that popular culture was recognized. Until then the vast lower layers of society had been regarded as barbaric. It was taken for granted that the concept of civilization was to be identified with the élite. Commentators, such as the historian Michelet[4] , not only identified themselves with the victims and the oppressed but also made the common people the driving force of history and the primary factor in the development of civilization. This popular culture was placed largely in the context of the nation. The concept of civilization, which until then had been almost synonymous with Europe as a whole, was now eagerly aligned with national borders. European civilization was subdivided into various national cultures.

The increasingly louder call for an extension of the right to vote and for social reform also had a largely national framework of reference. Many advocates of democracy hoped for the elevation of the people on a national scale.

During the first half of the nineteenth century, national movements had a predominantly romantic bias. While the reactionary romanticists glorified the Catholic Middle Ages and praised the union of throne and altar, the progressive romanticists found their inspiration in the ideals of the French Revolution, ideas let loose by the French Revolution. A good example is Giuseppe Mazzini (1805–72), the champion of the Italian *Risorgimento*. His ideal was that of an independent (anti-Habsburg), liberal (anti-clerical) and classless (anti-feudal) united Italy. After the failure of the 1830 revolt, he fled to Marseilles where he founded the Young Italy Movement. In 1834 he started an International of progressive nationalists in Switzerland. This movement, which took the name *Young Europe*, included such groups as *Young Germany, Young Poland* and *Young Italy*. Like the Jacobins of the French Revolution, they believed in universal human rights and the equality and fraternity of all peoples (*Histoire de l'Europe*, p. 325, *cf.* Gollwitzer, pp. 304–6).

We have already noted (see above) that the national awareness and ideals of cosmopolitanism of the late-eighteenth century revolutionary mentality seemed to leave hardly any room for the idea of Europe. It is remarkable, therefore, that half a century later the concept of Europe has a very prominent position in the men-

---

[4]   Jules Michelet (1798–1874) at one time collaborated with Guizot at the Sorbonne. His greatest works were his monumental *Histoire de France* (24 vols, 1833–67) and *Histoire de la Révolution* (7 vols, 1847–53).

tality of the revolutionaries of 1848. The liberation of the citizen is to take place within the nation and vast layers of the population are to take part in the national culture: the country should reconcile the social classes with one another. Subsequently, however, these reborn nations should become part of the brotherhood of European peoples.

Democrats therefore see Europe not as a balance of powers according to the views of political realism, but as a federation of nations: there was no place for hatred among the individual nations, the ultimate aim being fraternization. Michelet even went as far as to describe the relationship between France and its major rival, England, as '*deux amants opposées, deux électricités, positive et négative*' ('two opposed lovers, two electricities, positive and negative'), which should not be mixed and interchanged if progress was to be made (Michelet, *Le Peuple*; in Morazé, 1962, p. 224).

Under the influence of democratic ideals, an important change took place in the historical perspective of the idea of Europe. Until the middle of the nineteenth century, the origin of Europe was inevitably linked with the demise of the Roman Empire. The establishment of Christianity towards the end of that Empire was considered to mark the starting point of European civilization. This was not only the standard idea among conservative Catholics but also among liberals, for example Guizot. George Grote (1794–1871), an English banker and member of a small but influential group of radicals, published a history of Greece (part one appearing in 1846), which brought about a fundamental revaluation. It was no longer the establishment of Christianity, but Athenian democracy, which was to be regarded as the cradle of European civilization. Grote, who had been a Member of Parliament and a fervent advocate of widespread democratization, was the first to point out the political significance of Athens as the cradle of democracy.

It is true that Greek civilization had been hailed for a long time as the mother of philosophy, science, literature and art, but its political heritage had been largely ignored. As a result of Grote's position, however, the history of Greece came to be viewed in a different light (Gooch, 1913, pp. 291–97). It was emphasized that the highest achievement of the Greeks was to have established political freedom in a type of democracy which had for centuries been unsurpassed. The fact that women and slaves were excluded from the Athenian democratic system did nothing to tarnish the revolutionary appeal of the concept of the history of a European civilization, with its earliest roots in Athens rather than in Rome.

We have come full circle. Europe initially no more than a geographic indicator, was first identified with freedom in the context of the Persian wars. Centuries after this identification had disappeared, it was replaced by the identification of Europe with Christendom and subsequently, in the eighteenth century, with civilization. During the first half of the nineteenth century, the concept of Europe was given a historical perspective. We can see a detailed awareness of the history of Europe emerging, with Christianity and liberty as its leitmotifs and with civilization as a kind of all-embracing concept. As the call for political democratization grew louder and the concept of liberty became radicalized, it becomes useful to extend the history of Europe further into the past and to make Athenian democracy and Greek liberty the memorable starting-point of Europe.

Europe in the grip of nationalism (1848–1914)

The 1848 revolution sent a tremendous shockwave through Europe. Barricades were thrown up almost simultaneously in many capitals.

This development illustrates the solidarity and cohesion which had emerged on the European mainland. The issues, however, were not always the same. In Paris, the emphasis was on social issues, while elsewhere the main point was the introduction of a liberal constitution or, first of all, national independence. The Habsburg Empire was shaken to its foundations. Metternich fled to England; revolts broke out in Vienna, Prague and Budapest. The Austrians were driven from Milan, while Naples, Florence, Rome and Turin adopted liberal constitutions. In Prussia, Bavaria and the Netherlands the liberal demands were also met. The reformists, however, largely inhabitants of the cities, constituted an intellectual élite lacking wide public support and with little influence among the peasantry, who still made up the majority of the population in most European countries. A successful reaction soon followed. The Habsburgs restored their power in Prague, among the Czechs, and in Vienna. Assisted by the Russians, they succeeded in suppressing the Hungarians and Northern Italy was reoccupied by the Austrians.

The era of romantic idealism was over. The second half of the nineteenth century was dominated by political realism. The national liberation movements also ceased dreaming and started to adopt a pragmatic approach.

After a series of confusing events, Italian unification was achieved in the 1860s, led by the small kingdom of Sardinia-Piedmont. In 1866, the same year the Habsburgs had to cede Venice to Italy, Prussia gained a decisive victory (against Austria) and the Prussian monarchy took control of the newly established North-German Federation. German unification was then brought about within a few years.

Until German unification, France was the most powerful state on the European mainland. After winning the elections, with universal suffrage (for men), Napoleon's cousin established the Second Empire. As Napoleon III, he played a decisive role in the process of Italian unification and annexed Nice and Savoy. In 1870, the driving force behind German unification, the Iron Chancellor Bismarck, challenged Napoleon III into declaring a war which marked the end of French supremacy. The French suffered a crushing defeat, Napoleon III was captured and Paris was besieged. A national defence was organized, but Paris had to capitulate. In Louis XIV's palace of Versailles, the King of Prussia was proclaimed Emperor of Germany. Alsace-Lorraine was annexed by Germany.

More than ever before, Europe came into the grip of nationalism. It was not only the unification of Italy and Germany, but also the rivalry among the individual nations within Europe and abroad (in the colonies) that created a climate in which the idea of belonging to a European community was pushed into the background.

The vigorous process of national unification extended beyond Italy and Germany; people living both in rural communities and in cities in old political nations such as France, England and the Netherlands were turned into national citizens from the second half of the nineteenth century onwards. The entire educational system, from primary school to university, was stimulated and influenced by nation-building. Historical education played an important role in this process. The study of history had expanded enormously during the nineteenth century and was now being greatly encouraged and financed by national governments. Historiography and the teaching of history were given a national resonance in the countries of Europe, which they still retain. Reflecting on the past was inseparable from the pervasive process of nation-building. Historiography became a kind of national genealogy, with contemporary politics as the starting-point and the history of literature and art being viewed through the nineteenth-century nationalist looking-glass.

The period between 1871 and 1914 was one of armed peace. The issue of Alsace-Lorraine prevented a good relationship developing between France and Germany. At the beginning of the twentieth century, we even see the emergence of a true arms race, fuelled by the aggressive foreign policy of the German Empire. In this strained nationalistic climate, it seemed as if many were consciously aiming at a great European war.

Political thought, dominated by national self-interest, could be very cynical about Europe. This is illustrated by Bismarck's statement that to him, the Chancellor of the newly-established German Empire, Europe was merely a geographical expression. And when Bismarck, having explained Prussian plans to the English ambassador, was told that 'Europe would not allow it', he replied with the question 'Who is Europe?' (Gollwitzer, p. 340). In 1876, Bismarck wrote that he continually heard the word Europe being used by politicians to demand something from other powers which they were afraid to ask for on their own behalf (Gollwitzer, p. 447).

This man, who had enforced German unification, was not concerned with Europe. German unification was brought about against the wishes of the other European powers. For centuries, Europe had ignored Germany. 'As Europeans we were always made to do the donkey-work for others', said Bismarck, 'but as Germans we have no intention of playing this role'.

There were, of course, alternative voices to those proponents of *Realpolitik*. Even in Germany, there were those who remembered what Immanuel Kant had written as early as 1795 in a theoretical treatise entitled *Zum Ewigen Frieden* (Towards Eternal Peace). In this treatise, he stressed the need for the creation of a league of nations and sketched a federal Europe (Gollwitzer, p. 90, Denis de Rougemont, *L'Europe, invention culturelle, History of European Ideas I* (1980) 33). Kant argued that from the point of view of Reason there was no other way to legalize the relationship between states than through the creation of a community of peoples (in the same way as individuals have to abandon total freedom, which leads to anarchy, and obey certain rules).

The creation of a 'United States of Europe' was propagated with enthusiastic *élan* in 1848, but such ideas were voiced even much later, for example when the Polish revolt was crushed by the Russians in 1863 and when the Serbians rose against Turkish domination in 1876. The latter bloody event prompted Victor Hugo to argue once more in favour of the necessity of creating a European federation, 'on which necessity all philosophers agree'. The acts of cruelty committed in Serbia prove that Europe needs 'une nationalité européene, un gouvernement uni, un immense arbitrage fraternal, la démocratie en paix avec elle-méme...' ('a European nationality, united government, great fraternal arbitration – democracy at peace with itself'). And Victor Hugo would not have been a true Frenchman if he had not suggested Paris as the capital (*Histoire de L'Europe*; Carpentier and Lebrun (eds), 1990, pp. 363–64).

There were other pleas like Victor Hugo's, but they had little effect on European politics. Leading politicians considered them unrealistic ideas from the past, originating from the naïve idealism of 1848. That these ideas of a United States of Europe, however old-fashioned, would become very relevant again in the twentieth century, after the horrors of two world wars, could not be anticipated. During the heyday of nationalism, there was no room for supranational organizations.

This did not mean, of course, that Europeans lacked self-confidence as Europeans. It is remarkable that in Germany, France, England, Italy, and elsewhere, there existed a deep-rooted awareness of one's own nation sharing a vague but common European destiny. Even the most ardent nationalistic polemics contained an element of what one might call a 'European sous-entendu' (implicit understanding about Europe): the idea that the European nations had in common their superiority over non-European nations provided the impetus for their rapid expansion outside Europe.

This leads to the paradoxical conclusion that the era of rising nationalism is also the time of boundless belief in European supremacy and unlimited European self-confidence. It was the era of unprecedented European expansion. Progress came to be regarded as almost synonymous with European civilization. The idea was widely held that the history of the world had reached its highest level of development in European civilization. Europeans were to lead the way elsewhere as the world moved towards progress and civilization.

While Europe's self-confidence flourished, however, the secret undermining of cultural assuredness had begun. Both within and outside Europe, new civilizations were discovered. We have already noted the emergence of popular culture in Europe during the 1840s. At the end of the nineteenth century, non-European peoples became the object of extensive ethnographic studies, which accompanied the colonization process. These peoples also appeared to possess civilization in some form or other.

At the beginning of the nineteenth century it was highly unusual to use the plural form of the term 'civilization'. During the second half of the nineteenth century, however, the morals and customs of 'primitive' peoples also came to be worthy of the name *culture*. Besides European civilization, there is a *Primitive Culture*, which is also the title of Edward B. Tylor's famous anthropological work. It must be admitted, though, that in the England of 1871 this was still regarded as an unusual application of the word culture. Cultural relativism was absent in Tylor's work and he remained faithful to the idea of progress and European civilization. To him and most other ethnologists, ethnology was a science which served the laborious, but necessary and steady elevation of primitive peoples towards the blessings of European civilization. (E.B. Tylor, *Primitive Culture, Researches into the development of mythology, philosophy, religion, art and custom*, 2 vols. London 1871). *Cf.* J. Leopold, *Culture in comparative and evolutionary perspective: E.B. Tylor and the making of primitive culture* (Berlin, 1980).

It was not until the Great War of 1914, however, that the simple equation of Europe and civilization ceased to exist as a dominant idea. The awareness of crisis was all-pervasive, even in those countries not directly involved in the war. Could anybody be so insane as to still believe in uninterrupted progress and the values of so-called civilization after the hell of Verdun? A sense of doom pervaded Europe. Europe was associated with degeneration and decline. Yet even this feeling of despair, that touched so many, was a form of European self-awareness.

References

Author's note: The author would like to acknowledge the debt he owes, in particular, to the work of Denys Hay (on the Middle Ages), Heinz Gollwitzer (on the nineteenth century) and Frederico Chabod (on modern history).

ACKERMANN, H. C. and GISLER, R. J. (eds) (1988) *Lexicon Iconographicum Mythologiae*, vol. IV, Zurich, Artemis Verlag.

ADAM A. (ed.) (1966) Voltaire: *Le siècle de Louis XIV*, Paris.

ALVAREZ, M. F. (ed.) (1975) *Corpus documental de Carlos V*, vol. II (1539–48), Salamanca, Gráficas Europa.

ARNAUD-LINDET, M. P. (ed.) (1990–91) Orosius: *Histoira contre les paiens* (trans. of *Historiae adversus paganos*), Paris, Les Belles Lettres.

'Attributen' (1967) in *Reallexicon zur deutschen Kunstgeschichte V*, Stuttgart, Metzler.

AUGUSTINE, SAINT see: SANFORD, E. M. and GREEN, W. MCA. (trans.) (1965).

BAGROW, L. (ed.) (1930) A. Ortelii: *Catalogus Cartographorum*, Gotha.

BLOCH, M. (1939; 1968 edn) *La société féodale*, Paris, Michel.

BOER, P. DEN (1989) *Europese cultuur: de geschiedenis van een bewustwording*, Nijmegen, SUN.

BRINCKEN, A. D. VON DEN (1965) 'Das geographische Weltbild um 1300', *Zeitschrift für historische Forschung*, Beiheft 6, Berlin.

BRINCKEN, A. D. VON DEN (1973) 'Europa in der Karthographie des Mittelalters', *Archiv für Kulturgeschichte* 55, pp. 289–304.

BULL, G. (intro. and trans.) (1966) Machiavelli: *The Prince*, Harmondsworth, Penguin.

BURN, A. R. (1972 edn) Herodotus: *The Histories*, Translated by Aubrey de Sélincourt, Harmondsworth, Penguin.

CARPENTIER J., and LEBRUN, F. (eds) (1990) Victor Hugo: *Histoire de l'Europe*, Paris.

CHABOD, F. (1963) *Der Europagedanke: von Alexander der Grossen bis Zar Alexander I* (transl. from Italian), Stuttgart, Kohlhammer.

CHAPMAN, R. W. (ed.) (1953; 1957 edn) *Boswell's Life of Johnson*, Oxford, Oxford Standard Authors Series.

CHATEAUBRIAND see: REBOUL (1966).

DEROLEZ, A. (ed.) (1968) *Liber floridus*, Ghent.

ERASMUS see: FESTUGIÈRE, A. J. (ed.) (1971).

FESTUGIÈRE, A. J. (ed.) (1971) Erasmus: *Enchiridion militis Christiani*, Paris, Vrin.

FISCHER, J. (1957) *Oriens–Occidens–Europa: Begriff und Gedanke 'Europa' in der späten Antike und im frühen Mittelalter*, Wiesbaden, Steiner.

FREMANTLE, K. (ed.) (1977) *Beelden kijken. De kunst van Quellien in het Palais op de Dam*, Amsterdam.

GERLO A. (ed.) (1979) *La Correspondence d'Erasme*, vol. VIII (1529–1530), Brussels, Presses Académiques Européennes.

GEURTS, P. M. M. (ed.) (1989) *Vrede's weeklacht* (trans. of *Querela Pacis*), Baarn, Ambo.

GILES, J. A. (ed.) (1847) *William of Malmesbury's Chronicle of the Kings of England, from the Earliest Period to the Reign of King Stephen*, London.

GODECHOT, J. (1970) *Les constitutions de la France depuis 1789*, Paris.

GOLDSCHMIDT, V. (ed.) (1979) Montesquieu: *De l'esprit des lois,* Paris, Garnier-Flammarion.

GOLLWITZER, H. (1951) 'Zur Wortegeschichte und Sinndeutung von Europa', *Saeculum 2*, pp. 161–65.

GOLLWITZER, H. (1951) *Europabild und Europagedanke: Beiträge zur deutschen Geistegeschichte des 18. und 19. Jahrhunderts*, Munchen.

GOOCH, G. P. (1913; 1952 edn) *History and Historians in the Nineteenth Century*, London, Longman.

GUIZOT see: ROSANVALLON, P. (ed.) (1985).

HAY, D. (1957; 1968 edn) *Europe: the emergence of an idea,* Edinburgh, Edinburgh University Press.

HERODOTUS see: BURN, A. R. (1972 edn).

HIPPOCRATES see: TOYNBEE, A. J. (ed., trans.) (1924).

HOFMEISTER, A. (ed.) (1912) *Otto of Freising: Chronica, Sive historia de duabus civitatibus V. Monumenta germaniae historica. Scriptores rerum germanicum*, Hannover.

HUIZINGA, J. (1950) *Verzamelde Werken*, vols. VI, VII, Haarlem, H. D. Tjeenk Willink & Zoon.

JOSEPHUS see: THACKERAY, H. ST J. (trans.) (1930; 1978 edn).

KAEBER, E. (1906) *Die Idee des europäischen Gleichgewichts in der publizistischen Literatur vom 16. bis zur Mitte des 18. Jahrhunderts*, Berlin.

Kataloge des Kunstgewerbemuseums, vol. I. (Berlin, 1963).

KLUCKHOHN, P. and SAMUEL, R. (eds) (1983) Novalis (pseud. Friedrich Leopold von Hardenberg): *Schriften*, vol. 3, Darmstadt, Wissenschaftliche Buchgesellschaft.

KNIPPING, J. B. (1974) *Iconography of the Counter Reformation in the Netherlands*, Leiden, De Graaf.

KRETSCHMER, K. (1891) 'Eine neue mittelalterliche Weltkarte der vatikanischen Bibliothek', *Zeitschrift für Erdkunde,* 26 , pp. 371–406.

LAARHOVEN, J. VAN (1991) *Europa in de bijbel*, Nijmegen.

LECLERC, J. V. (ed.) (1826) Montaigne: *Essais*, Livre I, Paris.

LEOPOLD, J. (1980) *Culture in Comparative and Evolutionary Perspective: E. B. Tylor and the making of primitive culture*, Berlin.

LINDSAY, A. D. (ed.) (1947) Thomas Hobbes: *Leviathan*, London.

LINDSAY, W. M. (ed.) (1957) Isidori Hispalensis episcopi, *Etymologiarum sive originum libri XX*, Oxford, Clarendon Press.

MABLY, ABBÉ DE (1773) *Le droit public de l'Europe fondé sur les traités*, Amsterdam/Leipzig.

MACHIAVELLI: see BULL, G. (intro. and trans.) (1966).

MERCATOR, *Europa* (1st edn Duisburg, 1554); Facsimile Lichtdruk Reichsdruckerei nach dem Original in der Stadtbibliothek zu Breslau, herausgegeben von der Gesellschaft für Erdkunde zu Berlin (Berlin, 1891).

MEYER, J. P. (1952) (ed.) Alexis de Tocqueville: *L'Ancien Régime et la Révolution*, Paris, Gallimard.

MICHELET see: MORAZÉ, C. (ed.) (1962).

MILLER, K. (ed.) (1898) *Mappae Mundi*, vol. VI, Stuttgart.

MONTAIGNE see: LECLERC, J. V. (ed.) (1826).

MONTESQUIEU see: ROGER, J. (ed.) (1964).

MORAS, J. (1930) *Ursprung und Entwicklung des Begriffs der Zivilisation in Frankreich (1756–1830)*, Hamburg.

MORAZÉ, C. (ed.) (1962) Michelet: *Le peuple*, Paris.

NAPOLEON see: WALTER, G. (ed.) (1963–64).

NOVALIS see: KLUCKHOHN, P. and SAMUEL, R. (eds) (1983).

OROSIUS see: ARNAUD-LINDET, M. P. (ed.) (1990–91).

PHILIPS GALLE (*c.* 1580) 'Philips Galle after Marcus Gheeraerts', in *Europe circa 1580*, Rijksprentenkabinet, Rijksmuseum Amsterdam.

POMEAU, R. (ed.) (1963) Voltaire: *Essai sur les moeurs et l'esprit des nations*, Paris, Garnier.

RAUHUT, F. (1953) 'die Herkunft der Worte und Begriffe Kultur, Zivilisation, Bildung', *Germanisch-Romanische Monatschrift*, pp. 83–7.

RAUMER, KURT VON (1953) *Ewiger Friede: Friedensrufe und Friedenspläne seit der Renaissance*, Freiburg/Munchen.

RAYMOND, I. W. (ed.) (1936) Orosius: (*c.*417 AD) *Historiae adversus paganos*; Eng. trans. by King Alfred.

REBOUL, P. (ed.) (1966) Chateaubriand: *Génie du Christianisme*, Garnier-Flammarion, Paris.

RICHARDSON, G. (London 1779; 1979 edn) *Iconology*, New York, Garland.

RIPA, C. (Rome, 1593; 1976 edn), *Iconologia*, (English trans.) New York, Garland.

RIPA, C. (Amsterdam, 1644; 1971 edn), *Iconologia*, (Dutch trans.), Soest, Davaco.

RIQUETTI, V. (1758 1759) *Marquis de Mirabeau. L'ami des hommes ou traité de population*, vols. 1–4, The Hague.

ROGER, J. (ed.) (1964) Montesquieu: *Lettres persanes*, Paris.

ROGERS, H. (ed.) (1850) *The Works of Edmund Burke*, vol. 2, London.

ROSANVALLON, P. (ed.) (1985) Guizot: *Histoire de la civilisation en Europe*, Paris.

ROUGEMONT, D. DE (1980) 'L'Europe, invention culturelle', *History of European Ideas*, **I**, pp. 31–38.

SANFORD, E. M. and GREEN, W. MCA. (trans.) (1965) *The City of God Against the Pagans*, vol V, London/Cambridge, Mass., Harvard University Press.

SCHMIDT, H. D. (1966) 'The Establishment of Europe as a Political Expression', *The Historical Journal*, **9**, pp. 172–78.

SCHMITT, O., GALL, E. and HEYDENREICH, L. H. (eds) (1967) *Reallexicon sur deutschen Kunstgeschichte*, vol. V, Stuttgart, Metzler.

SELIGMAN, E. R. A. (ed.) (1947) Adam Smith: *Inquiry into the Nature and Causes of the Wealth of Nations,* London.

SMITH, ADAM see: SELIGMAN, E. R. A. (ed.) (1947).

SOUTHERN, R. W. (1953) *The Making of the Middle Ages*, London, Hutchinson.

STUBBS, W. (ed.) (1889) *Willelmi Malmesbiriensis Monarchi De Gestis Regum Anglorum Libri Quinque,* vol II, London.

THACKERAY, H. ST J. (trans.) (1930; 1978 edn) Josephus: *Jewish Antiquities* Book I–IV, Cambridge, Mass./London, The Loeb Classical Library.

TOCQUEVILLE, ALEXIS DE see: MEYER, J. P. (1952) (ed.).

TOYNBEE, A. J. (ed., trans.) (1924) Hippocrates: 'Influences of atmosphere, water and situation', Chapter 16 in *Greek historical thought. From Homer to the age of Heraclius*, London/Toronto, Beacon Press.

TYLOR, E. B. (1871) *Primitive Culture, Researches into the Development of Mythology, Philosophy, Religion, Art and Custom*, 2 vols, London.

VIVES, JOANNIS LUDOVICI (1964 edn) *De Europae dissidiis et bello Turcico dialogus* [1526], in *Opera omnia*, tomus 6 (Valentiae, 1784), pp. 452-481; also in *Obras Completas II* (Madrid, 1948).

VOLTAIRE see: POMEAU, R. (ed.) (1963).

VOLTAIRE: see ADAM A. (ed.) (1966).

WALTER, G. (ed.) (1963–64) Napoleon: *Le mémorial de Sainte-Hélène [par] De Las Cases,* Paris, Gallimard.

Essay 2
The nation supreme
The idea of Europe
1914–1945

*Prepared for the Course Team by Peter Bugge
Senior Research Fellow, Slavisk Institut, Aarhus
Universitet*

Introduction

Professor den Boer demonstrated in the first essay how, from the late eighteenth century onwards, a notion of Europe emerged in the shape of *ideas*. It was a notion that consisted of a plurality of conflicting interpretations of Europe, each drawing on a specific set of historical references.

'Europe' has proved to be a highly potent, if imprecise, political concept – hence the frequent attempts at definition:

- Who belongs to Europe and who can be excluded?

- Which values are genuinely (and uniquely) European?

- Is there a threat towards Europe and where does the threat come from – from within or from without?

All the answers to such questions have immediate political consequences and begin to explain why the interpretation of the term 'Europe' has been so disputed.

So, one must be keenly aware that Europe is always seen and interpreted *from somewhere*, from a particular national or political viewpoint. Europe depends on the eye of the beholder and it is not just a problem of, say, competing French, German or Russian versions of the concept or plans for Europe's future. Any thinking about Europe – no matter how much it tries to remain above the level of national self-interest – is likely to be so embedded in a specific cultural, political or religious tradition that its outcome may be incompatible with other, equally sincere ideas, even if they are both expressed in seemingly identical terms. Thus, not only are a Catholic's and a socialist's projects for Europe likely to be different, but so are their perceptions of Europe itself.

I have just drawn a distinction between *perceptions of Europe* and *projects for Europe* and this will shape the argument throughout this essay. By *perceptions of Europe* I mean how Europe is seen, how it has been described and analysed. And since we restrict ourselves to discussing how Europeans themselves have looked at Europe, I could also say that the image covers a European self-understanding, or self-concept.

In contrast, *projects for Europe* is meant to cover political manifestations of feelings of unity and plans for the organization of the continent. Of course, no clear-cut boundaries between the two concepts can be found. All projects are nourished by perceptions of Europe and these perceptions again, at least implicitly, contain suggestions for change.[1]

In short, for the purposes of this essay, we should bear in mind that a host of polemics and special pleading clusters around the term 'Europe'; it may help to clarify the distinction between 'perceptions of Europe' and 'projects for Europe' by drawing attention to the intellectual context in which the political visions, which have most often been the focus of discussion, emerged.

The nation supreme: the idea of Europe 1914–1945

In my search for the idea of Europe in the three decades from the outbreak of one disastrous European conflict to the end of another I will divide my argument in two: first some *projects for Europe* launched between 1914 and 1945 are discussed to see how people sought to counter the perils of two great wars and an unstable peace. However, without a deeper knowledge of the era's *perceptions of Europe*, i.e. the way people looked at Europe, its trends of development, its state of health, and its relations to the surrounding world, we can only get a superficial understanding of these projects and their origins and scope. This complex and often contradictory pattern of perceptions is treated in the second half of the essay. But, before this, I will briefly present some preconditions of the pre-war era and give a short summary of the historical setting, which shaped the era's notions of Europe.

The end of innocence?

To many post-war observers, the last decades before the outbreak of war in 1914 looked like a haven of innocence. These years have been described as a golden era: 'obviously the happiest time in the development of the European society' (Krejčí, 1931, p. 214). There is definitely more than a tinge of nostalgia in such statements, but the contrast in atmosphere before and after the war must have been huge. At the turn of the century, a feeling of optimism and firm belief in progress seems to have prevailed in most European countries: impressive technological and scientific advances allowed for a huge overall increase in wealth, which gave the

---

[1]   The use of the two concepts has been inspired by Heinz Gollwitzer's distinction between *Europabild* and *Europagedanke* (Gollwitzer, 1964, p. 12). 'Europabild' translates approximately from the German as 'image of Europe', while 'Europagedanke' becomes 'idea of Europe'.

growing middle classes a chance to enjoy such luxuries as medical care, bathrooms, and telephones. The poverty of the proletarian masses remained immense, but in many countries social legislation had been adopted and as the social democratic parties turned 'reformist' and were tolerated in the political system, sympathetic intellectuals could even see a 'new proletarian European type' emerge in the disciplined worker organized in the non-nationalist, all-European Second International.

A new brotherhood of man looked plausible: newspapers, telegraphs, trains and travel brought people closer to each other and the world almost visibly seemed to shrink. Stefan Zweig gives an excellent description of the intellectual mood:

> In Vienna we shouted with joy when Blériot flew over the Channel as if
> he had been our own hero; because of our pride in the successive
> triumphs of our technics, our science, a European community spirit, a
> European national consciousness was coming into being. How useless,
> we said to ourselves, are frontiers when any plane can fly over them
> with ease, how provincial and artificial are customs-duties, guards and
> border patrols, how incongruous in the spirit of these times which
> visibly seeks unity and world brotherhood! This soaring of our feelings
> was no less wonderful than that of the planes, and I pity those who
> were not young during those last years of confidence in Europe.
>
> *(Zweig, 1943a, pp. 153–4)*

However, this was only half the truth. The process of rapid industrialization, which revolutionized all aspects of life in the nineteenth century, helped both to create and to destroy a feeling of 'European-ness'. It fostered it through such things as compulsory schooling and improved communications, which gave increasing numbers of people a rudimentary knowledge of European geography and politics. It also helped to undermine it because, as we have seen in Pim den Boer's essay, industrialization was bound up with the process of nation building – and this did not lead to European solidarity but to a fierce nationalism, replacing the *cosmopolitanism* of earlier centuries.

Politically, these trends expressed themselves across Europe in a vociferous nationalistic jingoism at home and a ruthless imperialist race abroad; the new European *internationalism* of the liberal intellectuals or socialist workers was in fact the privilege of a minority. Politically (and partly also intellectually) the sense of Europe as a unity became eroded. Bismarck precisely described the situation when, in 1876, he dryly remarked 'Qui parle Europe a tort' ('Who talks about Europe is wrong' – quoted from Barraclough, 1963, p. 33).

Pim den Boer has well described the paradoxical link between rising nationalism and unlimited European self-confidence. In spite of the growing number of warning voices, we may accept the term 'innocence' as representing a situation where few people could foresee the devastating consequences of the slumbering forces in society, once the war came. These contradictions are summed up by Henry Cord Meyer:

> The age that disappeared into the chasm of the First World War was the
> golden nineteenth century. It was that great European era, so

internationalist in spirit, despite the lack of international organization. In this happy epoch, as it appears to us in retrospect, the intellectual, cultural, and material progress – combined with an unusual diversified balance of diplomatic strength – blinded most men of the century to the full ethical and practical dangers to Western Civilization of reliance upon the cult of naked force in international relations. True, nineteenth-century constitutionalism and respect for the law appeared to contribute an effective safeguard of internal liberty and security. Yet, if the international system was exposed to the caprice of force, internal economic and political security was inevitably jeopardized.

(Meyer, 1955, p. 336)

Europe 1914–1945: some history

What started in 1914 as a traditional European war turned into long years of hitherto unseen mass destruction and deprivation. It ended in 1918 in revolutionary upheaval, turmoil and chaos, which also left the European self-consciousness in ruins. In the meantime the war had become a world war and, not accidentally, the two most spectacular peace plans were launched from outside the traditional European centre: by Lenin's Bolsheviks and by the American president Woodrow Wilson (1856–1924).

The intervention of the USA on the side of the Allies had a decisive impact on the war and demonstrated that the old European era was gradually giving way to a new Western or Atlantic one. Also, Wilson introduced a new element in world politics: politics based on moral principles, rather than on traditional power. To him, the goal of the war was not so much to defeat Germany as to 'make the world safe for democracy', i.e. to create a new, just, world order. This was most profoundly expressed in Wilson's highly idealistic 'fourteen points' speech to Congress of 8 January 1918, which demanded an open diplomacy, respect for the principles of national self-determination both in Europe and in the colonies, free trade and disarmament and finally the creation of a *League of Nations* to protect the liberty of all nations and to secure world peace. Though based in Geneva and heavily dominated by the European powers, the League of Nations represented an attempt at a global peace order rather than a specifically European solution. The League had a certain modest success during the 1920s, but as international conflicts got tougher in the mid-1930s its impotence became obvious. And from the very beginning it was a severe blow to Wilson and the League that the USA refused to ratify the covenant. Instead the USA withdrew into isolationism for two decades.

The Covenant of the League of Nations was part of the Versailles Treaty, but in spite of the rhetoric the peace treaty was written more in the traditional spirit of winners and losers than in the spirit of idealism. Britain and France insisted on imposing very harsh conditions on the beaten enemy with the purpose of weakening Germany as much as possible. Germany was given the whole responsibility for the war, and the country had to accept to pay enormous reparations to the victorious powers. Furthermore, bits of what had traditionally been regarded as German territory had to be ceded to Poland and severe restrictions were put on the size of the German army. Not surprisingly, the Versailles

Treaty was almost uniformly felt as a great injustice in Germany and its re-vision became a major political objective all through the inter-war period.

The restoration of Poland was part of a national reconstruction of Europe, which took place in the name of the Wilsonian principles of national self-determination. A whole number of small nation states were created on the ruins of the Tsarist and the Hapsburg Empires; but, often, their borders were drawn to weaken the losers – Germany, Hungary, and Austria – rather than to satisfy ethnic criteria. In fact, the establishment of a smaller Austria was a se-vere violation of the principle of national self-determination since an over-whelming part of the country's population preferred an *Anschluss* (connection) with Germany.

The immediate result of both the war and the following peace treaty was complete chaos in Germany and most of the newly established countries. For four years the French remained intransigent in their demands for reparations although it was ob-vious that a Germany ridden by hyperinflation and extreme political instability could not possibly pay. In January 1923 French troops even occupied the Ruhr Basin, but it was an operation from which they reaped nothing positive.

But a new factor gradually demonstrated, even to traditional nationalists, that Germany could not forever be treated as an enemy. As the Bolsheviks in Russia managed to stabilize their regime (in spite of not achieving world revolution) a new element was brought into the European reality: instead of war between the nations, the Bolsheviks called for a class war in every country, and so the mere existence of the Soviet state became a direct challenge to liberal democrats and to nationalists of all kinds.

Communism presented itself as a modern phenomenon, an ideology that offered a prescription for the future. The same is true for Fascism, the most radical anti-Bolshevik movement born after the war. Fascists in Italy and elsewhere, and later National Socialists in Germany, considered themselves to be the most efficient and potent opponents of Communism. These two opposed ideologies shared a con-tempt for liberal democracy, which they regarded as decadent, false and outdated. Still it seems right to say that they – unlike the traditional absolutist regimes – were a *perversion* of democracy rather than a *denial* of it: both regimes were un-thinkable without mass involvement and both tried to legitimize their rule as an expression of a mythical will of the people.

Mussolini seized power in 1922, but it took some years before his Fascist regime found its shape. In the meantime a predominantly democratic and relatively peace-ful Europe seemed set for recovery and stability. But the world crisis in the late 1920s destabilized most European economies and led to mass unemployment and depression. Before the crisis was over, many European countries had abandoned democracy, most notably Germany with the Nazi triumph in January 1933. In sum, three ideologies were striving for hegemony in Europe: Communism, Fascism, and liberal democracy, the last of which for a long time looked the weakest. This condition led the German historian Ernst Nolte to describe the era as 'The European Civil War 1917–1945'.

A civil war with European implications (though fought more in the name of ideologies than in the name of Europe) did take place in Spain 1936–1939. All the major European powers were involved. The Soviet Union and Nazi Germany gave active support to the Republican and Fascist causes respectively, but the liberal democracies refused to help the Republican government in Madrid and, accordingly, were accused by pro-Republican activists of indirectly supporting Franco. The end result was a complete victory for Franco.

In September 1939 a new European war broke out when Hitler attacked Poland. This move had been preceded by a strange *rapprochement* between Germany and the Soviet Union, as Molotov and Ribbentrop in August 1939 signed a treaty of non-aggression, which secretly divided Poland and the rest of east-central Europe into 'spheres of influence' and paved the way for Hitler's war. In spite of fierce British resistance it looked as if Hitler was close to complete victory, but his assault on the Soviet Union in June 1941 proved less successful than first expected. The British-Soviet alliance that ensued was reinforced by the USA after the Japanese attack on Pearl Harbour on 7 December 1941. Once again Europe had to rely on outside forces until American and Soviet soldiers shook hands in Berlin (May 1945), thereby signalling the complete defeat of Nazi Germany and the end of the Fascist epoch. (Franco's regime persisted in Spain until his death in 1975, but it became increasingly obvious that its survival was an anachronism, and the same might be said of Salazar's Fascist regime in Portugal, which crumbled after his retirement in 1968.)

Projects for Europe

We can now turn to some of the most important projects for Europe launched in this period. First, I will discuss the scope of two conflicting plans for Europe proposed during the First World War. Then I will consider several proposals, made in the relatively stable period of the mid-1920s after the initial post-war chaos, for a united democratic Europe. However, Fascism and Nazism posed a formidable challenge to democratic forces in Europe, so it will also be necessary to discuss the solutions to the European 'menace' offered by these ideologies as well as the opposition and resistance to them, both before and during the Second World War.

The effects of the Great War

The First World War sent millions of young men to their slaughter; but in addition, on the home fronts, the whole populations of the warring countries were mobilized and involved to a degree hitherto unknown.

This had severe ideological repercussions. The values of nineteenth-century liberalism were swept aside as war hysteria gripped the combatants. Nationalists saw in the war an opportunity to purify the nation and to find a new spiritual community above the trite and petty conflicts of everyday life. National self-worship and the call for unity led to demands for discipline and strong men. The enemy was smeared in every possible way: in Germany, a 'Hassgesang gegen England' (i.e., 'chorus of hate against England') became immensely popular, and a racist interpretation of the war as a conflict between primitive Slavs and superior Germans was used in the propaganda against Russia. The Germans were not alone in these facile denunciations of the enemy; the British, for example, were exhorted to fight against 'the Huns'.

This led to the near collapse of two networks of European solidarity. The *brotherhood of European intellectuals* was profoundly shaken as all too many writers and artists tried to exceed each other in patriotism. Appeals from the few moderates or pacifists who remained loyal to the ideals of pre-war Europeanness were received with suspicion and incomprehension. The notion that one had to be loyal only to one's fatherland was widespread even in neutral countries, so when the French writer Romain Rolland (1866–1944) published his pacifist article *Au-dessus de la mêlée* ('above the conflict') in 1915 he was condemned as a traitor not only by official France, but also by conservative newspapers in neutral Denmark (Boll-Johansen, 1988, p. 162).

Also *socialist internationalism* as expressed in the Second International quickly evaporated as the parliamentary Social Democratic parties all voted for war. Some socialists, especially in the strong German and Austrian parties, even saw the war as a short cut to socialism since wartime economy would require strong state planning and control. And so the war – and a German victory – could be justified as an historically progressive and necessary step towards the desired goal. In the first years of the war, socialist opposition to it was insignificant.

As the war went on and the senseless horrors of battles such as Verdun piled up, the feeling became widespread that something more than a traditional war between states was taking place. The need for a global interpretation grew and, for instance, the question of *guilt* was intensively discussed on all sides, although few still denied sovereign states the right to protect their interests by military means (Nolte, 1991, p. 124). The Allies were uniformly convinced that Germany bore the whole responsibility for the war; accordingly they tended to interpret the war as a conflict between civilized democracies and barbarous Prussian militarism. In Germany the spectrum of opinion was wider, ranging from truly imperialist calls for a total German victory, which would secure the country its rightful place in the sun, to interpretations of the war as a defence of German identity against the threat from British capitalist utilitarianism.

It is debatable whether any 'true' Europeanism was at all possible under these circumstances. Jean-Baptiste Duroselle simply states that 'De 1914 à 1918, il n'y a plus d'Europe' ('From 1914 to 1918, there was no Europe'; Duroselle, 1965, p. 261) and skips the war years completely. However, I will present two programmes for a new Europe – one from each side of the front line – which, in spite of their obvious bias and political utilitarianism, both contain an element of idealism that at least partially transcends the narrow national interests of their proponents. Both focus primarily on central Europe and, in spite of the political obsoleteness and oblivion to which they were soon exposed, they have retained their ideological relevance: the two positions reappeared with new strength seven decades later in the lively debate of the 1980s on Central Europe (see Ole Wæver's following essay).

Friedrich Naumann's 'Mitteleuropa'

Since Friedrich Naumann (1860–1919) is the first author presented in this essay, we must put his contribution into perspective. To begin with, Naumann was not the first German to think in 'Mitteleuropean' terms, although he definitely added much to the potency and popularity of the concept (Meyer, 1955, pp. 106*ff*). And secondly, Mitteleuropa was just one among many German foreign policy options and not the most influential. Wilhelmine policies during the war had other aims, which modified the direct political impact of Naumann's proposals. We will in fact meet a poetic vision of Europe rather than a full political project.

A German 'Mitteleuropa' or a 'Mitteleuropean' Germany? Friedrich Naumann's intentions have not stopped puzzling both adherents and opponents of his visions. Nor has the fundamental question of Germany's role in Europe lost any of its relevance (credit: Bildarchiv Preussischer Kulturbesitz, Berlin).

However, the immediate success in Germany and Austria in 1915 of Friedrich Naumann's book *Mitteleuropa* (variously translated as 'Mid-Europe' or 'Central Europe'), proved how much people were longing to find some higher meaning in the ongoing war. Naumann very persuasively managed to see something positive in the deprivations and to present a vision for a happier future. Naumann was a theologian who had also studied national economy. He was a member of the Reichstag and he was known as a spokesman for liberal causes, but before the war he had shown little interest in central Europe or models for supranational cooperation, as he eagerly favoured a German overseas colonial expansion.

The war forced him to look in new directions. The last words of Naumann's book clearly describe the experience that gave birth to his vision:

> Mid-Europe [*Mitteleuropa*] is the fruit of war. We have sat together in the war's economic prison, we have fought together, we are determined to live together!

> *(Naumann, 1915; 1916 edn, p. 287)*

The 'war's economic prison' mentioned is the economic blockade upheld by the *Entente* powers, and primarily Britain, against the Central Powers. It added economic warfare to the long list of means employed in the conflict and contributed severely to the want and starvation in Germany and Austria in the later years of the war. The blockade meant an end to Germany's colonial dreams and demonstrated how much Germany and Austria were dependent on domestic resources.

Naumann propounded that the more or less accidental military union of Germany and Austria-Hungary could be turned into associations of real solidarity leading to a better post-war order in central Europe. Mitteleuropa, he argued, would become a political necessity. Trenches would remain the predominant form of defence in the future, and such defensive structures would be reflected in the patterns of economic cooperation. Naumann did not expect the war to lead to lasting peace or harmony in Europe, and though he would not exclude a reconciliation with France in some distant future, France seemed to be too closely tied to Britain for the time being. So he envisaged a post-war Europe with two 'Chinese walls' of economic and military character running from north to south through the continent, one between Germany and France, the other somewhere between Germany and Russia. Naumann's main concern was to avoid a third wall between Germany and Austria-Hungary, which would weaken both powers. As for the smaller nations in Europe, Naumann expected defence needs and economic centralization to make it impossible for them to survive without alliances with the great powers, so he welcomed the Balkan States and, perhaps later, belligerent Italy in his Mitteleuropa.

Naumann was careful not to go into constitutional niceties and left questions such as nationality problems to the separate states, but the *Oberstaat* ('overstate') he envisaged was a somewhat loose confederation dealing first of all with economic matters – creating a huge Central European common market – and defence. Naumann anticipated that military imperialism (the 'Chinese walls') would lead to a highly controlled and integrated economy in peace as well as war. Mitteleuropa was very much the means to justify these economic ends.

Naumann found historical justification for his project in the mediaeval Holy Roman Empire of the German Nation. In his mind's eye he saw a Central European community of culture and politics, re-emerging in a modern, liberal democratic form under a natural German supremacy. Goodwill was needed for the project, but economy would be the driving force of integration and Naumann was in no doubt that German efficiency, organizational skills and work ethics would set the standard for the whole region. Naumann admitted that this firm regime in all spheres of life would seem to many like an unattractive loss of individual freedom and that it would contribute to feelings of German unpopularity common in other countries. But he nevertheless considered this trend towards an *Organisationsstaat* ('organizations state') to be a historical necessity as was the concentration of humanity in large competing units until the emergence (in some unspecified future) of a 'United States of the Planet'. Austria-Hungary could first of all contribute to this economic *Grossraum* (a kind of extensive market or arena) with its sense of good taste and quality to soften up the harshness of the North German rationalism.

Naumann preached tolerance towards the smaller nations in *Mitteleuropa*. He found demands for a forced 'Germanization' of these nations both harmful and unnecessary and even praised the Jews for being good mediators and teachers of the correct approach to cooperation in work and business. The Jews and all the small nations, he observed, were fighting loyally in the war and had therefore to be fully respected. Naumann went so far as to suggest that some supranational Mitteleuropean identity should be created, arguing that the central European peoples – unlike their French and British counterparts – were still young and therefore flexible. The 'Mitteleuropeans' were to feel loyal both to their nation and to the broader fatherland – a model he somewhat naïvely found at least partially realized in Austria-Hungary.

Here we find the main problem in Naumann's argument: Naumann himself does not make it clear whether the confederation envisaged was a goal in itself or a means to secure German interests. Naumann took German hegemony so much for granted that he was completely unable to persuade the non-German central European peoples that the foreseen German *Vorherrschaft* ('predominance') would not lead to a direct German *Herrschaft* ('rule'). In this quotation the ambiguity is obvious:

> Mid-Europe will have a German nucleus, will voluntarily use the German language, which is known all over the world and is already the language of intercourse within Central Europe, but must from the outset display toleration and flexibility in regard to all the neighbouring languages that are associated with it. For only so can that fundamental harmony grow up which is essential for a Great State, pressed and threatened from all sides.
>
> *(Naumann, 1915; 1916 edn, p. 108)*

The ambiguity of Naumann's argument was reflected in critiques of his book. Nationalists attacked him for giving up 'natural' German imperialist demands and for weakening the German race, whereas the Social Democrats found his project imperialistic, even though they were generally moderate in their condemnations. Yet others criticized him for striving so hard for Mitteleuropean self-sufficiency that it would leave the region isolated from international free trade, an argument Naumann later tried to parry. In spite of such criticism and his own political misfortunes, Naumann never gave up his vision. In an article written after the collapse of Germany and Austria-Hungary he very unsentimentally bade 'auf Wiedersehen' to Mitteleuropa while still believing that the lives and economies of Germans, Czechs, Hungarians and South Slavs would continue to be sufficiently intertwined to make some kind of supranational cooperation necessary (Naumann, 1918, 1964 edn, pp. 976*ff*).

T. G. Masaryk's 'New Europe'

Naumann's book was almost immediately translated into English. In Britain and elsewhere, *Mitteleuropa* was presented as a piece of extreme German imperialism and a pan-German threat to Allied national interests. The main war objective of the Entente powers was to prevent German hegemony in Europe, but when it came to Austria-Hungary their intentions were less clear. The general trend was to support any split between the two Central Powers but not to allow for the complete destruction of the old monarchy. But to the representatives of the small, non-privileged peoples of Austria-Hungary who demanded autonomy or full independence for their nations, Naumann's book was a gift from heaven. The more Austria-Hungary could be presented as eternally dependent upon Germany, the easier it would be to argue for its dismemberment.

One of the leading figures in this struggle was the Czech philosopher T. G. Masaryk (1850–1937), who in 1914 had gone into exile to fight for an independent Czechoslovakia. Masaryk knew very well that without a complete re-organization of east-central Europe his dream for an independent Czechoslovakia would remain unrealized, so he tried to present his objectives in a broader European framework. From February 1916 the historian R. W. Seton-Watson and other British supporters of the small Slavic peoples published, at Masaryk's request, a journal, *The New Europe*. However, for a long time it was hard to supplement the anti-Austrian propaganda with viable alternatives, since Britain, France and Russia had conflicting ambitions in the region. But the collapse of the Tsarist regime and Woodrow Wilson's appearance on the world stage gave Masaryk an opportunity to present both an explanation of the war and a post-war programme for Europe, which he did in a book, once again called *The New Europe*, published in 1918.

Masaryk described a Europe in the midst of a huge cultural and political transformation – from medieval and authoritarian forms of rule (which he termed 'theocracy') to modern democracies. In modern democracy, he said, freedom was expressed both on an individual level and collectively, as every nation's right to self-determination. So, for instance, the Germans were fully entitled to unite, but in this process the 'Reich' had isolated itself from the general European trend towards democracy: undemocratic at home, Prussian absolutism also perverted the nationalist principles abroad in a wild imperialist *Drang nach Osten* ('yearning for the East'[2]). Next to Germany, Austria had proved unable to modernize and grant its people the rights they were entitled to, and the Habsburg monarchy had degenerated into an 'artificial' and authoritarian regime, totally dependent upon Germany.

In contrast, Britain, France and, not least, Wilson's USA were presented as embodiments of modern democratic principles at all levels of society. So Masaryk could interpret the war as nothing less than the logical culmination of the conflict between 'theocracy' and democracy. So long as Russia had a Tsarist regime, his theory did not fully hold. Hence the Russian revolution of March 1917 was highly welcomed by Masaryk. Russia could now be presented – with a lot of wishful thinking – as being on the road to democracy. Also the Bolshevik takeover in November 1917 was a further boost. The Bolsheviks initially supported the principle of national self-determination, and the revolutionary chaos in Russia made it acutely necessary for the Allies to have reliable friends between hostile Germany and red Russia.

---

[2] 'Drang nach Osten', originally meaning *yearning* for the East, has also come to mean *expansion*, a 'push' towards the East, with the sense of breaking out of a restricted area into a place where there will be more space and freedom, or *lebensraum* (living space).

So Masaryk finally suggested a 'new Europe' consisting of an elongated zone of small nation states between Germany and Russia. He presented it as a fulfilment of the national aspirations inherent in modern democracy, but the pragmatic security considerations against German and Russian expansionism could not be overlooked. Still, Masaryk repeatedly insisted that the new European order would have to be democratic in Wilsonian terms of cooperation, open diplomacy and disarmament.

First of all, Masaryk wanted an independent Czechoslovakia. But he also envisaged a future trend towards regional and later all-European cooperation. He argued that only free and independent nations could join any such supranational structures as equal partners and insisted that there could be no conflict between collective (national) and individual democracy. Of course, he knew that it would be impossible to create ethnically pure nation states, so to make his scheme acceptable he introduced a distinction between *nations* (those entitled to their own state) and *nationalities* or *national minorities* (those ethnic groups too small for independence, or segments

T. G. Masaryk, philosopher and founding father of the modern Czechoslovakia. His programme for a 'new Europe' was a curious mixture of democratic idealism and political expediency (credit: Bildarchiv Preussischer Kulturbesitz, Berlin).

of a larger nation living outside their compatriots' territory, who in the interests of full nations would have to accept minority status) and suggested that full protection of these minorities' rights would suffice to avoid conflicts.

In fact, an attempt was made in 1918 to unite the anticipated new states of central Europe. In October 1918 a *Mid-European Democratic Union* was formed in the USA with representatives from twelve European peoples and Masaryk as its chairman. The union, however, was mostly a propaganda tool and as the organization had no clear mandate from Europe it restricted itself to calls for economic cooperation as a basic condition for later federal measures. It soon fell apart when news about clashes between rival national interests in Europe reached the delegates.

Though making plans for Europe, Masaryk put great emphasis on America's political role in the common Euro-American civilization, and in this respect his views are more 'Western' than traditionally 'European'. But like most of his contemporaries, his horizon never transcended cultures based on Christianity and European traditions. He condemned Turkey as *kulturfremd und barbarisch* ('alien to culture and barbarian'), and said nothing about the colonial system or about extending the principle of national self-determination to non-European cultures.

In both Naumann's and Masaryk's programmes the elements of expediency and national(ist) interests are of course highly visible. But both men tried to face key problems emerging in Europe. To Naumann, modernization was the motor of history and he expected it to require centralization and large-scale economic (and military) cooperation. His Mitteleuropa-project tried to create the appropriate political structures suitable, in the first instance, for the Germans. The problems of economic and military interdependence addressed by Naumann remained real enough, but he clearly underestimated the strength of a subjective factor – Nationalism – both among his German (and German-Austrian) countrymen, who proved very reluctant to share any power with the 'inferior' peoples of the East, and among those small nations who preferred independence to an unbalanced partnership.

Masaryk also focused on modernization, but he put all his emphasis on the factors omitted by Naumann. For him, modernization was essentially a moral and political process towards individual and national self-fulfilment. In the spirit of the German poet and philosopher J. G. Herder (1744–1803) he saw the nation as the 'natural' unit for the organization of society, and he wanted the state to be a mere servant of the individual and the nation. Masaryk was convinced that, if they attained their freedom, all nations would welcome a 'brotherhood of man'. Masaryk was clearly sincere in his desire for international cooperation. But he obviously underestimated the potential for conflict of national tensions in a world not ruled by goodwill alone; and, in the event, his exclusive focus on the notion of national independence compelled him to postpone his supranational schemes for conflict resolution.

Post-war plans for European unity (1923–1930)

Masaryk got his 'new Europe' – or rather one half of it: a whole lot of nation states were created in what looked like the culmination of a process which, in the revolutionary year of 1848, had been coined *the springtime of nations*. Supposedly, this national freedom should lead to the full bloom of a plurality of culturcs – a feature often associated with Europe. However, in reality minority problems, mutual distrust and post-war economic collapse soon exposed the difficulty of drawing the line between national self-realization and nationalistic expansionism. Little became of disarmament plans and economic cooperation as the thousands of miles of new borders in Europe were soon fortified with armies and customs barriers. The liberal Italian ex-premier Francesco Nitti in 1922 lamented the *thorough Balkanization* of Europe (Nitti, 1922, p. 53) and post-war Europe seemed hardly on the verge of becoming a pluralistic and prosperous community.

Nevertheless, the principle of democracy *was* strengthened in Europe after the First World War, and optimistic spirits could hope that war and the succeeding difficulties had made all Europeans understand the need for cooperation. In the years of European recovery after 1923 a number of programmes for a united Europe was introduced, the most influential being the one sponsored by the founder of the *Pan-European Union*, Count Richard Coudenhove-Kalergi (1894–1972). We will first of all examine Coudenhove-Kalergi's ideas and then show how his proposals were given political weight by the French politician Aristide Briand.

Coudenhove-Kalergi's Paneuropa

Coudenhove-Kalergi had an impeccable background for working on behalf of transnational understanding. His mother was Japanese and his father was an Austrian diplomat; and he spent his early, pre-war years in bilingual Bohemia, then in cosmopolitan Vienna. The war and the collapse of Austria that followed was a shock to say the least but, nonetheless, in 1918 he had high hopes that Wilson's peace programme and the League of Nations would secure a better, peaceful world. He was, however, soon disappointed by both the League and the disruptions in Europe and he became convinced that only a politically united Europe could overcome the continent's troubles. A convinced activist, Coudenhove-Kalergi argued for the creation of a *Pan-European Union* as an international pressure group, in his influential *Paneuropa*, first published in 1923.

Coudenhouve-Kalergi's approach was essentially political: although he frequently used historical analogies and arguments, he did not use the past itself as a basis for his ideas. He seemed to take Europe so much for granted that he never had to ask *why* this entity ought to be strong. He observed that the historical era of European world supremacy was over and that the supremacy of the white race had been broken. But the decline of Europe both could and should be halted in order to prevent the continent from becoming a mere plaything of world politics. In an indirect reply to the German philosopher Oswald Spengler (1880–1936) and his immensely popular book *Untergang des Abendlandes* (*The Decline of the West*, 1918), he alluded to the root of the problem as well as the cure:

> The cause of Europe's decline is political, not biological. Europe is not dying of old age, but because its inhabitants are killing and destroying one another with the instruments of modern science... The peoples of Europe are not senile – it is only their political system that is senile. As soon as the latter has been radically changed, the complete recovery of the ailing Continent can and must ensue.
>
> *(Coudenhove-Kalergi, 1923; 1926 edn, p. xii)*

The necessary modernization of the political system of Europe would have to consist in large-scale cooperation instead of the traditional anarchy, since technical progress had made small and conflicting states obsolete. Even the so-called European great powers were by now insufficient, as the world was about to be divided into global power fields. The old European powers were replaced by federally organized world powers, as could be seen in America (both in the USA and in the 'Panamerican' union), in the new Soviet Russia and in the British Empire. Only Europe was lagging behind.

Coudenhove-Kalergi knew the difficulties of defining Europe. Geographical criteria seemed immediately inappropriate, since Europe was merely the western part of the huge Eurasian continent with no natural eastern border. Furthermore, cultural and political definitions had been open to historical revision from the time of the ancient Greeks onwards. Culturally, Europe had spread to all continents, which allowed for several new 'global power fields' with roots in the same culture, but in sharp contrast to this apparent cultural success, Europe as a political entity did not exist. *Paneuropa* was the name given by Coudenhove-Kalergi to this aspirant political Europe to distinguish it from geographical and cultural Europe.

This Paneuropa excluded both Britain and Russia. In Coudenhove-Kalergi's view, Britain had 'grown out of Europe' and become a political continent in its own right, too big and powerful to be included in Paneuropa. However, relations between the two were to be based on cooperation and mutual defence guarantees, and both were to share 'the European cultural task' – i.e. the Europeanization of

*Count Richard Coudenhove-Kalergi in his heyday in the late 1920s –
indefatigable in his agitation for a united Europe (credit: Süddeutscher Verlag,
Munich).*

other parts of the world. Britain by controlling the colonies, and Paneuropa by providing the human raw material for their development. Britain also was to serve as a mediator between Panamerica and Paneuropa, since all three shared the same culture and the same democratic values. And if Britain should somehow lose its empire, its inclusion in Paneuropa would seem natural and obvious.

Coudenhove-Kalergi was much more critical towards Russia. By choosing the Bolshevik way Russia had turned its back on the democratic principles now pre-dominant in Europe, and so the borderline between the newly founded eastern European democracies and Russia should mark the eastern end of Paneuropa. Also, Russia saw itself more and more as a specific *Eurasian* entity and as an in-dependent global power field. Coudenhove-Kalergi was not in any doubt that Russia would soon recover after its devastating civil war, and that it would pursue its traditional politics of expanding to the West. Whether red or white, Russia would always seek hegemony, and only through mutual cooperation would the small European countries stand a chance of resisting this pressure. Coudenhove-Kalergi prophesied that a Russian Napoleon would arise from the revolutionary chaos and – if Europe did not unite – would push the borderline of Europe all the way back to the Rhine. The same would be the result if a revanchist Germany tried to unite with Russia instead of with France and the rest of demo-cratic Europe. In spite of his severe critical stance towards Russia, Coudenhove-Kalergi allowed for the possibility that – if democracy proved vic-torious – Russia might some day return to the pro-European line of Peter the Great.

Unquestionably, Paneuropa's main function was to secure the peace: internally in Europe by creating a supranational structure based on obligatory arbitration and multilateral cooperation, thereby reducing the risk of border conflicts by diminish-ing the importance of borders; and externally through a Pan-European defence al-liance protecting the small European nations against threats from outside, primarily from Russia. The hope was that, in the fullness of time, a united Europe could also secure a global balance of power allowing for large-scale disarmament.

Next to security (and tied to it) the European economy was fundamental to Coudenhove-Kalergi's argument. As he saw it, economic autarky and a devastat-ing arms race between the many small European states would keep the continent in a permanent state of crisis and prevent its recovery from the war. On the other hand, Paneuropa could render much of the defence expenditure obsolete and pro-mote economic growth by creating a 'common market' without internal customs barriers. Thus united, Paneuropa would be in a very favourable position in the glo-bal economy.

Coudenhove-Kalergi obviously had to take into account the new post-war Europe with its trend towards small nation states rather than huge supranational units. In addressing this problem, he chose to follow a line of historical reasoning similar to Masaryk's. Nations were not dismissed as irrelevant to Europeanness; on the con-trary, all modern culture was rooted in nationhood and the principle of nationality was to be revered. In the nineteenth century the competition between dynastic-imperial and national liberal principles had divided Europe. But the war had led to a complete victory of the principles of the latter over the former. Masaryk was even called the 'spiritual heir' of Mazzini[3] and 'the executor of his will' (Coudenhove-Kalergi, 1934, p. 84). Coudenhove-Kalergi found this link helpful. The principles of democracy and nation states had achieved widespread recognition: by now – he said – no European 'Kulturnation' ('culture–nation') was without national sovereignty.

Clearly, the potential for conflict, primarily in Eastern Europe with its many national minorities, was still very strong; and Coudenhove-Kalergi could see both the injustices of the system of borders imposed by Versailles and the protracted problems that would arise if the borders were to be redrawn. To solve this dilemma, Coudenhove-Kalergi pragmatically suggested that the status quo of postwar borderlines was to be respected, but that national minorities were to be protected by a common European 'Magna Carta of Tolerance'. In a wider perspective, nationality problems would be diminished by means of both economic and political integration and by the penetration of democratic principles: the bonds between citizenship and national affiliation would be lessened and borders would gradually lose their importance.

In his book *Europa erwacht!* (*Europe Awake!*, 1934), Coudenhove-Kalergi in a sharp engagement with Nazi theories rejected all notions about nations being objective, naturally-given entities. He dismissed all theories of consanguinity as nonsense, noticing that there were no such things as pure races in Europe. Ethnically all Europeans were cousins, and any attempt to divide the white race (whose existence he accepted as fundamental to Europe!) into sub-groups was both utterly unscientific and anti-European. Nor could families of language have anything to do with similarities of race or origin and, as Switzerland and Belgium proved, Coudenhove-Kalergi argued, nations could exist and flourish even without a common language. In short, the concept of a nation was both indeterminable and changeable.

Nations could best be compared to schools, since they were essentially spiritual communities shaped by common teachers and leaders. Few of these founding fathers had actually been nationalist, but nationalism had become an *Ersatzreligion* ('substitute religion') for the bourgeoisie in its emancipation from the nobility and the church. Later, compulsory school attendance had helped to make nationalism a mass phenomenon, as the illiterate and unaware masses learned about the virtues of their own country's culture, but not about its broader international context. This led to nationalist megalomania, but true education could highlight the common European roots of all national cultures and show that the different national schools were just branches of the same tree. People would then feel patriotism at many levels, harmoniously organized in concentric circles,

---

[3]   Giuseppe Mazzini (1805–72) organized the Young Italy Association in 1831, which aspired towards a free and united Italy. He was a restless conspirator and untiring political agitator for this cause. In 1849 he was a member of the revolutionary triumvirate that proclaimed a brief Republic of Italy but, in spite of this failure, it was Mazzini who prepared the ground for eventual Italian independence. He also co-founded the Young Europe Movement and the republican European Association and organized the Society of the Friends of Italy.

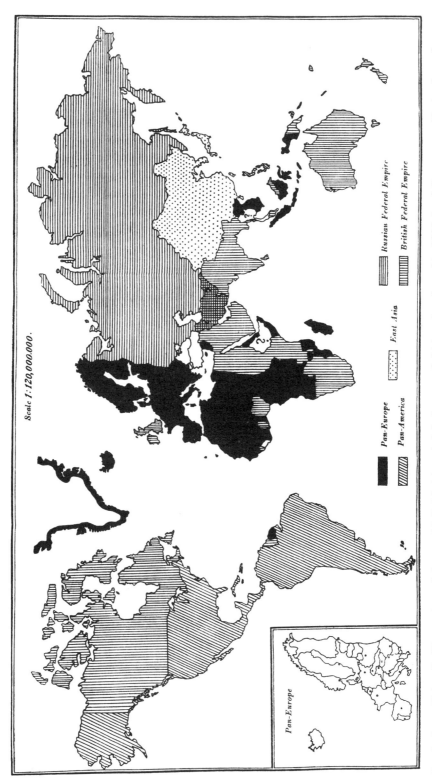

Coudenhove-Kalergi's illustration of the world divided into 'global power fields', taken from his 1923 book Paneuropa. Notice how, for instance, British and French colonies are attributed to the different power fields. Political Paneuropa was not meant to remain within the borders of geographical Europe (credit: R. N. Coudenhove-Kalergi, Pan-Europe, A. A. Knopf, New York 1926).

ranging from the family and village to the home county and country and then to Europe – their real motherland – and through her to the whole occidental civilization and race and in the end to all of mankind. The similarities with Herderian philosophy are obvious, but Coudenhove-Kalergi makes Europe – not the nation – the constituent socio-cultural entity and he does allow for historical change: in 1923 he was in doubt about where to place Turkey, but in his 1934 book Kemal Atatürk's new Turkey is bade welcome in political and cultural Europe!

Coudenhove-Kalergi expected Paneuropa to be the programme of every democrat and patriot. For small concessions of sovereignty all countries would prosper economically and obtain a lasting peace, and their national cultures would benefit from the free exchange with all the other European schools. Conversely, the enemies of Paneuropa would be found to the extreme left (among the Communists) and to the right (among the militarists and national chauvinists), but predominantly among those groups who were economically dependent upon customs borders and economic protectionism. Coudenhove-Kalergi had great confidence in the social democrats, so his main appeal in 1923 was to the democratic non-socialist parties in Germany and France to abstain from revanchism or revenge. A huge coalition of democrats across all European borders was needed in a common defence against destructive extremists.

In sum, Coudenhove-Kalergi's Paneuropa was an astonishing mixture of large-scale Utopianism, potent political analysis and clear-sighted pragmatism: for instance, he suggested the use of English as a common second language in Europe, since it would be impossible to solve the rivalries between the major continental languages and he predicted that English would become the pre-eminent global means of communication anyway. Idealistic in his belief in European brotherhood and in the possibility of global harmony through some balance of the superpowers, he also unhesitatingly accepted the colonial system, perhaps with some underlying assumption that Africa (plus native America and Australia) had produced no culture comparable to the four world cultures that he recognized: European, Arab, Indian, and Chinese.

Aristide Briand's proposals for a united Europe

Perhaps most characteristic of Coudenhove-Kalergi's whole argument was his firm belief that the world could be changed through political agitation and action – his tremendous voluntarism. The Pan-European Union founded in 1923 soon had local branches in all European countries and great efforts were made to persuade politicians and opinion-makers to support the movement.

The strategy of influencing first of all the political and cultural élites proved fruitful, and in France Coudenhove-Kalergi managed to win the sympathy of two leading politicians, Édouard Herriot (1872–1957) and Aristide Briand (1862–1932). Briand in 1927 even accepted the position of honorary president of the Pan-European Union. And generally, from the mid-1920s France pioneered political efforts to establish networks of broad, institutionalized European cooperation.

The First World War had a profound impact on French notions of Europe. For four years, French territory had been the main battlefield and the country had suffered

Aristide Briand, French premier and the first leading politician in the inter-war era to place European unity on the political agenda (credit: Roger-Viollet, Paris).

heavy losses. Consequently, French post-war Europeanism was first of all security-oriented and gravitated around Franco-German relations. Inevitably, the immediate post-war years were dominated by an anti-German nationalism. The nationalists dismissed visions of a broader European cooperation as self-delusive and dangerous and saw the road to French security only in national strength and German weakness. However, rather than strengthening France's economic position, the chaos in Germany seemed to weaken it.

In 1924 there was a radical change of emphasis as elections brought a left-wing co-alition led by Édouard Herriot to power. Herriot was an ardent supporter of the idea of

Édouard Herriot, Briand's close ally, in front of the Brandenburger Tor in Berlin – a symbol of the Franco-German reconciliation so vital for any programme for European cooperation and stability (credit: Roger-Viollet, Paris).

European cooperation, and in January 1925 he made a speech in which he formulated the notion of a 'United States of Europe' growing out of the cooperation introduced with the League of Nations. His speech evoked no immediate response, but the politics of reconciliation was continued in 1925 – now with Painlevé as premier and Briand as foreign minister – in the *Treaty of Locarno*, which paved the way for Germany's admission to the League of Nations in 1926 and guaranteed the borders in western Europe. The agreement was signed by France, Belgium, Italy, Germany and the UK. Of course, the French *rapprochement* was impossible without German benevolence and abstention from 'revanchism'. The symbol of this reconciliatory approach in Germany was foreign minister Gustav Stresemann (1878–1929), who for many years closely cooperated with Briand.

Serious pan-European initiatives had to wait until Aristide Briand took the lead in the late 1920s. In a speech to the League of Nations in Geneva on 5 September 1929 he called for the creation of a sort of *federal link* between the European nations. Briand first of all stressed that the time was ripe for closer economic cooperation. Four days later, the speech was followed by a direct political initiative as Briand invited all European foreign ministers represented in the League of Nations to informal discussions on the subject of European unity. Briand's proposals were well received in a noncommittal way and he was authorized to prepare an official memorandum with specific proposals for the European governments to consider.

Briand's memorandum was ready by 1 May 1930. In his prefatory remarks, Briand mentions the danger to stability and security inherent in the present division of Europe into a large number of competing small states. Awareness of such factors as common racial background, common civilization and geographical proximity should point these states in the direction of cooperation rather than contention. However, despite his high-flown visions, Briand's specific proposals were modest.

First, the European governments were to prepare and ratify a treaty, establishing the principle of a European 'moral union' and confirming the solidarity of the partners involved. Further, the treaty was to oblige the European governments to hold regular meetings. The main organ for this cooperation was to be a 'European conference' for all participants. Between its sessions a smaller, permanent 'Political committee' with its own secretariat was to take care of day-to-day business. Finally, the goals and the motives behind this cooperation were to be formally confirmed, and Briand listed a whole number of issues ranging from customs arrangements to hygiene to academic and political exchange programmes, which could be treated in this European forum. Unlike his Geneva speech, Briand now gave absolute preference to political issues, especially peace and security, and demanded the subordination of economic matters to politics. A political *rapprochement* was seen as a precondition for the creation of a European common market.

But surprisingly, Briand hardly gave the proposed European association any competence at all. First of all, Briand repeatedly stressed that by no means was his association to compete with the League of Nations. On the contrary, he demanded a 'subordination of the European association to the League of Nations', and made membership of the League a prerequisite for participation in the Union. Nor was the European association to take over any responsibilities of the

League in its capacity as mediator between conflicting nations. Furthermore, he underlined that the purpose of the cooperation was to be 'agreement, not unity' and called for feasible procedures. Briand rejected any restrictions upon the unconditional sovereignty and full political independence of the European states, which made the arrangement look at most like a loose confederation.

In his political designs, Briand put great emphasis on British involvement in the process of European cooperation. This – as indeed the whole venture – was undoubtedly rooted in French security interests. The UK, as a signatory of the Locarno agreement, was committed to securing the status-quo in western Europe, which made France most reluctant to cut ties with the UK in favour of some continental association largely dependent on a fragile alliance with Germany. Also, by proposing a sort of European federation Briand could assure his eastern European allies, notably Poland and Czechoslovakia, that the Franco-German *rapprochement* would not take place at their expense.

Briand's memorandum was passed to the European governments, who were asked to respond. Simultaneously, supporters of the proposal campaigned widely on its behalf and debate in the European press was lively. Briand was helped by his colleague Édouard Herriot, who published a lengthy and detailed study in support of Briand's proposals (*Europe*, 1930). At the very least, the supporters of the pan-European idea were successful in making all European governments give serious consideration to the question, and in the following months replies were received from all the twenty-six governments who had been asked.

The result was presented by France in a report of 8 September 1930. Generally speaking the reception was polite, but far from overwhelming. There was a willingness to go on with the talks, but it was obvious that the adherents of the League of Nations felt no need to support a potential rival. Technically, most governments criticized the subordination of politics to economics. Some demanded that economic issues be accorded a clear priority. Others stressed the interdependence of economics and politics. A number of states asked for the inclusion of Turkey in the process, while Germany and Italy requested the inclusion of the Soviet Union as well. Most hesitant in their overall approach to Briand's suggestions were Italy and the UK. A few days later in Geneva, Briand tried to persuade the League of Nations to establish a 'European Council' as a first step in the process, but British resistance allowed for no more than a 'Study Commission for the European Union' under the auspices of the League and with Briand as president. The commission had a couple of meetings over the next year before it wound up its activities.

Henri Brugmans lists five reasons why nothing came of this pan-European initiative (Brugmans, 1965, pp. 56*ff*.):

1 The main advocates of the proposal quickly disappeared from the scene: Stresemann died in 1929, and Briand gradually faded from the political scene before dying in 1932.

2 The project showed a lack of political courage and realism by demanding European union while at the same time promising to leave national sovereignty untouched.

3   British resistance was especially hard to overcome, and few were willing to go on with the project against the wishes of the UK.

4   The economic world crisis set in causing mass unemployment and unrest and forcing governments to take protectionist measures.

5   Partly as a result of this, National Socialism began to gain ground in Germany with its virulent nationalism and revanchism. Once the Nazis seized power in January 1933, there was no room left for the federal ideas of a Briand or a Coudenhove-Kalergi.

To these five reasons we must add a sixth – the resistance of the League of Nations bureaucracy to a potential rival.

Fascism, Nazism and Europe

It may seem paradoxical to talk about 'Europe' or even 'Europeanness' in connection with Fascism and Nazism. Both movements were strongly nationalist and deeply rooted in the specific historical developments of their home countries. But, on the other hand, Fascist parties soon appeared in most European countries and, though heterogeneous or even nebulous, Fascism presented itself as a universal ideology capable of replacing liberal democracy or Communism. Mussolini could claim that his new, strong Italy, through its Fascist revolution, had shown the twentieth century a way out of the miseries of liberalism, parliamentarianism, democracy and socialism, and that it had thus become the vanguard of Europe. This allowed for a certain Europeanism in Italian Fascism. Italian delegations visited Coudenhove-Kalergi's Pan-European congresses and in 1932 an international congress on European culture was organized in Rome (de Meijer in Rijksbaron, 1987, p. 64).

However, Hitler's seizure of power soon demonstrated the narrow limits of any Fascist Europeanism as Germany and Italy clashed over national interests, most notably in Austria. Fascist internationalism was hampered by mutual aggression and distrust: a 'Fascist International' remained stillborn (Woolfe, 1981, p. 3) and because many minor Fascist parties, most notably in east central Europe, had to look to Germany or Italy for support they were open to criticism from ultra-nationalists at home (Wipperman, 1983, p. 198). Only the war and the early German triumphs allowed for the possibility of a new Eurofascism and a belief in the birth of a new Europe. But, generally speaking, Fascism remained blind to its transnational possibilities as the British Fascist leader, Sir Oswald Mosley, was later to lament:

> Confronted with a clear choice between pursuing national ambitions or promoting some form of European union through the universalism of Fascism, the national socialist and Fascist leaders invariably chose the former course. Whenever Fascism was really beginning to succeed throughout Europe, it always received a knock-down blow from the leaders already in power prancing into some territory or another in service of purely national interests... Never talk to me of a Fascist International, for the peace of Europe might have been maintained if such an organization had existed.
>
> *(Mosley, 1968, p. 292)*

It could be claimed there was more scope for discussions about Europeanism in Mussolini's Italy than in Hitler's Germany. Although Mussolini boasted about the creation of a *stato totalitario* ('totalitarian state'), the intensity of totalitarian control in Italy never got near the level experienced in Germany. But, on the other hand, the war soon demonstrated that only the opinion of Nazi Germany mattered.

Nazi 'Neuropa'

Basically, National Socialism was a programme for Germany and not for Europe. Hitler had two primary goals: to cleanse the German race from inferior elements, such as Jews and Gypsies (and German life from the influence of Jewish-Bolshevik thinking) and to create a German *Lebensraum* by expanding to the East. This extreme *Blut und Boden-nationalism* ('blood and soil nationalism') could not tolerate ideas of trans-national communities, and 'Paneuropa' and similar projects were condemned by Hitler as degenerate Jewish attempts to subvert the German people by racial mixture.

The quest for racial purity was so extreme that Hitler condemned any integration even between 'blood related' peoples like the Germanic. He dismissed suggestions that one of the 'racially valuable' European great powers could by force and assimilation create a united Europe with the argument that such a mixture – even if it only included related races – would lead to the degeneration of the ruling race and thus deprive the project of any possible value (Foerster, 1963, p. 247).

Hitler rarely used the concept of 'Europe' and the little he said, other than in propagandistic connections, is fully in accordance with his racial philosophy and the *Drang nach Osten*. In a private conversation in 1941, Hitler stated that the real border between Europe and Asia was the one that 'divides the Germanic from the Slavonic world', and that thus 'it is our duty to put it where we want to have it (i.e. the frontier)' (quoted from Kluke, 1955, p. 260). Only Germanic Europe was real Europe, and the Slavs were to be annihilated or expelled from whatever land the Germans might need. As to the Romance peoples of Europe, Hitler's notions are marked, most of all, by lack of interest. He seemingly foresaw a division of Europe into two living spaces, a pan-German and a Mediterranean pan-Italian, but he cared little about the south. To Hitler, only a German dimension mattered; the efforts of the SS-ideologists to racially determine and assess the quality of the different Germanic tribes in Europe was more to Himmler's taste than to the Führer's.

With this in mind, one may legitimately ask why we should bother to take Nazism seriously here, particularly as little of the most extreme wartime racial planning was known to the public. The answer lies in the fact that the Nazis frequently and very efficiently used the concept of Europe in their propaganda both before and during the war. Also, the very success of early German wartime operations in a way created a united continental Europe in which Germany managed to secure a high degree of economic coordination. This efficiency led many – even honest and serious – people in the occupied countries to believe that a new federal or united Europe could and should be created in cooperation with and under the hegemony of National Socialist Germany (Brugmans, 1965, pp. 69*ff*; Lipgens, 1968, pp. 7*ff*).

During the war, the concept of Europe appears to have been used more frequently in German propaganda than by the Allies.

Initially, following the Nazi seizure of power in 1933, Germany tried to present itself as the only efficient bulwark against Communism. Versailles had left Europe weak and all Germany wanted was to undo the injustice of 1919 and see all Germans united in a common state. A strong Germany would be beneficial for all of Europe, and in a 1936 speech Hitler even used an expression that, much later, would become popular: 'the European house' – a house in which Germany was to keep the order.

In many countries, and not least in Britain, this propaganda was not without success. In 1918–19 Britain had been more reluctant than France and the USA to endorse the splitting up of central and eastern Europe, and comprehension of this 'New Europe' remained low. The incalculable consequences of the principle of national self-determination looked rather less attractive than the re-establishment of some European great power accord or equilibrium. In 1938 several attempts were made to persuade Germany to accept her share of responsibility for the European order, culminating in the Munich crisis of September 1938, when Germany, Italy, France, and Britain decided upon the fate of independent Czechoslovakia without reference to that unfortunate country. Two comments illustrate the level of official British engagement in Europe at that time: Neville Chamberlain, talking about Czechoslovakia, referred to 'a quarrel in a far-away country between people of whom we know nothing', and his brother Austen Chamberlain, echoing Bismarck, had earlier spoken complacently of a place 'for which no British Government ever will or ever can risk the bones of a British grenadier' (he was referring to the Polish corridor in 1925). The destruction of democratic Czechoslovakia was not considered an issue big enough to justify a new war.

German occupation of what was left of Bohemia-Moravia in March 1939, the pact with Stalin in August, and the attack on Poland in September demonstrated the level of sincerity of previous talk. But the war and the seizure by 1940 of much of the continent only forced the Nazis to adjust their European propaganda to the new needs of Germany. In order to mobilize all continental economies for its war effort, Germany had to present a programme for a 'new order in Europe' to those countries under German occupation or control. As in the First World War, the need for a continental European common market was stressed (although with much more emphasis on the necessity of planning than for instance by Naumann), and the military and economic virtues of 'European autarky' were praised. Propaganda stories described the advantages of organizing the 'European family of nations' in a political and economic union after German principles and under German supremacy. Against rotten old Britain a young and healthy 'united front of the different peoples of the Continent' should arise to secure Europe's freedom. (All these expressions are taken from a Nazi leaflet, published in Denmark in 1941.)

After some initial success, the ability to mobilize people in the occupied countries declined as it became evident that slogans about the common European economy masked an ever more ruthless German exploitation. The propaganda was remarkably hazy about questions concerning the level of political independence that would be granted to the non-German countries. And references to a common Europe were systematically omitted from domestic German propaganda.

The attack on the Soviet Union brought about yet another change, again purely instrumental, in Nazi European propaganda. Kluke notes (1955, p. 259), that the

'Behind the enemy powers – the Jew.' Germany's political and military enemies might change, but Nazi propaganda never forgot the racist core of its ideology (credit: Bildarchiv Preussischer Kulturbesitz, Berlin).

motive of 'the struggle of the peoples of Europe against bolshevism'[4] did not appear in German propaganda until it was reported that some non-communist circles in the occupied countries welcomed the assault. From then on, Hitler could be 'marketed' as the standard-bearer of European culture and, after Stalingrad, as Europe's defender from the Eastern menace. In a speech in Berlin on 30 January 1942, Hitler said:

> This time it is not a war we are fighting just on behalf of our own
> German people, but a struggle for the whole of Europe and thus for the
> whole of civilized humanity.
>
> *(Hitler, quoted in Schlie, 1992)*

In this way German soldiers, and SS-volunteers (Waffen SS) from other countries, were actually sent to die 'for Germany and for Europe' at Stalingrad and in Berlin.

Once again, the Nazi use of 'Europe' had no other purpose than to justify an unlimited centralist German rule on the continent. But we should not fail to notice how attractive this propaganda was in its various phases.

Antisemitism was not confined to Nazism, and calls for dictatorial law and order in the building of a new Europe or in the struggle against Bolshevism appealed to all too many. Mosley lamented the missed opportunities to found a new Europe on such principles – but his belief in the existence of such opportunities serves as a salutary warning.

Opposition and resistance

Soon after Hitler's seizure of power the German branch of the Pan-European Union was dissolved and its literature outlawed. In Coudenhove-Kalergi's words, the anti-European revolution had conquered Germany:

> It was from then on that Germany cut itself off from Europe more and
> more decisively: in external affairs through pan-German policies, in
> internal affairs through racist policies, morally by depriving people of
> their human rights, legally by rewriting the laws and economically by
> notions of self-sufficiency.
>
> *(Coudenhove-Kalergi, 1934, p. 151)*

Coudenhove-Kalergi and other adherents of a federal Europe had to face the fact that, as long as this regime was in power in Germany, no such union was possible – apart from under Nazi rule. The Pan-European Union with its headquarters in Vienna concentrated in the following years upon preserving Austrian independence and establishing regional economic cooperation among the Danube countries backed by Italy and France. In doing so, the movement had to compromise with forces far from the democratic ideals of the programmes of the 1920s, and a split occurred between Coudenhove-Kalergi, who remained fiercely anti-Bolshevik as well as anti-Nazi, and left-wing intellectuals who saw in the Soviet Union a fo-

---

[4]   Spain, Italy, Slovakia, Hungary, Rumania and Finland took part in the war against the Soviet Union, together with representative military units drawn from other countries which did not formally commit themselves.

cus for Europe-wide, anti-Fascist agitation. Generally speaking, public interest in and support for federalist programmes for Europe reached an absolute low in the 1930s.

Only the war led to a revitalization of the plans for European unity. Walter Lipgens, in a very thorough study (Lipgens, 1968), describes how the voice of unity was echoed in almost all European resistance movements and how the demands for a federal European order were expressed with quite a different accent from that of the interwar years. They were all primarily motivated by moral or ideological arguments, which stressed the need to overcome the narrow and destructive power of the nation state and the need to secure human rights and individual freedom against all institutions.

The new, emphatic and highly idealistic approach to European unity was a product of two interrelated experiences: the atrocities of the Nazi regime and the complete political and military collapse of almost all the states that were at war with Hitler. Their collapse, which profoundly demonstrated the inadequacy and weaknesses of the old Versailles system, had at first created illusions – even among people who were not pro-Fascist collaborators – about the viability of creating a new Europe in cooperation with Germany.

As the consequences of Nazi rule became obvious, the experience of the collapse of the old order led to the inevitable conclusion that national pride and vanity were the real culprits. The nation state had been discredited in every possible way: morally, by its nationalistic chauvinism; economically, in its inability to avoid crisis and secure cooperation; and militarily, as it had proved unable to secure the safety of its citizens. To most of the non-communist Resistance leaders, the only solution seemed to be a European federation or even a 'united states' of Europe. In many clandestine documents the need was stressed to include the Germans and to avoid nationalistic revenge. The *Manifesto of the European Resistance*, published in Geneva in July 1944 by members of the Resistance from nine separate countries, called for a federal union of the European nations; the main arguments were:

(a) the necessity to have the Germans participate in European life without threatening their neighbours;

(b) the need to protect national minorities and avoid the abuse of minority interests; and finally

(c) the demand for cooperation in the economic reconstruction of the continent after the war, without which any democratic political order would be threatened (Brugmans, 1965, p. 81).

This 'Resistance philosophy' manifested itself in almost all the countries under German occupation or Fascist rule, with one exception: in Scandinavia, the Resistance movements seemed more in favour of an 'Atlantic' order. Italy had a particularly strong federalist movement, supported by many who came to play a role in Italian post-war politics, perhaps a reaction against the long experience of Mussolini's Fascism. Lipgens observes (Lipgens, 1968, p. 251) that Resistance movements in smaller countries, such as Belgium, were generally more reluctant to commit themselves to large-scale post-war planning than their colleagues in

Italy or France – probably a result of small countries having been more objects than subjects of history. The highly limited access to archives in the countries under communist rule has made it difficult to follow the programmes of the non-communist Resistance in Eastern Europe, but Polish and Czechoslovak material indicates that their political élites were at least as interested in federal structures as the Western Resistance leaders.

The main problem for the federal minded Resistance leaders was, of course, how to realize such a programme. Hitler could only be defeated with help from abroad, and much was done both to persuade the Allies of the virtues of a federal Europe and to identify signs that this message was appreciated. Actually, until 1943 the notion of a regional union or the idea of closer European cooperation did play a role in British and American post-war planning. Churchill seemed especially to favour a 'United States of Europe', although the Americans were reluctant to give the issue a high priority.

The attitude of the USSR was the main obstacle to the realization of any plans for the federalization of Europe. Theoretically the question was settled by Lenin in 1915 in his article, 'On the slogan for a United States of Europe', in which he condemned any such project as 'either impossible or reactionary'. The argument ran, that under capitalism the 'United States of Europe' could be nothing but an agreement about how to share out the colonies and how to strengthen reactionary, decrepit and monarchic Europe in the struggle against the USA and Japan. Only after the worldwide victory of socialism would some 'United States of the World' be possible, but then, with the establishment of Communism, the state as such would 'wither away'. But in the interim phase, when socialism had won in *some* capitalist countries, a strong centralization of the proletariat would be necessary in these countries' struggle against the forces of capitalism (Lenin, 1915, pp. 339–43).

As Soviet rule became a reality, such theses proved highly adaptable to the foreign policy interests of the Soviet Union. In 1929 Stalin vehemently condemned the Briand plan as being a reactionary attempt to intervene against the Soviet Union, and all regional plans for Eastern Central Europe were dismissed on similar grounds. Not without reason, one must admit, since the creation of a *cordon sanitaire* between Germany and the Soviet Union was part of the security arrangement desired by France and its allies. The Soviet attitude remained unchanged during the war: in 1943 Stalin even used the threat of a separate peace with Germany to dissuade the Western Allies from pursuing these schemes. The Soviet Union not only wanted to keep all territories occupied according to the Ribbentrop-Molotov agreements of August 1939, it also protested against the attempts to establish a Danube federation or similar structure involving Poland and its neighbours, and furthermore suggested a new dismemberment of Germany into several small independent units (Lipgens, 1968, p. 22).

The Western Allies – with the USA in the vanguard – eventually yielded to these demands because of the necessity to maintain cooperation with the Soviets. The USA further hoped to create a global security organization, and in this scheme of things a united Europe was deemed counterproductive. The end result was the division of the continent into 'spheres of influence' and – without regard for wartime visions – the restoration of the nation states in Europe after the Soviet Union had taken its share. The Resistance in Europe had no influence on these events and frustration grew from 1944, as the intentions of the Allies became more obvious. Outcries were heard protesting against the way the continent was to be split into two halves, but the war ended in exhaustion, explosions of hatred and revenge against the Germans and a growing communist influence in the Resistance movements. The rapidly declining influence of pro-federal Resistance chiefs was accentuated by the return of old political leaders from exile or prison and the rapid re-emergence of traditional lines of political division.

Supporters of formalized European cooperation seemed to have advanced no further than in 1919, but nevertheless a lesson had been learned. The discrediting of the ultra-nationalist order of the inter-war period was not forgotten and – as Europe obviously could not jump directly from the horrors of war to a federal paradise – the need for a functional approach focusing, first of all, on economic collaboration in the reconstruction of Europe began to be stressed at the expense of grander political visions.

Perceptions of Europe

We have seen how in the nineteenth century rival perceptions of Europe were constructed, each of them drawing on a specific set of historical references. The confusion has not diminished since then. Many themes presented here have roots in previous times, but I will try to emphasize what is specific or new in their use as appropriate. First, we will consider how 'culture' and 'civilization' – two concepts traditionally connected with Europeanness – were given new accentuation during the war. Then we shall see how people with different norms (norms interconnected with the perceptions of Europe identified by Pim den Boer as freedom, Christianity, civilization and democracy) faced the new post-war Europe, and finally we will turn to questions of European regions and borders.

Culture versus civilization

We have seen, in Pim den Boer's essay, how in the late eighteenth century the concepts of culture and civilization were nearly synonymous. However, in Germany, the French term 'civilisation' was considered a rather unfortunate import, and through the nineteenth century a contrast between 'Kultur' and 'Zivilisation' was gradually introduced (Elias, 1939, Chapter 1 for the standard discussion), which in the First World War was heavily exploited to explain and justify the war. The distinction survived the war and it appears in discussions of Europeanness even today – an indication of its relevance in frequent attempts to define the nature of Europe. We meet the distinction in Edgar Morin's *Penser l'Europe* from 1987: 'culture', in his terminology, means the Jewish–Christian–Greek–Latin cultural foundations of Europe, whereas 'civilization' covers humanism, rationality, science and freedom. In this sense, civilization comes after culture.

But Morin also accepts the *related German use*, which reserves the word 'Kultur' for what is peculiar and characteristic for one specific community and 'Zivilisation' for what is transmittable to other communities. There is, then, a dichotomy between what is unique and spiritual and what is common and interchangeable. According to Morin, culture develops by faithfully drawing from its own particular principles whereas civilization develops by gathering and comparing the results of culture (Morin, 1987, p. 72). So, essentially, our present global civilization is the spoiled and powerful child of the European culture(s), or at least that is how it looks in Morin's 1987 perspective:

> ...that if European *culture* has become a civilization by spreading throughout the world, European *cultures* have remained cultures henceforth menaced by the civilization that issued from Europe itself.
>
> *(Morin, 1987, p. 73)*

Let us have a closer look at the wartime use of these concepts.

Culture, civilization, and the First World War

As we have seen above, the Allies uniformly interpreted the war as a conflict between civilization and barbarism. 'Barbarism', not 'culture', was antonymous to civilization. The French philosopher Henri Bergson (1859–1941) in a 1915 leaflet, *La signification de la guerre*, saw only barbarism in the German war effort. To him it was a terrible assault on civilization and on associated attempts to solve the crisis of the modern world through greater freedom, brotherhood and justice. Germany – or rather Prussia, which had ruined what was traditionally good in Germany – ruthlessly sought the complete destruction of the enemy, and in its effort to militarize all of society – to 'mechanize the spirit' – it had abused the forces of civilization by espousing a 'systematic barbarism', an 'empire of death'. But since only life could be creative, Bergson was convinced that the forces of life and decency would win this final battle (Nolte, 1991, pp. 127*ff*).

If we disregard the element of war propaganda, Bergson's theories do point to a problem that was to culminate three decades later in Nazism and Stalinism (and to which he himself, being of Jewish origin, would fall victim): it is that the forces of civilization are Janus-faced, both liberating and destructive. If these forces are in the hands of a regime with a totalitarian ideology, which exploits modern techniques while simultaneously suspending individual responsibility by transferring truth, justice, and power to one supreme rule (the 'Führer' or 'the Party'), they can lead to a *scientific barbarism* that would be unthinkable outside a European frame of mind. Some of the roots of this 'reactionary modernism' can be found in German wartime propaganda.

Max Scheler

During the First World War, frequent attempts were made in Germany to explain the war – not as a clash between civilization and barbarism, but between 'Kultur', represented by Germany, and 'Zivilisation' represented by the liberal West. In *Der Genius des Krieges und der deutsche Krieg* (1915), the German philosopher Max

Scheler (1874–1928) presented a sophisticated expression of a line of thought that was often treated much more crudely (and with greater popular appeal) in ordinary war propaganda. However, the intellectual quality of his argument and the questions addressed make Scheler relevant to us, and his philosophical line of thought with its critique of modernity and positivist science has inspired people as different as Heidegger (1889–1976) and Havel (1936–).

To Scheler the war was a conflict between Russia and Europe, in which Germany and Austria had become the main defenders of the common European heritage. Scheler defined Europe as a primarily spiritual brotherhood based on 'a distinctive spiritual structure – for example, a certain form of ethos, a certain kind of ideology and the active way of forming the world' (Scheler, 1915, p. 294), rooted in Greece, Rome, and Christianity. He rejected all definitions of Europe in terms of geography or race.

Scheler goes to great lengths to show that Russia is an independent cultural sphere (*Kulturkreis*), fundamentally different from Europe, and that Russian expansion to the West would mean the end of the unparalleled creativity of the European spirit. To him, the different world cultures are *unique* and incompatible and marked by a high degree of stability and permanence. So Scheler finds it absurd, for instance, that Japan could become 'European' simply by assimilating European technology, a factor that would have only a superficial bearing on the Japanese way of life; and the same is true for the 'Europeanization' of Russia. This forces all sincere thinkers to recognize that their world view – their whole cognition – is embedded in the spiritual structure of the culture within which it exists. In other words: there is no 'neutral' perception – all we see, we see with European eyes, and so we should speak of a 'multiverse' rather than of a 'universe' (there are some similarities here to Herder's understanding of the uniqueness of each nation). In reality, we only have the European world to live and work in, and this world existed long before we became aware of it.

So all of Europe should have cooperated in self-protection against the new wave of militant Russian expansionism, but unfortunately Europe was weakened from inside by the great villain Britain as the main representative of capitalist civilization. According to Scheler, the British capitalist spirit was marked by a profound utilitarianism which eroded all higher values and preferred what is useful to what is noble. Britain accepted only the principle of expediency, and this has led to a ruthless imperialism and a destructive policy towards Europe. In addition, Britain embodies an artificial, cynical, and rational *society* (*Gesellschaft*) against the German (and to Scheler hopefully also European) principle of a true, emotional, inner *community* (*Gemeinschaft*). Philosophically, Scheler puts the blame on naturalism and positivism, since they refuse to recognize the true ethical and spiritual dimensions of cognition. This primitive, materialist 'objectivism' sees the world as only an 'economic world catalogue', i.e. as consisting purely of material objects for exploitation, which leads to a complete instrumentalization of both the world and its inhabitants.

To Scheler, this 'English capitalist disease' had spread dangerously all over Europe. Even Germany had not been left unaffected as the country's imperialist and nationalist sentiments proved. It had been sad to see how most European *Kulturträger* ('carriers of culture') renounced all common transnational religious and moral authority. This decline had reached its nadir in the war, which threatened to destroy all transcendentally anchored values. But Scheler found it completely mistaken to blame the war itself for this misery. The ruthlessness of war was not a product of decent militarism, but of convenient peacetime utilitarianism, which left no room for what was noble in humanity.

Scheler hoped for the war to become a purifying flame, in whose bright light the true spiritual values of Europe would become clear again. Idealistic German soldiers would soon understand the values they risked their lives for, and hopefully the equally idealistic young soldiers on the other side of the front line would recognize the deceit that had led them to war and demand an all-embracing European brotherhood.

The war would lead either to the renaissance of Europe or to its fall, depending upon whether the German or the English spirit won. Germany still had an anticapitalist, heroic community spirit which, in combination with the cosmopolitanism of the German national spirit, its sense of responsibility for the fate of all of mankind, made it natural for the country to lead the struggle for the spiritual and political unity of Europe. Scheler calls such a brotherhood based on higher values a *Liebesgemeinschaft*, and he hopes that the Catholic church – spiritually reformed and renewed – will again become the common moral authority of Europe. In this, the Church can find inspiration in the deep, inner religious form of Catholicism felt in Germany.

Against a nightmare vision in which the world is divided into three – a Mongolian-Japanese empire ruling in the East, a culturally uncreative Russian empire expanding to the West, and finally a mechanical, capitalist America as the heir to British utilitarianism – Scheler puts his positive vision of a spiritually united continental Europe under German military supremacy:

> A Europe in which the rich, unique characteristics of its disparate
> peoples work together in a harmonious and complementary fashion,
> preserving the great traditions of the mighty Mediterranean culture, so
> as to build a culture of freedom, of the spirit, and of individuality. This
> will be a Europe which will cleanse its blood of the foreign poison of
> English-American capitalism and its Calvinistic, puritanical distortion of
> Christianity, and at the same time a Europe which reverses the
> movement of expansion from East to West into West to East.
>
> *(Scheler, 1915, p. 249; see also p. 353)*

In sum, Scheler sees the spread of capitalist civilization as tragic and destructive to a Europe based on culture, i.e. a unique nobility of thought and deed, a true community of love. He wants Catholicism to deliver the spiritual recovery, but he appeals to Germany, not the Church, in defence of Europe. This gives Scheler a problem: was not Germany at least as capitalist as Britain, or put differently, at least as industrialized? How can Germany save itself from capitalism and at the same time exploit the virtues of technology? Scheler finds the answer in the German state. Germany (and Austria) have kept antiquity's idea of the state alive:

their state is an 'überindividuelle Willensrealität' ('trans-individual reality of will'), which preserves a genuine, organic community of the whole people and thus a true culture. He believed these states to be spiritual in a European sense, since they supposedly had not submitted to any petty nationalism or to other kinds of utilitarianism.

Scheler was not alone in his celebration of the German state as a bulwark against civilization. Thomas Mann (1875–1955) in his *Betrachtungen eines Unpolitischen* ('reflections of a non-political person') from 1917 lamented civilization's imperialism towards German culture and expressed his horror over the thought that the Prussian spirit could be defeated by the philosophy of the business world. Unlike Scheler, he foresaw this tragic end and described ironically the trivial, empty convenience of life in the post-war democracies. It must be said that both men later deeply regretted their adulation of the war and the Wilhelmine state.

To return to the question of 'scientific barbarism': Scheler condemned capitalism and liberalism for reducing everything to mere objects. But when primitive versions of his own logic (and they were frequent both during the war and after) at times glorified the German state as *the* authority which could dialectically transcend the conflict between culture and civilization, they came dangerously close to delivering ideological ammunition to totalitarian methods. If the state is presented as 'spiritual', it – and not its inhabitants – becomes the subject that can 'save' people from the otherwise seemingly inevitable nihilism of industrial life. In this process, the state as the incarnation of higher values also has the right to dispose of whoever it considers to be enemies of these values – Jews, Gypsies, capitalists and so on.

A Communist interpretation

It is no accident that one can find interesting parallels to this (see Bělohradský, 1990, p. 16) in Communist thinking, and one of its most important philosophers in this century, the Hungarian György Lukács (1885–1971), directly addressed himself to the same problem. As the First World War broke out, Lukács was put in a dilemma: he definitely did not approve of the emperors of Germany and Austria, but if they should lose, who then could save the world from Western 'civilization'? In 1917 he found the answer in Soviet Russia.

In 1919 he gave a fascinating interpretation of the case in his article 'Old and New Culture'. Capitalism, Lukács noted, was the culmination of civilization so far, but at the same time it was a force that destroyed all genuine culture. 'Culture', we should notice, is not used here in the German sense; Lukács defines it as *everything that is aesthetically and ethically valuable in products and abilities beyond their functional necessity*. There were several reasons for this:

(a) Capitalism allowed humanity to control nature, but at the same time becoming subservient to the means that made this emancipation possible in the first place. All people – even the ruling class – were now directly involved in production and, in a sense, they had become the functionaries of production rather than its controllers. Economic growth had become a goal in itself.

(b)   As all products in a capitalist society – even cultural products – were dragged into economic circulation, they became commodities. And if the only value they ended up having was their commodity value, they lost the cultural autonomy necessary for them to preserve any genuine, inner value.

(c)   In pre-capitalist modes of production culture was of course the privilege and product of the ruling classes, but it did have an inner autonomy as the ruling classes were still above the system of production, not just agents of it, which enabled them to appreciate genuine value and allow for its creation.

(d)   All historic periods culminated culturally in times of harmony between their ideology and the mode of production[5]: culture could then develop in organic correspondence with the life surrounding it and equally organically attach itself to the totality of the cultural tradition. The capitalist revolution had destroyed this, both by destroying the tradition of craftsmanship (making all products anonymous) and by eliminating any organic continuation of traditions: now hectic, superficial and empty-headed fashion had to substitute for real culture.

(e)   Since no class in capitalism had a role in the mode of production which would allow it to create culture, the last valid cultural epoch had to be found in the days when capitalism was still young and the idea of individual freedom still genuinely emancipating for the emerging bourgeoisie, i.e. in the classical idealism of the nineteenth century. Since then, culture had either been dissembling (by not showing the misery of exploitation) or was so ruthlessly critical that its inner harmony had disappeared.

In sum: to Lukács, capitalist civilization fully emancipated humanity from the tyranny of nature, but at the same time it exposed us to tyranny of an economy, which brutally erased the beauty of pre-capitalist culture. This dilemma seems to me to be strikingly similar to the one faced by the admirers of German spirituality and, like them, Lukács tried to overcome the problem dialectically with the help of a 'final solution' (though for him, unlike Scheler, it was not the Prussian state). Lukács instead expected the dictatorship of the proletariat (in reality of the Party) and the emerging Communist society to put an end once and for all to the conflict between culture and civilization:

> Communist society … wishes to create a societal order of a kind that will entitle everyone to a lifestyle that was led only by the ruling classes *before* capitalism, but which was not available to any single class *during* capitalism.
>
> *(Lukács, 1919, p. 134)*

Through state planning the perversions of capitalism (and the capitalist perverts!?) could be eliminated and humanity reinstated in control of the economy, not vice versa. Thus, freed of superfluous worries, people could return to the truly existential questions of life and produce culture in abundance. This is a digression, since

---

[5]   For example, in the years after the French Revolution there briefly existed a balance between the political, ideological emancipation of citizens and the destruction of feudal ties in the economy.

Lukács says little about Europe, but the structure of the argument demonstrates how much Communist thinking, in spite of its 'anti-European' universalism, is indebted to European traditions both in its diagnosis of the modern era and in its solution to its dilemmas. Attempts have been made to describe Bolshevism as inherently Russian and therefore non-European, but without firm roots in European thinking the great appeal of Bolshevism to many European intellectuals would hardly have been possible.

Der Untergang des Abendlandes

During the First World War and after, it was very popular to speak in biological metaphors: cultures were compared to living beings and were supposed to go through a cycle of childhood, youth, adulthood and old age. Suddenly, new connotations were added to the metaphor of Europe as 'the old world', as numerous commentators seemed to agree that Europe had reached its final stage. Descriptions of Europe as a patient lying feverishly on the deathbed were numerous, ranging from the Danish literary critic Georg Brandes during the war to the French writer Jules Romains more than two decades later (Boll-Johansen, 1988, p. 163). Young intellectuals were just as convinced about the near collapse of European civilization as their parents had been about its continuous progress.

One book became an immediate symbol of all these sentiments: first published in 1918 and revised a few years later, Oswald Spengler's *Der Untergang des Abendlandes* (*The Decline of the West*) became a bestseller – perhaps not the least because of the superbly compelling title which gave name to the mood of a whole generation.

Spengler's book was a highly ambitious attempt at an all-encompassing philosophy of history. By comparing different world cultures (operating, like Scheler, with a multiplicity of apparently incompatible cultures) Spengler believed he had found a 'morphology of world history', according to which all cultures were deemed to go through a number of phases compared sometimes to the four seasons, at others to a life cycle. On the basis of this analysis, Spengler even considered himself able to *predict* developments over the next two centuries. Culture, like youthful spring, is the time of a powerful mythical-religious blossoming which, at its zenith, takes on a fuller and a more serene appearance. In the autumn, the creativity of any culture is most sublime with a sweetness not untinged by melancholy. But in the end, the fire of the culture's soul dies out and the culture transforms into a civilization.

So here we meet yet another use of the terms 'culture' and 'civilization'. In Spengler's terminology, civilization is the inevitable *last phase of a culture*, its logical culmination and demise. Spengler draws examples from all major cultures in world history, but his main theme is given by the title of his book, and his most compelling comparisons are made between the life cycle of antiquity (leading to the decline of the Roman Empire) and the development of the occidental (European) culture which, according to Spengler, had completed its transition from culture to civilization in the nineteenth century. When the Romans are called barbarians –

> unspiritual, unphilosophical, devoid of art, clannish to the point of
> brutality, aiming relentlessly at tangible successes, they stand between
> the Hellenic culture and nothingness.
>
> *(Spengler, 1918; 1928 edn, p. 32)*

– no one could miss the point.

At first glance, Spengler gives the impression of being just another cultural pessimist. His main symbol of civilization was the metropolis, the cosmopolitan centre of rootless, depersonalized masses. His epoch was characterized by a loss of religiousness and sense of purpose. Money ruled supreme, accompanied by political cynicism and philosophical scepticism.

But civilization was not only the manifestation of decay and disaster; its end was also the birth of something new. Spengler held that civilizations could manifest themselves actively: if 'civilization-man', as Spengler called him, could not direct his energy inwards, an outwards expansion was possible – its name being imperialism. To Spengler, Cecil Rhodes was the first herald of a new age which was to culminate in the next two centuries. Also, occidental culture had certain unique features in being future-oriented and with aspirations towards eternity. Its spirit had manifested itself in a technical inventiveness, which has allowed European culture in its civilized phase to spread all over the world. Since the spreading of civilization was inevitable, one could just as well make the most of it, for instance by engaging in imperialist conquest rather than succumbing to decadent pseudo-philosophies like pacifism or scepticism. Spengler did in fact find a timeless truth beyond all morphological change, a principle that offered a last resort from the decadence of world history. This truth had a lot in common with the then fashionable Social Darwinism (Nolte, 1991, p. 221), dressed up in Nietzsche. In Spengler's words:

> Ever in history it is life and life only – race-quality, the triumph of the
> will-to-power – and not the victory of truths, discoveries, or money that
> signifies.
>
> *(Spengler, 1922, 1928 edn, p. 507)*

Spengler's book (whose first edition was published early in 1918 – the first volume only; the second volume was published in 1922 – in expectation of a German victory) can therefore also be read as a piece of wartime propaganda giving philosophical absolution to the German war effort. In common with his above mentioned colleagues, Spengler considered the conflict to be the inevitable result of the historical transformations of the time, a conflict in which 'money' (the UK) was fighting against 'blood' (Germany). Spengler was not in doubt about the outcome:

> The coming of Cæsarism breaks the dictature of money and its political
> weapon democracy. After a long triumph of world-city economy and its
> interests over political creative force, the political side of life manifests
> itself after all as the stronger of the two. The sword is victorious over
> the money, the master-will subdues again the plunderer-will. If we call
> these money-powers 'Capitalism', then we may designate as Socialism
> the will to call into life a mighty politico-economic order that

transcends all class interests, a system of *lofty* thoughtfulness and duty-sense that keeps the whole in fine condition for the decisive battle of its history, and this battle is also the battle of money and law.

(Spengler, 1922; 1928 edn, p. 506)

Spengler's socialism, to be sure, has little to do with Marxism and even less with the Utopian socialism of the nineteenth century. It found its true expression in the Prussian *Organisationsstaat* with its ability to mobilize all resources in the imperialist struggle. So, contrary to traditional interpretations, Spengler was not a pessimist. His historical determinism was not defeatism: he had written off one culture, but only in the hope that a new one – vital, dynamic, and ruthless in a Nietzschean way – could be born in Western Europe. This is the essence of his recommendation to young generations to give up culture and philosophy in favour of technology, military force, and the politics of power (Spengler, 1918, p. 57).

Facing post-war Europe

The horrors of the war, America's intervention in Europe and the post-war near collapse of the European economies convinced most observers that the days of a self-evident European world supremacy were over. All 'European-minded' intellectuals had to face this relative decline in Europe's global position, and both Catholics and liberal democrats were confronted with the growth of powerful new trends in European politics, which rejected most of Europe's past: to the adherents of Communism or Fascism in its various national versions, 'the old world' was totally discredited and both ideologies tried to exploit the metaphors of youth and vitality to increase their popularity.

Many young intellectuals, who had either witnessed the senseless losses at the front line, or the famine, deprivations and corruption at home, felt that the liberal system that had led to this warfare had lost all credibility. These feelings are strongly expressed in a poem by Ezra Pound (1885–1972) and in the harshness and ugliness of the immediate post-war drawings of George Grosz (1893–1959). Consequently, both men (and with them many of the new, young generation) looked for radical solutions, Pound in Fascism and Grosz in Communism.

Hugh Selwyn Mauberley

IV

These fought in any case,
and some believing,
               pro domo, in any case...

Some quick to arm,
some for adventure,
some from fear of weakness,
some from fear of censure,
some for love of slaughter, in imagination,
learning later...
some in fear, learning love of slaughter;

Died some, pro patria,
                    non 'dulce' non 'et decor'...
walked eye-deep in hell
believing in old men's lies, then unbelieving
came home, home to a lie,
home to many deceits,
home to old lies and new infamy;
usury age-old and age-thick
and liars in public places.

Daring as never before, wastage as never before.
Young blood and high blood,
fair cheeks and fine bodies;

fortitude as never before

frankness as never before,
disillusions as never told in the old days,
hysterias, trench confessions,
laughter out of dead bellies.

V

There died a myriad,
And of the best, among them,
For an old bitch gone in the teeth,
For a botched civilization,

Charm, smiling at the good mouth,
Quick eyes gone under earth's lid,

For two gross of broken statues,
For a few thousand battered books.
                    (Ezra Pound, 1920; 1952 edn, pp. 207–8)

Liberal programmes for a united Europe such as the ones of Coudenhove-Kalergi and Briand had trouble gaining mass attraction in competition with nationalistic slogans, echoed in pamphlets with such titles as *Schluss mit Europa* ('Enough of Europe', mentioned in Schulze, 1990, p. 36). Generally the public interest in a 'European dimension' was low in these years and, with some noticeable exceptions, the same can be said about the level of intellectual engagement. No wonder, then, that Duroselle has reached this conclusion about the mood of the European-minded intellectuals:

> Widespread pessimism was the dominant characteristic of European thought between the two wars.
>
> *(Duroselle, 1965, p. 287).*

We can find exceptions, but everywhere we meet a feeling of uncertainty which is far from the complacent optimism of the previous century.

The comfort of European culture

After 1918, a liberal's belief in Europe could hardly anymore be a faith in unlimited progress. In fact, it was hard not to overlook how the USA rather than old Europe was becoming the vanguard of invention and modernity. In this situation, in the relatively peaceful years from 1924 to 1930, European intellectuals could use features from the dichotomy of culture versus civilization to support their somewhat flawed feelings of superiority.

With an ambiguous attitude, both affirmative and sceptical, to modern civilization they noticed that this fruit of the European mind had spread all over the world and permitted non-Western countries to make impressive progress. Japan had become a strong industrial power and 'in Central Africa the negroes also ride in motor-cars and dose themselves with aspirin', as the Spanish philosopher José Ortega y Gasset (1883–1956) remarked in his *Revolt of the Masses* (Ortega y Gasset, 1930, p. 66). Still, only the immense success of America meant a real challenge to the European self-consciousness. But, no matter what they did, there was one thing the Americans could never have: and that was the European cultural heritage.

Scheler in 1915 was sure that if North America should suddenly cease to contrib-

Some got slaughtered and others got rich. George Grosz graphically illustrates the horror and the corruption of war (credit: Akademie der Künste, Berlin).

123

ute to the field of culture, the loss would be minute in comparison to the loss of a European nation such as France or Italy, at least so far as quality was concerned (Scheler, 1915, p. 287). Fifteen years and a peace settlement later, Ortega y Gasset noted (ibid., p. 20), that the living standard of the average American might be higher than in Europe but, by comparison with Europe, the level of their 'select minorities' (i.e. their intellectual élites) was still relatively low.

Despite this, Europeans still felt somewhat defensive: the Czech writer Karel Čapek (1890–1938) in a letter to the *New York Times* tried, in 1926, to explain why he would find it dangerous if American ideals were to spread to Europe. Some aspects of the American way of life particularly alarmed him. First, the speed and bustle, since for Čapek work efficiency was not the be-all and end-all in life, and also because most of what was valuable in Europe was the product of people who were not in a hurry:

> Europe wasted its time for thousands of years; that is where its inexhaustibility and fertility comes from.
>
> *(Čapek, 1926, p. 48)*

It takes a certain laziness to fully appreciate life, Čapek noted, and in the same vein he complained about the American cult of success. Europeans used to have a heroic tradition, they died for their faith, for love, for truth or for similar irrational things. In its craziness Europe had managed to care for thousands of other things besides success, and while these things remained, the devil took whatever there was of success in history. Finally, Čapek found it hard to accept the cult of quantity:

> The Creator of Europe made her small and even split her up into little parts, so that our hearts could find joy not in size but in plurality.
>
> *(Ibid., p. 50 – author's translation from Czech)*

Čapek was a liberal democrat, a pragmatist, but this did not preclude a touch of nostalgia and romanticism intruding in his view of Europe. Once again, one wonders if capitalism was not after all a European invention.

Facing the same problems, and explicitly basing his analysis on the dichotomy of culture and civilization, Čapek's countryman, the writer and literary critic F. V. Krejčí (1867–1941), in his book *Czechhood and Europeanness* (1931), tried to analyse the essence of Europe.

Civilization, he said, was easily transferable as could be seen from the way European civilization – in its specific Anglo-Saxon version – had conquered all continents. Culture in contrast was specific and historical, it was a structure of aesthetic, ethical and intellectual norms and practices generated over centuries. According to Krejčí Europe, since antiquity, had proved to possess a special ability to open new dimensions for all humanity and even now its moral and social thinking incarnated the conscience of humanity. Always – and the exact sciences had added new dimensions to this – Europe had sought to make the fruits of its spirit become a *lived experience*, a daily affirmation of the virtues of Europeanness. When successful in this, culture and civilization became one, as could be seen in Western Europe and parts of Central Europe.

The difference between culture and civilization was very visible in the case of the USSR and the USA. Both of them had daringly adapted the newest ideas of European civilization and even added new dimensions to them, but in spite of these efforts they were not even getting close to the level of European culture. Krejčí found proof of this in the barbarian practices of the Bolsheviks in Russia and in the violence, racism, and fierce antisocialism of American society. Krejčí was a social democrat, and socialism in the basic sense of care for the weak and the poor was to him the culmination of European humanism, which consciously strove to make European culture a 'lived experience' for everybody. To him, the USA and the USSR were strikingly similar in spite of their antagonistic social systems, since both adhered to principles of empty materialism and primitive utilitarianism, principles alien and dangerous to true European values (Krejčí, 1931, p. 175).

I chose to present two Czech voices to show that Europe was not only the concern of the great nations of the West. And their views were definitely shared by many people in other European countries as can be seen from the great popularity of Georges Duhamel's *Scènes de la vie future* (1930; immediately translated into English and published in the USA as *America: the Menace!*), a travel report from the USA describing it in terms evoking some gigantic purgatory. The whole book is a powerful plea for Europe to avoid the dangers of 'Americanization'. We see in conclusion that even good democrats and liberals in the inter-war era began to seek refuge in history and tradition from the strange fruits of the export of Europe's own civilization. A few decades ago the authority of the whole world, now the shaken European ego found comfort in the cosiness of the past.

Europe and the Nazi myths

From an ideological standpoint, Fascism and National Socialism were, as previously mentioned, highly heterogeneous and even contradictory in their curious blend of anti-modernism with a technocratic modernizing ethos, their search for roots in ancient myths and history and their claims to represent the youth and the future, their 'anti-capitalist' anti-socialism and so on. Can one really speak of reactionary revolutionaries?! If we are to attach this ideology to any of Pim den Boer's different identifications of Europe we must – however paradoxical it may sound – see Nazi self-perception in the tradition of 'Europe as freedom'.

At least, that is how the Nazi ideologist Alfred Rosenberg (1893–1946) presented Nazism in his book *Der Mythus des 20 Jahrhunderts* (1930). Rosenberg conjures up a powerful myth of the blood – the blood in which the soul of every race is expressed. Extensively mixing myths and legends with pseudo-science, Rosenberg attempts to demonstrate how the unalterable racial soul and the values attributed to it have ruled the life and history of the races. In Europe, Rosenberg sees three principles fighting a life-and-death struggle: the authentic Nordic *Abendland* resting on freedom and honour struggles with both the Catholic church, this child of decay and racial chaos in Rome with its tyrannic dogmas and demands for submission, and the heralds of chaos – the Jews and their adherents with their materialist individualism, Marxism, and mock democracy which only hides the rule of Jewish money.

In Rosenberg's eyes, these three powers were fighting 'um die Seele eines jeden Europäers' ('about the soul of every single European' – Rosenberg, 1930, p. 118), and the war had shown that no coexistence between them was possible. Everywhere, all forces had to concentrate on cleansing the national spirit of ideological dregs and the national body of racially alien elements. France, for instance, would have to desist from racial degeneration before the country could rightfully claim its natural position in Europe. In this racial and ideological struggle, Rosenberg called all 'real' Europeans to arms:

> Europe's states were all founded and maintained by Nordic peoples. This Nordic man has been in part poisoned and in part exterminated by alcohol, world war and Marxism. It is clear that the white race cannot maintain its position in the world unless it creates order in Europe...If Europe is to be preserved, the first priority must be to revive the Nordic sources of Europe's power – these are Germany and Scandinavia, with Finland and England.
>
> *(Rosenberg, 1930, p. 640)*

Alfred Rosenberg, Nazi ideologist, who drew a racial (racist) interpretation of Europe to the extreme (credit: Bildarchiv Preussischer Kulturbesitz, Berlin).

Rosenberg tolerated no racially mixed 'Franco-Judean' Paneuropa, nor the 'rasse-und volksloses Mitteleuropa' ('a Mitteleuropa void of races and peoples') suggested by Naumann. Instead, a Nordic Europe was envisaged with Scandinavia guarding the north-east and a strong German Central Europe with the necessary *Lebensraum* for future German generations as its core. Britain was to secure the West and the oceans, and in the south, Italy was supposed to lead some vague Mediterranean alliance. Russia, if it ever recovered from Bolshevism, would have to accept a future as an Asiatic power.

Two years later, at a conference on Europe in Rome, Rosenberg in his lecture, *Krisis und Neugeburt Europas* ('The crisis and rebirth of Europe'), was more open towards the southern European people. He calls for a European unity based not on an abstract assumption of one uniform principle for all peoples, but on a respect for the distinctive characteristics of the four great nations of Europe. Small nations have the right to exist and their qualities recognized, but only as long as they accept the primacy of those who really shape Europe. Italy, with its proud notion of the state as the highest possible value, will need to expand along the Mediterranean; France, with its idea that French soil shapes the mind of the French people, will for a while have to defend Europe from African penetration; Britain, with its traditions and understanding of the nation as society, will represent Europe abroad; and finally Germany, with its belief in the blood, will have to see all Germans united in one state before this Germany can fully recognize Europe. Only if these four nations respect each other will Europe be able to defend itself against Bolshevism and the threats from the awakening inferior races, and at the same time avoid unnecessary wars dictated by the interests of a national plutocracy without national identity.

Here, one can still hear a remote echo of an older, conservative nationalism, according even small peoples the right to some existence (as long as they got rid of the Jews); but as *Ostminister* during the war, Rosenberg did not stick to his own principles. He led an *Ostpolitik* marked by the most ruthless genocide and terror, and was sentenced to death at the Nuremberg trials after the war.

The revolt of the masses

Fascism and Communism were mass movements – or at least they tried intensively to exploit and evoke the masses. The whole phenomenon of masses – so different from the upper-class individual liberalism of the nineteenth century – provoked a host of reactions and studies by such people as Sigmund Freud, Elias Canetti, Hermann Broch, and many others. One such study from 1930 gained much attention, perhaps because its author, José Ortega y Gasset, in *The Revolt of the Masses*, had found yet another very seductive title. Ortega y Gasset's diagnosis was clear: Europe was experiencing a severe crisis because the masses had penetrated into all spheres of life, including those that in earlier days had been reserved for a privileged minority. Politics ought to be the domain of a qualified minority offering a selection of programmes to the masses, but today the masses ruled alone although they were by nature unable to rule. The result was a threatening decay of norms. However, there were also positive features in the process that had brought the masses to their new position. Ortega y Gasset welcomed the technical progress that had allowed many people to obtain a standard of living, which only a few decades ago would have been the exclusive privilege of the wealthy few. Now nothing seemed to prevent a life of freedom and luxury.

But if the masses possessed modern techniques, they still lagged far behind in moral upbringing. They were like spoiled children who considered the whole complicated material and social organization of society, from which they benefited, natural like fresh air, instead of realizing that it was the frail product of a specific civilization. Only the combination of nineteenth century liberalism, capitalism, and experimental science had made the explosive social progress possible. But 'mass-people' hated the nobility and generosity of liberal democracy, since they had an antipathy to values that were different from their own, to everything that was unfamiliar to them. They refused to listen and learn and favoured the tyranny of mediocrity, devoid of ideas and values. Politically, they could only express themselves in 'direct action' or violence, since any dialogue would imply some higher 'rules of the game' – a principle unacceptable to 'mass-people'.

No wonder, then, that 'mass-people' felt attracted to the nihilism of Fascism and Bolshevism, two movements cynically mocking the principle of freedom that had made them possible. Bolshevism and Fascism were symptoms of decay; they were anachronistic and offered nothing but a return to an outlived archaic world, which had once been defeated by liberalism. They were empty, but dangerous since the masses could now usurp the state apparatus (which had grown alarmingly in importance) and turn it into a perfect apparatus of violence and exploitation. If it happened, it would be the end of historical spontaneity and the death of Europe.

But the masses alone were not to blame. Ortega y Gasset was a staunch supporter of liberal democracy, to which he saw no alternative. He called it 'the loftiest endeavour towards common life' and a noble act of self-limitation and tolerance (Ortega y Gasset, 1930, p. 58). Liberalism was to him the essence of civilization, and civilization the negation of barbarism. Still, liberalism had obviously suffered from 'certain radical vices', since it had brought into being such characters as 'mass-people' who were in revolt.

Liberalism had somehow lost its alertness and forgotten its need of a dynamic programme; probably it had been too complacent. It was symptomatic how specialization had made even scientists 'mass-people', absorbed in their own little worlds without knowing the inner philosophy of the science they cultivated. The lack of elementary historical knowledge left people without firm guidelines; they had become rootless, aware of their possibilities but uncertain of how to use them. Petty nationalism, which had become so influential after the war, was just one proof of this.

Ortega y Gasset was convinced that the decline of Europe was essentially a myth perpetuated by the Europeans on themselves, and that it only revealed their own lack of a programme. Without the will to progress, all European values and all its creativity would disappear. It would not have mattered so much if only some other authority had been ready to take over, but so far nothing new was in sight. Europe had landed itself in a vacuum, but perhaps the present crisis could lead to a renewal of its most valuable principles. Europe still had a mission to perform; it only needed a new philosophy and a goal.

Ortega y Gasset suggested a programme of large-scale political reform aiming at the creation of a 'United States of Europe'. Technical developments and the steadily growing exchange of ideas had made the nation state obsolete, and since a national community was basically a future oriented ideological product it ought to be possible to make Europe into a national concept. This would be the only way to revitalize Europe and to present a genuine, morally superior alternative to Soviet Communism.

In sum, although Ortega y Gasset blamed modern civilization and the technical specialization inherent in it for the rise of the new barbarians – the 'mass-people' – he mainly sought a solution on the political level (ascribing only a minor role to the detrimental effects of technological development itself) through the unification of Europe in a new nation state. 'Mass-people' were more a symptom than the cause of the crisis, he said, but he abstained from detailed analysis of the flaws in modern European culture that were really to blame.

In a brilliant essay, *Achtung, Europa!* (1935), Thomas Mann unmasked the brutality and the lies on which Fascism was built. Accepting Ortega y Gasset's main analysis of the revolt of the masses, he directly attacked the question only hinted at by his Spanish colleague. Mann saw the roots of the present miserable state of Europe in the way in which the bitterly idealistic nineteenth century seekers after truth had torn apart the idealistic philosophy of liberalism. In a tragic way, reason had undermined its own foundations: Marx and Nietzsche were noble idealists, but they (or rather their later interpreters) had lacked a sense of responsibility since they did not see the danger of anti-intellectual romanticizing inherent in their thinking. As the masses learned about the dethroning of spirit and reason, nothing could prevent them from revelling in cheap irrationalism and intellectual fraud. To Mann, the cult of the irrational of the 1920s and 1930s was utterly pathetic.

Today's masses had no ambition but to escape from the 'I' (and thus from morals and reason) and take refuge in collective ecstasy. Of course their totalitarian masters knew what kind of ideologies to feed them with in order to control them (Marx in his day wanted to enlighten the masses, the Nazis had no such ambitions), since the masses were sentimentally romantic and took pleasure in a vocabulary of blood and soil in spite of their thoroughly modern trappings. The traditional European ideas of truth, freedom and justice were replaced by 'myths', i.e. by a destruction of the borderline between truth and falsehood. There was nothing Christian in this revolt of the poor in spirit, since all they preached was the destruction of human rights; nor was there any heroic ethos, since heroism demanded higher moral values than lies and murder.

Mann was in no doubt that if the rule of the masses and their masters lasted for any length of time in Europe, war would follow and bring about the end of civilization as we knew it. But what frightened him most of all was the weakness of the old, educated world when confronted with this new barbarism. He saw in all humanism an inherent weakness caused by its own good nature and called for a renaissance of a new *militant European humanism*, ready to fight resolutely against fanaticism devoid of shame and doubt. Without this rebirth, Europe would be destroyed to the point where only its name was left.

Mass people in an impoverished mass society was a harsh reality after the First World War. The picture shows a crippled ex-serviceman begging: left-hand side of the triptych 'Metropolis' by the German Otto Dix (1891–1961) (credit: Otto Dix Stiftung, Vaduz; photo: Galerie der Stadt, Stuttgart).

As mentioned above, Mann had in 1917 been an ardent defender of culture (authenticity) in its struggle with civilization (political convenience without deeper spirituality). It is therefore tempting to interpret this later defence of civilization as a 'defection' to the other side, but Mann's later work can be seen as an attempt at a synthesis (Nolte, 1991, p. 616). In a speech in the USA in 1937, *Vom kommenden Sieg der Demokratie* ('The Coming Victory of Democracy'), Mann compared democracy to the temporary attraction of the novelties of Fascism (the only quality of Fascism being its 'youth'). In contrast, democracy was 'timeless-human' and contained a potential youthfulness stronger than any ephemeral fashion. Violence too was part of human nature, but what really separated people from animals was a consciousness of the frailty of being, which gave birth to conscience and to a link to something inherently absolute. True democracy saw and honoured this secret dignity ('Geheimniswürde') of humans. And without this spiritual dimension, mechanical democracy or 'the rule of the people' was not worthy of its name:

> We must define democracy as that form of government and of society which is inspired above every other with the feeling and consciousness of the dignity of man.
>
> *(Mann, 1937, p. 121)*

Democracy in this sense is no less the worldly agent of a transcendental principle than the Prussian state.

Catholic dilemmas

For a long time, the Catholic church had trouble finding the right attitude to the new phenomenon of Fascism. The main enemy of the Church for a century had been liberalism, later joined by socialism; and when nineteenth-century liberalism experienced its great crisis after the war, clerical conservativism saw its chance. In both Italy and Germany it chose to support the new Fascist movements (in spite of their anti-clerical rhetoric) as the most potent opponents to both socialism and liberalism. Later, in Spain and Portugal, the alliance with dictators who were probably more clerical conservatives than 'genuine' Fascists worked well, but in Germany and Italy the Church was to find out that no unholy alliances with such nihilist revolutionaries as Hitler and Mussolini were possible and that the Church could not hope to control them (Trevor-Roper, in Woolf, 1981, pp. 23–36).

Thomas Mann's thoughts indicated that there were intimate ties between a democratic humanism aware of its transcendental roots and Christianity. But the alliance was not an easy one. To some, for instance to many social democratic intellectuals, humanism and democratic socialism were the natural heirs to a Christianity that had had its day, and many Christians – especially in Catholic circles – were as likely to see the root of present evils in democracy rather than the reverse.[6]

[6]   A few words of terminology: in Catholic circles there has at times been a tendency to prefer the word 'Abendland' ('Occident' or 'West') to 'Europe', whereas liberals and socialists have almost uniformly preferred the last concept. No clear difference of definitions can be found, but 'Abendland' was obviously to evoke connotations of medieval Christendom in Europe (cf. den Boer above), united against the heathens of the Oriental world. In this view, only Mediterranean, Roman Catholic Europe was 'real' Europe (Gollwitzer, 1964, p. 15; Schulze, 1990, p. 18).

Definitely anti-totalitarian, but also sceptical towards liberalism, the British Catholic Christopher Dawson (1889–1970) presented a complex discussion of the problems of Europe in his book *The Judgement of the Nations* (1943). In 1945, his book was translated into German and published in Switzerland. With his thorough analysis of the dangers of a secular civilization and recommendations for Christian social politics, Dawson became an important representative of an *Abendland* trend in Catholic thought, which became influential in Western and Southern Europe after 1945 (Nolte, 1991, p. 455).

So far, little has been said about British views on Europe. Of course, British interest in questions of Europe and Europeanness was not absent, but all the literature I have consulted suggests that it was generally low. Europe was 'somewhere else', so to speak. Exceptions were mainly found among Catholics such as Hilaire Belloc and G. K. Chesterton (Duroselle, 1965, p. 283), as they had obvious religious ties to the Continent. Christopher Dawson, who had published his historical study *The Making of Europe* in 1932, was no exception to the rule. In contrast, most of their countrymen were more concerned about the future of the British Empire and the Commonwealth than about Europe.

To Dawson, the decades after the First World War had seen the total collapse of all the optimistic illusions of nineteenth-century liberalism. Western civilization – and through it all of humanity – was being exposed to a destructive totalitarian nihilism, which threatened to annihilate it. The threat left no room for neutrality: first, the evil came from inside Western civilization as a result of its own decay and, secondly, the totalitarian systems had the power to control minds as well as bodies, to brainwash people and destroy everything good in them. This danger was more serious for Christianity than any earlier invasion of barbarians, since the new evil was depersonalized and inspired not by the naïve cruelty of primitive warriors but by what Dawson called 'the perverted science of a corrupt civilization'. Civilization itself had become dubious, since its material power and wealth was growing rapidly while simultaneously its moral foundations were eroded. The more the power, the more complete the destruction, it seemed.

The evil threatening Europe was essentially of a spiritual kind; and Hitler and Stalin were its 'creatures, not its creators'. But since 1918, such evil had been institutionalized in the totalitarian state, which had come into being as two reactions against liberal democracy came together. Individual liberalism was threatened from inside by the mechanization of culture, and externally it was faced with national opposition in countries without democratic traditions. To Dawson, the totalitarian idea was distinctively Russian before it became German or Italian, and he explains the appeal of Communist collectivism by placing it in the context of Russia's theocratic ideals of Orthodoxy and Tsarism.

Dawson's 'real' Europe was only the parts with a Roman Catholic past, and even here he makes a distinction between 'Western civilization' and what is at times called Central, at times Eastern Europe, within which he includes Germany. Dawson was sceptical about this region, which he found culturally susceptible to the spirit of authoritarianism and collectivism:

> But for Western civilization as a whole the victory of such a spirit
> means death, because it is the denial and destruction of the spiritual
> principles by which the West has lived.
>
> *(Dawson, 1943, p. 48)*

Dawson uses the concepts of 'Europe' and 'the West' almost as synonyms, but while Britain (and the USA) are definitely part of the 'Western civilization' it is less obvious if 'Europe' also includes the British Isles.

Much of the blame for the present malaise was put on the unhealthy elements of Orthodoxy and Lutheranism (Dawson sees a direct link from Luther to Prussian militarism), and thus on the divisions of Christendom. If the splits had not arisen, no 'neutral territory' for a secular politics could have emerged and religion would not have been squeezed out of the public sphere and into the private. Still, Dawson does not consider the resulting humanistic liberalism (inspired first of all by Calvinism and the Free Churches) sinful; on the contrary, he is convinced that religion played a much greater role in this culture than is usually admitted. He even talks about the 'sublimated Christianity of the liberals and the humanitarians'. But liberalism forgot its roots in Christianity, which made it unable to reform itself when faced with the challenge of socialism and mass society:

> ...for Christianity and humanism and social freedom are not conflicting
> ideas that have alternately dominated the European mind, they have a
> spiritual affinity that was not apparent to the reformers and
> revolutionaries who were enveloped in the dust of conflict, but which is
> now becoming visible when all of them are threatened alike by inhuman
> forces that have no kinship with any of them.
>
> *(Ibid., p. 16)*

Therefore, friends of justice and liberty were natural allies of true Christians in the ongoing war, even if the reformers hesitated to recognize the Christian foundation of their ideals. But they would have to understand that humanity could not save itself by its own powers, as freedom alone would not bring salvation. A victory over Germany would be of little value if it was achieved by means that made the victor all too similar to the defeated. Only the restoration of a Christian spiritual order could save the world through a return to Christian unity. By recognizing that most schisms in the Church had been unnecessary, since they had their roots in national or political disagreement, a spirit of tolerance, accepting differences of rites and national cultures, should be possible within the same Christian faith.

Thus Dawson accepted a pluralistic Europe, and he was careful not to demand a universal return to the Catholic church. Without national differences, religious unity might have been possible, but European civilization would have been much poorer and religious life would probably have suffered as well. The national principle was to be respected as long as all Europeans remembered that they were part of a 'community of culture' that had been based on Christianity for a thousand years. Only modern nationalism had to be abandoned, morally because it did not respect the Christian–European community and politically because global trends had made whole civilizations, not nation states, the basic unit of international politics. Europe would have to organize in a free democratic federation, similar to the USA or perhaps first of all to the British Commonwealth. In the event, it is clear from the context that Dawson's vision of a 'Western European federation' does not include Britain, which politically was to remain outside Europe.

Europe's regions and borders

Dawson had little to say about Germany's eastern neighbours, and in most of the literature discussed so far, the European horizon has been essentially Western European. Ortega y Gasset understood Europe to be 'primarily and probably the trinity of France, England, Germany' (1930; 1961 edn, p. 103), and east of Germany, perhaps only enigmatic Russia was noted. We therefore need a discussion of Russia's complicated and ambiguous relationship to Europe as seen both with Russian and Western eyes. But before that, I will focus on the smaller peoples of Eastern Europe, since our understanding of what Europe has meant to Europeans would remain insufficient if we only entertained views from one dominant region. And finally I will discuss a fundamental, complicated and painful aspect of Europeanness: the Europeans' attitude to their colonies and to races: did race matter, and if so, who was 'allowed' to be part of the 'European race'?

Europe seen from Czechoslovakia

I have chosen to take a closer look at Czechoslovakia to see how intellectuals and politicians in this new state looked at the Europe of which they had now become a politically independent part. But Czechoslovakia is just one example, and in the East Central European region one can find a diversity of views on Europe – all of them probably very much determined by what we could call *formative events* in the history of these countries.

In Poland, the many *divisions* of the country and the permanent pressure from both East (Orthodox Russia) and West (Protestant Prussia) has been crucial in the formation of an ambiguous Polish attitude to Europe. On one hand, the Poles feel themselves to be a Western European nation, even the bulwark of (Catholic) Christianity against the barbarians from the East. But simultaneously there was the feeling that the unreliable West had all too often sacrificed Poland as a 'Messiah of the nations'. Politically, this has at times resulted in an almost 'schizophrenic' anti-Western attitude linked to the view that by comparison with the Lithuanians, the Ukrainians, and the Russians, the Poles *are* European. And at times, such sentiments led in the inter-war period to a self-assertive anti-Western nationalism (Krol in Herterich, 1989, pp. 102*ff*).

Hungary had also traditionally seen itself as a defender of Christianity against 'Oriental barbarism'. But the country's attitude to Europe was in the inter-war period totally dominated by the 'Versailles syndrome'. In 1919 Hungary lost most of its territory, and millions of Hungarians were included in the new neighbour states. A wave of emotional anti-Western nationalism ran through the country. Some stressed Hungary's links with the 'German Christian World' in order to seek justice through an alliance with Germany, others wanted to abandon Europe completely: in a reaction against the treacherous West a 'Turanian movement'[7] became popular. It stressed the Hungarians' Asiatic roots (based on an erroneous theory of a linguistic relationship

---

[7]   Turanian languages – the family of languages related to Turkish.

between the non-Indoeuropean Hungarian and the Turkish languages – in fact Hungarian is only related to Finnish and Estonian) and called for a union of all 'Turanian peoples' from Mongolia to Hungary (Varda, 1989, pp. 158*ff*).

By comparison, the Czechs felt unconditionally (Western) European. Before the war Czech patriots had striven to emancipate the nation from its solid embedment in German culture. In their sometimes exaggerated search for non-German inspirations, the Czechs turned in various directions from Russia to France and, as an independent national life began to flourish, the Czechs found themselves in the somewhat unenviable position of 'knowing all about Europe and being completely unknown to her' (Krejčí, 1931, p. 208). As the war changed that, most Czechs and Slovaks saw the creation of Czechoslovakia as a culmination of a progressive trend in the European civilization they felt part of[8]. They all knew that the survival of their state was dependent on the preservation of the post-war international order. So, politically, Czechoslovakia had great interest in European cooperation and the country played a very active role in the League of Nations and in different regional organizations.

Foreign minister Edvard Beneš (1884–1948) was honorary president of the Czechoslovak Pan-European Union, and another top politician, the Slovak Milan Hodža (1878–1944) was seriously involved in the 1930s in projects for an agrarian economic union in Central Europe. To him, regional structures such as this would be the best – and only viable – foundation for any 'Pancuropa'. Hodža argued that all Central European nations shared the same historical experience, in which they had been more objects than subjects of their own history and, to avoid nationalistic conflicts and economic chaos, the new nations in the region would have to unite spiritually and economically (Hodža, 1931, pp. 384*ff*). Without such cooperation, all Central European nations would some day be ground between the millstones of Russia and Germany.

Hodža's Central Europe was the land between Russia and Germany. The East begins with Russia, he stated, and Germany was presented as a part of Western Europe or perhaps as a regional entity in its own right. The agrarian character of central Europe should help it find its own identity, and Hodža expected it to develop a new kind of cooperative farmers' democracy in defence against the super-capitalist mechanization of America and Western Europe. To him, the West needed new vitality and he predicted that Central Europe could become such an inspiration. Politically and economically, Central Europe was to mediate between the West and the Russian East.

Hodža's plans for a Europe of regions were at times influenced by short-term political expediency, but his general line of thought was typical of most Czech writing. For instance, no Czech would regard his country as being part of 'Eastern Europe', and many voices predicted a shift of influence and energy from the West to Central Europe.

---

[8]   The Slovaks had been under Hungarian rule and a ruthless politics of 'Magyarization' had left the Slovak national movement very weak – the alliance with the linguistically very close, but culturally more distant, Czechs was therefore a necessity for Slovak national survival, in spite of later long-term Czech predominance in the relationship.

F. V. Krejčí in his above mentioned *Czechhood and Europeanness* also presents a Europe of distinctive cultural zones. In the controversial issue of Czech–German relations he accepts what Hodža perhaps for political reasons denies: the close Czech cultural affinity to the Germans. To Krejčí, the main axis in the long march of the European spirit stretched from Greek antiquity through renaissance Italy to France and England. The European lifestyles unfolding on these historical stopping-places were, in their heyday, objects of desire for all of cultural Europe. With Italy politically weak and England half withdrawn from Europe, France for two centuries became the incarnation of European cultural progress and was envied and imitated everywhere. But France had become decadent, seduced by its own splendour and careless about its cultural heritage. In Krejčí's words, France had become self-sufficient and, in so doing, had forgotten about Europe.

So adjoining this first axis, where Europe was a lived experience, a new Central European cultural axis passing from Scandinavia through Germany to the Austrian Empire began to make itself felt with Germany in the lead. The region's sincere, introverted and perhaps slightly gross spirit gave Europe the Reformation, for which the region paid dearly in the Thirty Years' War. As German culture finally recovered a century and a half later, the lifestyle of the German élites had none of the French *élan*. No wonder, then, that the culture of the region became speculative and romantic. In this axis, Europe was first of all an *idea* – a dream and a future project.

Tied to the continent, the Germans were fully aware of not being alone in Europe, and they soon became preoccupied with the principle of nationality. Knowledge of Europe became a means to realize the idea of Europe and, as Krejčí put it aphoristically, the French thought they *were* Europe, whereas the Germans tried to *know* her. Much of the same was true about the Czechs who could not escape a close cultural relationship with the Germans. The Czechs were put in a difficult situation since they were the Slav tribe that had penetrated furthest into the West. Though fully integrated in Western European culture since the acceptance of Christianity, the Czechs had been reluctant to accept Western civilization, as it usually came through German mediation and contained a danger of assimilation. Only in recent years had the Czechs become strong enough to give up romantic Pan-Slav nostalgia and vote for a fully integrated Europe.

To Krejčí, true Europeanness consisted in accepting a double adherence to one's own nation and to a shared European culture. In fine romantic tradition, Krejčí believed in the existence of 'national souls' and in tribal-linguistic national affinities. To him, all European nations had to appear on stage before a fully authentic Europeanness could evolve. He mentioned the recent wave of Scandinavian literature as proof of the richness of such a multi-cultural Europe, and he found the élites of small nations more European than those from the great powers, since they had to be 'transnational' and know foreign languages to enrich their own cultures. Like many of his compatriots, Krejčí saw no conflict between a culturally heterogeneous Europe and political integration, and his book ends on a note of support for Briand's plans for a European confederation.

Russia, the Soviet Union and Europe

To Poland, Czechoslovakia, and Hungary it was more difficult to be *discovered* than actually *accepted* as part of Europe, since for a thousand years they had been part of (Roman Catholic) Christianity. Russia's case was almost the opposite, and for centuries Russia's relationship with Europe had caused endless trouble both for the Russians themselves and for the (Western) Europeans. Most discussions of Russia's 'otherness' are based on the fact that Russia, for centuries, developed independently of (Western) Europe. In religion, the country went its own way since the breach between the Roman and Byzantine churches in 1054, and the Mongol invasion in the thirteenth century and later military pressure from the West kept Russia isolated and hence xenophobic. However, from the time of Peter the Great (1672–1725), Russian leaders made serious efforts to shape the Russian state in a European way. It was also in Peter's time that the notion of the Urals as the boundary between Europe and Asia was established in Russia (Bassin, 1991, p. 6). In politics, Peter and later tsars managed to make Russia a European power (cf. den Boer above), and during the nineteenth century Russia on several occasions intervened directly in (Western) European affairs.

Only then did Russia's relations with Europe become a problem to both sides. The whole discourse was of course highly politico-ideological and views often differed greatly on both sides. In Russia, 'Westerners' lamented the country's backwardness and isolation and wanted it to catch up with Europe as fast as possible: the reactionary government first of all wanted Western efficiency, Prussian style, liberals looked to the political freedom of England and France, and radicals found inspiration in Marxism or anarchism. They all shared the will to import ideas to overcome the menace of the 'lost' centuries (Schubart, 1938, pp. 279*ff*). But soon nationalist reactions to the admiration of the West set in. The 'Slavophiles' praised the uniqueness of the Russian national spirit and called Russia a world of its own. There was a deep historical and cultural gulf between Russia and Europe so it would be detrimental for Russia blindly to imitate the West. Somewhat inconsistently, this protective attitude was often combined with pan-Slav demand for a union of all Slav peoples, evidently under Orthodox Russian supremacy (Bassin, 1991, pp. 9*ff*). The denunciation of the West was primarily a critique of present-day European society in all its materialist degeneration. The common roots of Russia and Europe in Greek and Christian culture were stressed, and often Russia was accorded a messianic role as 'saviour' of Europe.

Western attitudes were at least as varied and may roughly be divided into four groups. One considered Russia European, due to Christianity, perhaps also to race and culture. Another saw Russia as Asiatic – primitive and oriental underneath a thin veneer of Europeanness upheld mostly by German, Baltic, or Jewish élites. A third saw in Russia a mixture of European and Asiatic elements and a bridge between the two worlds and, finally, many argued that Russia was a whole universe of its own, neither European nor Asiatic. It is interesting that the 'discovery' of the USA (as a strong independent power) also had repercussions for the perception of Russia. The Europeans began to see themselves as an entity *between* other powers, i.e. America and Russia, not just as the centre of the world. It was an early warning, when Alexis de Tocqueville (1805–59) predicted in 1835 that some day the two powers would each control the fate of their half of the globe (Tschižewskij, 1959, pp. 13, 108), but at the turn of the century such a notion was becoming increasingly common.

The Bolshevik takeover seemed to make the task easy for most European observers. A political and cultural pariah, Russia required little effort to be excluded from cultural Europe proper. Hardly any of the texts discussed here accept Russia unconditionally as part of Europe, the general tendency being to see in Russia a world of its own. Some took into account socialism's European origins, but dismissed the Soviet version as primitive and alien and deeply marked by the Asiatic or Orthodox traditions of Russian history.

Somewhat paradoxically, this repudiation of Russia took place at a time when the challenge of the revolution and the resulting wave of Russian immigrants greatly increased European interest in Russia and contact with its culture. Also the emigrants themselves had lively views and one group, represented here by the linguist N. S. Trubeckoj (1890–1938), brought the notion of the otherness of Russia to its logical extreme. For the first time Russians presented Russia as being fundamentally *outside* the European cultural world. Though politically often just as critical of the West as the Slavophiles, the 'Eurasians' used modern scientific methods in their analysis, which gave their work a curious blend of ideology and serious academic research. An area approximately coinciding with the Soviet territory was identified as a cohesive geographical unit that neither belonged to Europe nor to Asia and which was termed *Eurasia*. Furthermore, historically, culturally and anthropologically this Eurasian melting pot had formed an independent world, and Trubeckoj could quite agree with the Westerners who found that the war and the revolution had torn the European mask off the Russian face. He made a sharp distinction between the Russians (whom he called 'Turanian') and the Slavs and placed the border between the West and the East between the two (Trubeckoj, 1927, in Tschižewskij, 1959, p. 523).

But more influential in Western intellectual circles was a critic of Eurasianism, the philosopher Nikolay Aleksandrovic Berdyaev (1874–1948). Born an aristocrat, he had flirted with Marxism in his youth before turning to Christianity. In 1922 he settled in Paris, and two years later his book *The New Middle Ages* was published to great acclaim.

The book can be seen as a Russian parallel to the line in German thinking that disliked Western liberal civilization and preached its end. According to Berdyaev, history, like nature, moved rhythmically, and now the world (i.e. the Christian world – he has no interest in the rest) faced a new Middle Ages. The war and the revolution in Russia proved that the modern era was spiritually burnt out and that the old liberal principles could no longer be restored. Some good elements of the modern era would live on into the next epoch, but while humanism had liberated man *from* something – from the theocracy of the old Middle Ages, for example – it had been completely unable to raise man *to* a new spiritual awareness. The whole theory of democracy was based on the absence of any higher truth and humanism's pride had brought its downfall, since if God did not exist, neither did man.

This was reflected in Berdyaev's views on ideologies. Socialism was a logical result of capitalism, and both shared the cult of Mammon and the denial of God. But unlike capitalism, socialism was dynamic; it had a vision and was right in putting matter above form. But its messianism was false and allowed the proletariat – or rather its self-appointed vanguard – to become a monstrous, absolutist tyrant, destroying all spiritual freedom in the name of an empty goal.

Still, Communism had one foot in the new era since it was openly Antichrist and thus destroyed the liberal illusion of not-believing. From this perspective, Fascism also was a harbinger of the new era. In general, the loss of neutrality was a good sign, although Communism sought an international, sacral community with the devil. It demonstrated by negation the features of the new Middle Ages, which would be marked by a return to a transcendental spirituality in which the Kingdom of Christ was sharply opposed to Antichrist. Poverty and misery would follow, but through ascetic purification a spiritual community in Christ would arise. This community would be organic and hierarchical, ruled by a spiritual aristocracy and true parliaments of corporative guilds.

Berdyaev believed that Russia had a special mission to save the world. Unlike Europe, Russia had never fully left the Middle Ages or mastered the secular rationality of bourgeois society. Therefore, in 1918 the radical Antichrist of Communism had much more appeal than the lukewarm principles of liberal democracy: 'The Russians … are spiritually a non-political people who aspire only to the highest point of history, the actualization of the Kingdom of God' (Berdyaev, 1924; 1933 edn, p. 149). Apocalyptic as they were, the Russians wanted either a brotherhood in Christ or a comradeship in Antichrist. Berdyaev expected the terror of the revolution to make the Russians understand their sins and return to Christ, and this spiritual renewal would be an example to the whole world. A true universalism would have to waken in all peoples if Christendom was to triumph. And:

> The Russian people is by nature the most universalist of all the peoples
> of the world, the quality is part of the very framework of their national
> spirit, and their calling ought to be to work for world-unification and
> the formation of a single spiritual cosmos.
>
> *(Berdyaev, 1924; 1933 edn, p. 100)*

Berdyaev shared this messianism with the Slavophiles, but he condemned any nationalism or belief in a God with national affiliations. He rejected old forms of theocracy, and in his appeal to all individuals to make a personal choice between good and evil seems more inspired by Protestantism than by orthodoxy.

Berdyaev's apocalyptic visions and condemnations of the God-forsaken West appealed to flagellating natures, and even his belief that Communism, by negation, could bring the world closer to salvation through the reborn Russian people found some adherents in the West. Walter Schubart (1887–c.1940; he 'disappeared' in the USSR) in his *Europa und die Seele des Ostens* ('Europe and the soul of the East', 1938), with arguments curiously mixing Spengler and Berdyaev, predicted the end of the (Western, German, bourgeois, soulless, etc.) 'Promethean epoch' and the coming of a new era (Eastern, Russian, spiritual, brotherly, etc.) for which Bolshevism indirectly paved the way.

Europe, races, colonies

The reluctant or even dismissive attitude of most Western Europeans towards Russia suggests that the awareness of borders and non-'Europeanness' has been vital to the construction of a feeling of European community. Often the perspective of an imagined (a fictional traveller or inhabitant of some Utopia) or real outsider was needed to make visible a European identity. Max Scheler observed how Europeans had only come to notice their common identity when they discovered how similar they looked in the eyes of non-Europeans; he wanted the Europeans to utilize this experience in remembering their roots instead of naïvely believing in the global possibilities of European civilization (Scheler, 1915, p. 261) in a world of incompatible cultures.

The anti-liberal German stance with its emphasis on culture and tradition almost 'had to' produce theories of European singularity, but even in liberal thought we often meet notions of a unique – mostly superior – Europeanness rooted in culture or race. Aristide Briand's memorandum of 1 May 1930 mentions European 'racial affinities and common ideals of civilization' (quoted in Coudenhove-Kalergi, 1934, p. 115). In 1953, the first half of the same sentence in a publication from the German Foreign Office has 'technische Zusammengehörigkeit' ('technical affinities') (Europa, 1953, p. 33).

This piece of reinterpretation (or 'censorship') is hardly accidental. To any post-Auschwitz observer it is striking how frequently the concept of race appeared in pre-war texts. It was in no way taboo, nor was it reserved to the Nazis. Vital to some and marginal to others it was widely accepted as at least one element relevant to the understanding of Europeanness. Sometimes the concept was used at the level of nations (the German, Russian, French, etc. race), and some people spoke of a European (Caucasian, white, etc.) race as a whole. Some examples serve to illustrate this range:

> The whole of Europe forms one single race, one single blood fraternity, which is divided into many strains.
>
> *(Coudenhove-Kalergi, 1934, p. 273)*

> ...the disunity and lack of balance that marks the German national temperament is rooted in the racial and historical origins of the German national being.
>
> *(Dawson, 1943, p. 20)*

> ...even in the case of Eastern orthodox Jewry, where the weaknesses as well as the merits of the whole race are more intensely manifested...
>
> *(Zweig, 1943a, p. 20)*

> In all cases the bearer of the European intellect is seen to be of a generatively cohesive mixed race made up principally of Celts, Latins, Slavs and Teutons, plus a vanishing Judeo-semitic minority, which, when considered from a geographical point of view, can be divided into broad categories of the fair, Nordic, blond race, the Alpine race and the Mediterranean race.
>
> *(Scheler, 1915, p. 293)*

Of course there were also sceptics. Spengler accepted the idea of a subjective racial community, but virtually ridiculed biological racism:

> A strict classification of races – the ambition of all ethnology – is
> impossible. …Race, in contrast to speech, is unsystematic through and
> through. In the last resort every individual man and every individual
> moment of his existence have their own race.
>
> *(Spengler, 1922; 1928 edn, p. 131)*

Nevertheless, racial anthropology had become both academically acceptable and
popular in the late nineteenth century, and despite a huge growth in anti-racist
literature it had by no means disappeared in the period between the wars. Ortega y
Gasset:

> …the human species has flourished in zones of our planet where the hot
> season is compensated by a season of intense cold. In the tropics the
> animal-man degenerates, and vice versa, inferior races – the pygmies,
> for example – have been pushed back towards the tropics by races born
> after them and superior in the scale of evolution.
>
> *(1930; 1961 edn, p. 77)*

Not least, such theories of racial (biological) and cultural difference between
Europeans and non-Europeans were very convenient in granting legitimacy to
European colonial adventures. Generally, colonialism was found acceptable wherever the Europeans were unable to see any 'higher' culture (i.e. typically a culture
strong enough to make serious military or cultural resistance to the European penetration). China and Japan had won a certain respect, but nobody saw anything
wrong in the exploitation of Africa. To later observers the era's unreflected acceptance of colonialism gave the idea of Europe a tragic ambiguity, as the concept *in-
tramuros* often meant freedom, human rights, and democracy, but *extramuros*
domination, exploitation, and subjugation (Morin, 1987, p. 147; Duroselle, 1965,
p. 318). Only in the Resistance programmes do we find a denunciation of 'Euro-
imperialism' and calls for a release of the colonies (Lipgens, 1968, p. 18).

It is worth remembering that Europe between the wars was still overwhelmingly
'white' and in a 'global' sense ethnically rather homogeneous (though of course
migration took place, and Danes in 1910 felt no less distance from the alien Polish
creatures imported to pick sugar beet than they do to the Turks today). Japanese
tourists were not a frequent sight, and people from the European colonies had not
yet begun to move in great numbers to the colonial centres. This perceived homogeneity may be one reason for the great interest devoted to the 'Jewish question'.
These very visible 'internal foreigners' were (no matter for how many centuries
the Jews had been present in a country) a permanent reminder of the 'otherness' of
the world and posed a problem of interpretation. In the first half of this century
racial terminology was commonplace and, as the quotation above by Stefan Zweig
shows (he himself a Jew), this was once again no Nazi monopoly.

But for any discussion on the Jews in Europe it is helpful to go back to Friedrich
Nietzsche (1844–1900). Nietzsche, in his remarkably anti-nationalistic reflections,
introduced the concept of the 'good European' and he believed that the European
peoples would fuse into a new superior 'Mischrasse' (mixed race). This process

would also solve the 'Jewish problem', which he contended only led to conflicts in nation states. In the upbringing of this new European man, Nietzsche found the Jews as useful as any other national 'ingredient' (Gollwitzer, 1951; 1964 edn, p. 326), and the Jews had even won immortal merit by being the Best Europeans in the Dark Ages:

> In the darkest hours of the Middle Ages, when the bank of Asiatic
> cloud hung heavy over Europe, it was the Jewish free thinkers, scholars
> and doctors who kept aloft the banner of the Enlightenment and
> intellectual independence in the face of the most pitiless personal
> duress, and defended Europe against Asia. Even when Christendom has
> done everything possible to orientalize the occident, Judaism has played
> a major part in occidentalizing it again...
>
> *(Quoted from Gollwitzer, 1951; 1964 edn, pp. 327ff)*

In many ways the Jews (at least better-off emancipated Western European Jewry) formed a European élite, somehow *above* the (other) nations – at the same time 'foreign' and representing the essence of civilized Europeanness. In the characteristic language of the time, Walter Schubart explained that the obvious success of the Jews in the last 150 years came about less by their own efforts and more by the fact that European history was taking a shape very familiar to the deepest nature of the Jewish national character (Schubart, 1938, p. 24). Jews were often identified (and identified themselves) with cosmopolitanism, anti-nationalism, progress, and so on (of course also with money and commerce), i.e. with the principles of the liberal order and its socialist offshoot. According to Theodor Lessing (1874–1933, killed by Nazi extremists in exile in Marienbad), the permanent sufferings of the Jews had led many of them to identify with all oppressed peoples and thus to engage strongly in European revolutionary movements – an attitude in paradoxical contrast to the painfully conservative Jewish national soul (*Volksseele*) without which the Jews could not have survived for two millennia (Lessing, 1923, pp. 318*ff*). Though repeatedly referring to the Jewish *will* to be different Lessing, like Nietzsche and Spengler (Spengler, 1918, p. 399), assumed the disappearance of (Western) European Jewry through assimilation in the rising cosmopolitan, secular civilization.

But to those who did not believe in a liberal (socialist), European 'civilization' the Jews posed a problem. Of course racial anti-Semitism described the Jews as fundamentally non-European, but others also had problems of interpretation. The adherents of 'Europeanness' as 'Christendom' often found it hard to avoid anti-Semitism, and the heavy engagement of the Jews in secular capitalism and socialism led no less to their castigation than their role in the crucifixion of Christ. Berdyaev is one example of this and he manages to condemn both Jewish messianism (for being exclusive and collectivist) and racial anti-Semitism, suggesting that the two just mirror each other:

> One could call racial teaching a distorted, secularized, godless and
> biologized imitation of the Jewish national ideology. The Jews represent
> the only classical form of the racial idea... Judaism has in many periods
> of Jewish history ascribed a religious meaning to 'the people' and
> attached the religious inseparably to the national.
>
> *(Berdyaev, 1935, p. 125, author's translation from the Danish version)*

By contrast, Berdyaev said, Christianity could not preach exclusivity or hatred towards the Jews, since the religion was open to anybody willing to convert. But the Jews were rarely willing to give up their identity – a problem also faced by the adherents of a Herderian vision of Europe as a sum of nations. It was highly inconvenient to have contingents of Jews in all countries, when only the nation state could form the nucleus of an ideal Europe. And for those who neither wanted to give in to racism, nor to abandon the validity of nationality as *the* constituent feature of any culture, the only options were a politics of assimilation or a support of Zionism as an expression of Jewish nationalism. Masaryk, for instance, whose Czechoslovak republic was a haven of tolerance towards Jews compared to most neighbouring countries, was an ardent supporter of the Zionist movement.

Europe's pride, its belief in its own intellectual superiority, and its contempt for the 'lower races' is summed up in the quotation below from the Bohemian-German-Jewish philosopher Edmund Husserl (1859–1938). It also illustrates a typical feature of European self-understanding: in order to be part of the spiritual community you have to be settled and to 'build the European home', i.e. to contribute to the continued growth of a culture that considers itself unique – since it alone has defined itself as an 'historical teleology of an unending series of goals of reason'. The quotation can also remind us that the fate of European Jewry – this people 'above Europe' – was tragically mirrored in the fate of other 'internal foreigners', the Gypsies, invisible to most in their position 'below Europe'.

> In the spiritual sense the English dominions, the United States, etc., clearly belong to Europe, whereas the Eskimos or Indians presented as curiosities at fairs, or the Gypsies, who constantly wander about Europe, do not. Here the title 'Europe' clearly refers to the unity of a spiritual life, activity, creation, with all its ends, interests, cares and endeavours, with its products of purposeful activity, institutions, organizations. Here individual men act in many societies of different levels: in families, in tribes, in nations, all being internally, spiritually bound together and, as I said, in the unity of a spiritual shape.
>
> *(Husserl, 1935; 1970 edn, p. 273)*

Conclusions

Only thirty-one years separate 1914 from 1945. It is a short space of time, but it contained two world wars, a series of immense political and social upheavals and breathtaking transitions in all spheres of life. It was an era of extremes, and it took Europe from a state of self-confident global superiority to near exhaustion. Intellectual life was no less turbulent than the world surrounding it, and it may seem impossible to identify any prevalent notion of Europe in the midst of all this. However, in the material treated here, one single concept manifests itself with an overwhelming authority. Of all the aspects contributing to the era's notion of Europe, the *national dimension* was pivotal and it determined the character of most lines of argument.

First, the political life of the period was ruled by a disastrously triumphant nationalism. It accompanied if not fostered both the wars, and in the inter-war period it characterized the behaviour of most actors on the European stage.

Secondly, even people devoid of nationalistic chauvinism unconditionally accepted 'the national principle'. The Europe of Versailles was founded on it and was for many protagonists a vital step in the realization of the ancient European ideas of freedom and equality. If cultural Europe was primarily composed of its national cultures, then political Europe ought to be the sum of its nation states. We saw how the main political initiative towards European unity between the wars, that of Briand, did not even dream of violating the principle of national sovereignty, and the prestige of the nation in the hierarchy of values is perhaps best described by this quotation from Briand's loyal supporter, Édouard Herriot:

> [Briand] affirmed the necessity to preserve the sovereignty of different countries destined to become united in a federation. Occasionally, he blamed the fundamental differences of conception on certain internationalists who wished to suppress nations in favour of abstract notions, without having any point of contact with history and life.
>
> *(Herriot, 1930, p. 50)*

Thirdly, those who warned against nation state pettiness were also deeply influenced by this line of thought. Coudenhove-Kalergi and Ortega y Gasset – major advocates of a 'United States of Europe' – both considered the nation state as an intermediate step on the way to the creation of a common European nation, one to which all inhabitants were to feel *nationally* attached. In Italy in 1932, the influential liberal historian Benedetto Croce (1866–1952) wrote:

> …just as, seventy years ago, a Neapolitan of the old kingdom or a Piedmontese of the sub-Alpine kingdom became Italians, not by denying that which they had been, but by elevating it and incorporating it into that new existence, so will the French, Germans and Italians and all the others elevate themselves to become Europeans and their thoughts will turn to Europe, and their hearts will beat for it, as they had done for their smaller fatherlands, which they will not have forgotten, but love the more.
>
> *(Quoted from Rijksbaron, 1987, p. 67)*

Once again people's loyalties were seen to be arranged in concentric circles, and only after learning to behave as Europeans could there be a start to discussion about the possibility of a truly global civilization start.

Europe was regarded primarily as an interplay of nations rather than of, say, groups of consumers or producers, regional communities or interest groups devoted to specific issues, and so on. There were, of course, attempts to stress non- or trans-national communities of interests (for instance, the German Social Democrats had a 'United States of Europe' in their party programme) but, in general, the perspective in such claims as the solidarity of workers, Catholics, pacifists, and so on, almost inevitably ended up being global rather than European.

Nationality was a seemingly stable component, without which Europe at this time could not be imagined. Dynamically, most observers identified the *explosive growth in modern civilization* as the main *challenge* to Europe. No one was left unimpressed by the possibilities opened up by aeroplanes, radios, electric light, and cinemas, but the double-edged nature of technological progress had been demonstrated in the mass destruction of the war. In many texts we find a highly ambiguous attitude to a process that seemed to challenge everything known and established.

There was general consensus that Europe was not sufficiently prepared for changes of this magnitude, which threatened Europe both internally and globally. In Europe's 'internal' political life a conflict appeared between, on the one hand, the strong trends towards large-scale production, economic centralization, and international interdependence and, on the other, the seemingly untouchable 'national principle'. Stefan Zweig – one of the few intellectuals absolutely untarnished by nationalism – in an essay from 1932, *Der europäische Gedanke in seiner historischen Entwicklung* ('the idea of Europe in its historical development'), dedicated to the unifying elements in European culture, lamented the present strife between the peoples:

> ...if I were to try to formulate the intellectual situation today, I would say that the present drive to unite Europe has more to do with *things* than it has with *people*.
>
> *(Zweig, 1943b, p. 348)*

Most plans for European unity from Naumann to the propaganda of the Nazis stressed the need for economic cooperation and for an adjustment to a world of global competition. But at the same time, there was an unwillingness to give up any national sovereignty to create customs unions, or common markets. On the contrary, economic autarky had a high priority and dovetailed with political nationalism. Attempts at unification either neglected the dilemma (Briand's official memorandum), tried to eliminate it by moving national loyalties to a continental level (Coudenhove-Kalergi), or implicitly or explicitly counted on the hegemony of great power according satellite status, only, to smaller nations (Naumann, Nazi Neuropa).

Modern civilization did not restrict itself to undermining the foundations of national self-sufficiency; it also ruined the political values of nineteenth-century Europe. Mass production created a mass society with mass politics, which did its best to destroy the principles that had made it possible. Not everybody was willing to bury the 'decadent bourgeois liberalism' and opt for the totalitarian solutions, but many democrats did see some truth in Marx's dictum about the bourgeoisie being its own gravedigger, and were left irresolute when asked for a dynamic alternative to Communism or Fascism. 'Europas grösste Gefahr ist die Müdigkeit' ('The greatest danger to Europe is tiredness'), said Husserl (1935; 1954 edn, p. 348), but his calls for a rebirth of Europe through a 'heroism of reason' had no more effect than Mann's desired new 'militant European humanism'.

Finally, modern civilization mercilessly revealed to Europe that it was no longer the undisputed power centre of the world. Europe was now only one of several global powerfields, a condition often used in arguments for European unity, but not yet fully comprehended. Often, the traditional feeling of European superiority, in all its pride and arrogance, was mixed with an almost paranoid wish to protect a culture that had suddenly discovered intimations of its own mortality.

In my introduction I discussed the dichotomy between projects and perceptions of Europe, stressing the analytical purpose of the two concepts. The aim was to clarify different aspects of a complex phenomenon, but obviously the two dimensions were contained within each other. If the distinction has turned out to be reasonably applicable for the period treated here, it is perhaps because the political projects for Europe were so stunningly far from any practical realization that they could easily be singled out for analysis. Both politically and intellectually, 'Europeanness' experienced a strong recession, and the few who still cared enough to insist on seeing Europe as an entity were so preoccupied with making a diagnosis that they had little time for actually suggesting cures. Finally, in 1945, the 'doctors' moved in from abroad.

References

BARRACLOUGH, G. (1963) *European Unity in Thought and Action*, Oxford, Basil Blackwell.

BASSIN, M. (1991) 'Russia between Europe and Asia: the ideological construction of geographical space', in *Slavic Review*, **50** (1), pp. 1–17.

BĚLOHRADSKÝ, V. (1990) 'Je Masarykovo pojetí Německa ještě aktuální', in *Přítomnost* **1**, 1990, Prague.

BERDYAEV, N. (1924; 1933 edn) *The End of Our Time*, London, Sheed and Ward.

BERDYAEV, N. (1935) *The Fate of Man in the Modern World*, London, SCM Press.

BOLL-JOHANSEN, H. and HARBSMEIER, M. (Eds) (1988) *Europas opdagelse – historien om en ide*, Copenhagen.

BRUGMANS, H. (1965) *L'idée européenne 1918–1965*, Cahiers de Bruges.

ČAPEK, K. (1926; 1991 edn) *Amerikanismus* (First published in *The New York Times* 1926), printed in: *Od člověka k člověku* II, Prague.

COUDENHOVE-KALERGI, R. N. (1923; 1926 rev. edn) *Paneuropa*, Wien-Leipzig; translated (1926) *Pan-Europe*, New York, A. A. Knopf.

COUDENHOVE-KALERGI, R. N. (1934) *Europa erwacht!*, Zürich-Wien-Leipzig (*Europe Awake!*).

DAWSON, C. (1943) *The Judgement of the Nations*, London, Sheed and Ward.

DUHAMEL, G. (1930) *Scènes de la vie future*, Paris; translated (1931) *America the Menace*, London, Allen and Unwin.

DUROSELLE, J.-B. (1965) *L'idée d'Europe dans l'histoire*, Paris, Denoël.

ELIAS, N. (1939; 1980 edn) *Über den Prozeß der Zivilisation* I, Frankfurt-am-Main, Suhrkamp.

Europa (1953) *Dokumente zur Frage der europäischen Einigung*, Bonn.

FOERSTER, R. H. (Ed.) (1963) *Die Idee Europa 1300–1946*, Munich.

GOLLWITZER, H. (1951; 1964 edn) *Europabild und Europagedanke*, Munich.

HERRIOT, É. (1930) *The United States of Europe*, London, George Harrap.

HERTERICH, F. and SEMLER, C. (Eds) (1989) *Dazwischen – Ostmitteleuropäische Reflexionen*, Frankfurt-am-Main, Suhrkamp.

HODŽA, M. (1931) *Československo a střední Evropa* ('Czechoslovakia and Central Europe'), in *Články, reči, stúdie* IV, Prague.

HUSSERL, E. (1954) 'Die Krisis des europäischen Menschentums und die Philosophie' (1935), in *Die Krisis der europäischen Wissenschaften und die transzendentale Phänomenlogie*, Gesammelte Werke VI, Haag; English language edn: (1970) The Vienna Lecture, Appendix I: 'Philosophy and the crisis of European humanity' in *The Crisis of European Sciences and Transcendental Phenomenology*, Evanston, Northwestern University Press.

KLUKE, P. (1955) 'Nationalsozialistische Europaideologie', in *Vierteljahrshefte für Zeitgeschichte*, **3**, pp. 240–75.

KREJČÍ, F. V. (1931) *Češství a evropanství*, Prague.

LENIN, V. I. (1915), 'On the Slogan for a United States of Europe', originally in *Sotsial Demokrat*, No. 44, English edn in *Collected Works*, vol. 21, pp. 339–43.

LESSING, T. (1923) *Europa und Asien*, Hannover.

LIPGENS, W. (1968) *Europa-Föderationspläne der Widerstandsbewegungen 1940–1945*, Munich.

LUKÁCS, G. (1919; 1975 edn) 'Alte Kultur und Neue Kultur', in *Politische Aufsätze* I, Darmstadt 1975; originally published (1919) 'Régi kultura és uj kultura', in *Internationale*, Budapest, No. 6–7, pp. 6–12.

MANN, T. (1937) *Vom kommenden Sieg der Demokratie* ('The Coming Victory of Democracy') speech in USA, 1937.

MANN, T. (1935) *Achtung, Europa*; translated (1942) *Europe Beware*, in *Order of the Day: political essays and speeches of two decades*, New York, A. A. Knopf.

MASARYK, T. G. (1920) *Nová Evropa: stanovisko slovanské*, Prague; *The New Europe: the Slav standpoint*.

MEYER, H. C. (1955) *Mitteleuropa in German Thought and Action, 1815–1945*, The Hague.

MORIN, E, (1987) *Penser l'Europe*, Paris; translated (1991) *Concepts of Europe*, Holmes and Meier.

MOSLEY, O. (1968) *My Life*, London, Nelson.

NAUMANN, F. (1915; 1916 edn) *Mitteleuropa*, Berlin; translated (1916) *Central Europe*, London, P. S. King.

NAUMANN, F. (1918; 1964 edn) 'Vorläufiger Abschied' (1918), in *Werke*, IV, pp. 974–77, Cologne/Opladen, Westdeutscher Verlag.

NITTI, F. (1922) *La decadenya dell'Europa*, Firenze; translated (1923) *The Decadence of Europe*, London, T. Fisher Unwin.

NOLTE, E. (1991) *Geschichtsdenken im 20. Jahrhundert*, Berlin, Proplyaën.

ORTEGA Y GASSET, J. (1930; 1961 edn) *La Rebelión de las Masas*; translated (1961) *The Revolt of the Masses*, London.

PORTER, B. (1983) *Britain, Europe and the World, 1850–1982*, London, Allen and Unwin.

POUND, E. (1952) *Collected Shorter Poems*, London, Faber.

RICHTER, E. (1983) *Leitbilder des europäischen Föderalismus*, Bonn.

RIJKSBARON, A., ROOBOL, W. H., and WEISGLAS, M. (eds) (1987) *Europe From a Cultural Perspective*, The Hague, Nijgh and Van Ditmar Universitair.

ROSENBERG, A. (1930) *Der Mythus des 20. Jahrhunderts*, Berlin.

ROSENBERG, A. (1934) *Blut und Ehre*, Munich.

SCHELER, M. (1915) *Der Genius des Krieges und der deutsche Krieg*, Leipzig.

SCHLIE, U. (1992) 'Nur Fiktion und Rhetorik – Hitlers Vorstellungen von einem Neuen Europa', in *Frankfurter Allgemeine Zeitung*, 1 February 1992.

SCHUBART, W. (1938) *Europa und die Seele des Ostens*, Lucerne; translated (1950) *Russia and Western Man*, New York, F. Ungar.

SCHULZE, H. (1990) *Die Wiederkehr Europas*, Berlin.

SPENGLER, O. (1918, 1922; 1928 edn) *The Decline of the West: Vol. I, Form and Actuality; Vol. II, Perspectives of World-history*, London, Allen and Unwin. (First published in two volumes as *Der Untergang des Abendlandes: I Gestalt und Wirklichkeit* (1918)*; II Welthistorische Perspektiven* (1922), Munich, C. H. Beck'sche Verlagsbuchhandlung.

TSCHIŽEWSKIJ, D. and GROH, D. (Eds) (1959) *Europa und Russland – Texte zum Problem des westeuropäischen und russischen Selbstverständnisses*, Darmstadt.

VÁRDY, S. B. and VÁRDY, A. H. (1989) *The Austro-Hungarian Mind: at home and abroad*, New York, Columbia University Press.

WIPPERMANN, W. (1983) *Europäischer Fascismus im Vergleich, 1922–1982*, Frankfurt-am-Main, Suhrkamp Verlag.

WOOLF, S. J. (Ed.) (1981) *Fascism in Europe*, London and New York, Methuen.

ZWEIG, S. (1943a) *The World of Yesterday: an autobiography*, London, Cassell. (First published in 1943 as *Die Welt von Gestern*.)

ZWEIG, S. (1943b) *Zeit und Welt*, Stockholm.

Essay 3
Europe since 1945: crisis to renewal

Prepared for the Course Team by Ole Wæver
Senior Research Fellow, Centre for Peace and
Conflict Research, Copenhagen

Europe in the hands of the receiver

Sometimes apparently similar events can produce quite opposite effects. The First World War left the idea of common – European or universal – values in crisis. As described in Essay 2, the war was followed by *political* efforts towards creating or maintaining 'Europe' but, at the deeper emotional and philosophical level, a grave doubt was implanted as to the sustainability of any idea of given, absolute, human or European values, standards or principles.

After the Second World War, there was a different reaction. Writing in 1959, Isaiah Berlin asked:

> What has emerged from the recent holocausts? Something approaching a new recognition in the West that there are certain universal values which can be called constitutive of human beings as such. Romanticism in its inflamed state – Fascist, National Socialist, and Communist too – has produced a deep shock in Europe, less by its doctrines than by the actions of its followers – by trampling on certain values which, when they were brutally thrown aside, proved their vitality, and returned like war-cripples to haunt the European conscience.
>
> *(Berlin, 1959; 1991 edn, p. 202)*

The First World War followed a period of optimism and belief in progress, and thus it was a shock to see that humanity had not progressed beyond cruelty and barbarism. 'War', which had become in many quarters a heroic idea, was in reality shown to be nauseating. Twenty-five years later the general mood was much more pessimistic, the surprise was not war, nor that war was horrible – but that enlightened Europeans were able to reach – back or forward? – to an ultimate bestiality. This caused reflection on limits, on the absolute, on humanity, on Europe. The feeling of shock was overwhelming but hope was invested in the rational approach (heroic irrationalism was discredited). Such rationalism in Europe (in contrast to America of the 1940s and 1950s) was not a triumphant belief in the march of progress into a brilliant future controlled by enlightened science, but rather the understanding that irrationalism and romanticism had led the world into disasters via nationalism, the fascination of war and aesthetization of politics. Rationalism came back, as it were, by default.

Probably, one of the most decisive conditions for the project of European integration was the temporary rebuff of nationalism. In the defeated countries – Germany and Italy – nationalism had been associated with the regimes that had led the nations into war, defeat and destruction. In the words of Stanley Hoffman:

> The collapse of two national ideologies that had been bellicose, aggressive and imperialistic brought about an almost total discrediting of nationalism in every guise. Among the nations of western Europe that were on the Allied side, the most remarkable thing was that the terrible years of occupation and resistance had not resulted in a resurgence of chauvinism.
>
> *(Hoffman, 1966, pp. 870ff.)*

What was left behind, even among nations on the winning side, was a general feeling of defeat.

'Zero Hour' – tradition abandoned as legitimizing force

In the immediate post-war years, some Europeans were strongly influenced by a feeling that something special had been born in the resistance to Nazi oppression. One expression of it can be found in E. P. Thompson's description of the mood at that time, reflecting on the letters written in the last years of the war by his brother, who died fighting with Bulgarian partisans. The brother wrote in 1943:

> How wonderful it would be to call Europe one's fatherland, and think of Krakow, Munich, Rome, Arles, Madrid as one's own cities. I am not yet educated to a broader nationalism, but for a United States of Europe I could feel a patriotism far transcending my love for England.

This Union he saw as 'the only alternative to disaster'. And later in the same year he wrote:

> There is a spirit abroad in Europe which is finer and braver than anything that tired continent has known for centuries, and which cannot be withstood. You can, if you like, think of it in terms of politics, but it is broader and more generous than any dogma. It is the confident will of whole peoples, who have known the utmost humiliation and suffering and have triumphed over it, to build their own lives once and for all.
>
> *(Quoted in Thompson, 1982, p. 4)*

This aspect of resistance looked not towards the history of Europe, but rather to the *promise* of Europe – which might mean the possibility of freeing oneself from the old Europe. People were ready to learn something new; in certain quarters there was a feeling of general preparedness for redefining basic allegiances, for changing course. The first attempts to institutionalize a new European integration had very much the air of a cleansing exercise. As one recent commentator has put it:

> The new morality which the Resistance deemed necessary did not stop at national boundaries. Nationalism and national pride stood accused of being root causes of past European wars. Resistance views on the future therefore stressed the need to transcend historical national boundaries, dismissed as artificial and discredited, in order to rebuild a revitalised and genuine European community.
>
> *(Urwin, 1991, p. 8)*

If the late 1940s were marked by a certain anti-romanticism – a cool, not overly-emotional attitude was seen as the proper reaction to the strong emotions of nationalism and war – the 1950s and 1960s seemed to reflect a naïve belief in an enlightenment springing from science. The Atlantic area went through a period, sometimes called the second industrial revolution, when automation and consumerism became widespread. In the United States, the progressive and socially responsible had high hopes of social science solving such problems as war, injustice and criminality (for example, the numerous articles in the journal *Social Research* during the 1950s, which project an almost behaviourist belief in social science as a vehicle for social reform and progress; and in the 1960s the birth of peace research). In a parallel development, much of the political agenda in western Europe or at least north-western Europe was set by socialist and social democratic parties working for a form of welfare state which could be seen also as the rational planned society. Various studies in the US and in Europe presented Sweden as the actually-existing model of a social future. Scandinavia in the post-war period was marked by a certain anti-Europeanness (Wæver 1992) and the Swedish/Scandinavian model was seen less as a paradigm for Europe and more as an index of comparison with the United States. Sweden was in competition with the United States as the symbol of modernity. (Ruth, 1984, pp. 88 and 66)

Leading German social democrats, who had spent time in Scandinavia before and during the war, sought to implement some kind of Swedish/Scandinavian model in their own country. The truly 'European' society – belonging neither to the East nor the West – would be a rational society. Such a society would utilize planning to avoid the irrationality of United States 'jungle-capitalism', where aggressive market forces are allowed free rein, and it would use the market to avoid the irrationality, waste and rigidity of the Soviet system. As noted, this model is basically anti-nationalist – a sense of common purpose is installed without becoming imbued with romantic nationalism. Other political parties were important, but at a very general level it is still possible to describe these years as a 'social democratic epoch', where ideological hegemony was held by the concept of a 'package deal', including economic growth, equality, work, rationality, the state and internationalism.

Eastern Europe in the Soviet grip

In 1945, decisive power in Europe rested largely with the USA and the USSR. Most of what was soon to be called eastern Europe – the 'Iron Curtain' countries

– had been liberated by the Soviet Red Army and this would have a profound effect on the political realities of the region. The borderline between the USSR and the rest of Europe, which to many European observers in the inter-war period had been the border between Europe proper and some alien world, moved more than a hundred miles to the west. The Soviet Union kept what it had been granted by the Ribbentrop–Molotov agreements of 1939, and more. The Baltic republics remained firmly in the USSR, and parts of Germany (East Prussia), Poland, Czechoslovakia and Romania, too, were annexed. Poland, by way of compensation (probably as a means of weakening a future Germany and keeping Poland preoccupied with a possible German 'revanchist' threat) was granted much former German territory. Moreover, all the nation-states created after 1918 (except for the three Baltic republics) were allowed to re-establish their state sovereignty.

This sovereignty soon proved to have very narrow limits. Steadily, regimes totally loyal to and dependent on Moscow were installed in all countries liberated by the Red Army (except for Austria). In Czechoslovakia (the country with the strongest pre-war democratic tradition and the one that took the longest to become a 'people's democracy'), some non-Communists sought to adjust to the new realities by re-launching the idea of Czechoslovakia as a bridge between Russia and the West – and not just between their two social systems – but it soon became obvious that the Soviet Union had no intention of experimenting with any such east-central European 'third way'.

Politics in eastern Europe were subjected to an initial transformation according to the mould developed in the Soviet Union under Stalin. There has been much discussion amongst historians of the Cold War on the degree to which this shaping stemmed from action or reaction, from a Soviet drive for expansion or a western pressure on an essentially defensive Soviet Union. But even if one leans towards the latter interpretation as to security/power politics (i.e. the West being the stronger side), it is undeniable that the uniformization of 'eastern' Europe was driven also by the inner logic of 'Soviet-type societies' (Lemaitre, 1989).

The re-creation of east-central Europe in the image of the Soviet Union reflected the logic of Stalinist ideology. Holding a monopoly on truth derived from Marxist-Leninism, the Communist Party wielded absolute power. Whatever the effects of the Cold War, the uniformization of 'eastern europe' was deliberate and systematic. The Soviet Union had, since the 1930s, purged all 'eastern' European Communist Parties: for instance, most of the Polish party leadership was eliminated to ensure that no independent national leadership could emerge. Moscow never recognized the Polish government in exile in London and simply brought its own people to power in 1945, and in the case of Czechoslovakia, the threat to incorporate Slovakia as a Soviet Republic was used to secure the Communist Party a dominating role in the post-war coalition government (early in 1945 Ruthenia was simply taken over by the Ukrainian SSR). In 1947, when the Czechoslovak government with initial local Communist approval (the Soviet purge of the Party had to wait until after the seizure of power) accepted the offer of help under the Marshall plan, Foreign Minister Jan Masaryk was immediately summoned to Moscow and ordered to refuse the American offer.

From 1948 the Soviet model was implanted in all the countries in the Soviet sphere of influence, with the exception of Tito's Yugoslavia. It led to a high degree of uniformity in political, ideological, and economic structures – often with devastating results. Agriculture was collectivized and heavy industry was given top priority without any regard for the needs or traditions of industrial production in the relevant countries.

Soon – both in the Communist propaganda and in the eye of the western spectator – a homogeneous and uniform 'eastern Europe' emerged, which was to some a paradise of constructive work and fraternal co-operation, to others a totally uniform, grey and oppressed wasteland. Integral to Soviet strategy for achieving total hegemony in the region was the principle of *divide and rule* which made all the satellites directly dependent on Moscow and allowed for little transnational co-operation. The Warsaw Pact and Comecon (the CMEA – Council for Mutual Economic Aid) were founded in reply to western diplomatic and economic initiatives and contributed to the image of close integration. But beneath the blanket of uniformity, realities were more complicated, and the intended (and claimed) homogeneity never

Armed Volkspolizei guard East-German building workers during erection of the Berlin Wall, August 1961. The workers received an hourly rate of DM1.28 (photo: Deutsche Press-Agentur).

155

Windows were blocked up in buildings overlooking the Bernauerstrasse so that the occupants might not gaze upon – nor escape to – West-Berlin, October 1961 (photo: Deutsche Press-Agentur).

went below the level of the power élite (Kusy in Herterich and Semler, 1989, p. 190).

In the *economic sphere*, Comecon never led to a true internal 'socialist market'. The system of barter exchanges could not disguise the severe distortion of production and prices brought about by the central planning system. This alone made a severe limitation on travel in the eastern bloc necessary. Travel was of course restricted for political reasons. The attempt to prevent travel affected Soviet citizens most radically – in 1988 less than one per cent of the population (soldiers

excluded) had ever visited a foreign country. But economic problems contributed as well: the distorted price-system, shortages of various kinds, and the lack of convertible currencies made it necessary to prevent the 'exchanges' which would result from any unrestricted opening of the borders (ibid. p. 191). Even military co-operation was restricted to the top echelons. The Soviet troops installed in most of the satellite countries were kept strictly isolated from the local population.

The limited access to travel was one feature that helped to preserve the national peculiarities of the eastern European states. Another was the fact that, in the whole

The Berlin Crisis, October 1961: US and Soviet tanks face each other 200 metres apart in Friedrichstrasse (photo: Deutsche Press-Agentur).

157

Resistance fighters during the 1956 Hungarian uprising (photographs: Hulton/Deutsch).

region, the Jews and the Germans had disappeared. The Jews had been killed by the Germans (sometimes with local assistance), and later, if they had not already fled, the Germans were killed or expelled to the West. The process led to an 'ethnic homogenization' of the populations of Poland and Czechoslovakia especially (and to a lesser degree Hungary and Romania), and it severely weakened the cultural (as well as the economic) ties with the German speaking parts of Europe. For obvious reasons the Jews and the Germans had been the most 'transnational' groups in the region.

Finally, local Communist leaders often used nationalistic arguments in times of crisis to secure their position (Gomulka in Poland in 1968, Ceausescu in Romania in the 1960s and again in the 1980s, for example), though very rarely with an anti-Russian tone. The German threat was frequently invoked, in spite of the existence of the GDR, and in the case of Czechoslovakia internal rivalries were exploited to prevent reform-socialist co-operation developing. Little was done to eliminate national antagonisms hanging over from the inter-war period. The result of all these efforts to keep the eastern European countries isolated from each other (and of

course from the West) was a strange lack of interest in the struggles for freedom and independence in the neighbouring countries, a phenomenon which could be seen in 1956, 1968 and once again in 1980–81 in the behaviour of Hungary's, Czechoslovakia's and Poland's neighbours (Vajda in H & S, 1989, p. 129).

The surface uniformity and homogeneity of eastern Europe by no means implied any serious attempts to integrate countries at the social level. On the contrary, it might be argued that national varieties and stereotypes were preserved and sometimes even cultivated, while in western Europe, trade, travel and mass communication were spreading a greater uniformity of everyday habits and lifestyles.

Where does this leave the concept of 'Europe' in eastern Europe? Quite simply, repressed. As indicated in Essay 2, the attitude to 'Europe' had been different in each of the east central European countries in the inter-war period, partly as a result of their response to the Versailles settlement. Similar differences could be seen in 1945, but in general the prestige of the Soviet Union in these countries was greatly enhanced and western Europe was more or less discredited, being characterized as decadent and having shown itself to be impotent in the face of Nazism, a feature aptly used by the Communists to argue for a new (at times even 'Slavic') eastern brotherhood. In this kind of argument, 'Europeanness' was neither used, nor needed.

Thus the traditional problem of 'east-central Europe's' status as 'borderland' between the East and West seemed to be decided in favour of an 'eastern' attachment and it must be said that, initially, this association received domestic support, not least in intellectual circles. However, the harsh realities of 'Sovietification' soon led to a re-articulation of the border problem, since the new superimposed sociopolitical system (with its Stalinist terror and brutality) became unavoidably identified with the country from which it originated, that is to say the Soviet Union or, rather, Russia. Communism became Soviet Communism, and Soviet Communism was interpreted in terms of the Russian tradition of absolutism, orthodoxy (religious and later ideological) and brutality. Any rebellion against this system seemed (due to the bi-polar logic of the time) to imply a concession to (western) European values. Mihály Vajda accurately expresses this feeling when he writes that the goal of all the rebellions in east-central Europe (i.e. Poland, Czechoslovakia and Hungary) is not so much a challenge to the political status quo in Europe (with Hungary perhaps as an exception), but a means of 'die Ermöglichung des Europäertums' – 'making possible European-ness' (Vajda, 1989, p. 120).

In the particular case of Czechoslovakia, many reform Communists,[1] prior to the invasion of 1968, had returned to the traditional Czech idea of building bridges between East and West. Most notable perhaps was Milan Kundera, who, in a famous speech at the Fourth Czechoslovak Writers' Congress in 1967, argued that the combination of (western) European cultural roots and socialist principles gave Czechoslovakia excellent prospects of becoming a model for the whole world. Kundera was later to lose both his Party membership and many of his illusions about this kind of 'third way'.

---

[1]   'Reform Communism' refers to the wing inside the Communist Party that tried to carry out democratic and/or market reforms; most often the reference is to the Prague Spring of 1968, as it is in this case.

Within the regimes in eastern Europe, the concept of Europe was often met with suspicion, but allowed as a tactical tool for political developments or, to put it bluntly, as a foreign policy instrument for the Soviet Union in relation to western Europeans. Later such a stratagem could be deployed against other targets. For instance, Hungary and the GDR in the 1980s legitimized a foreign policy deviating from that of the Soviet Union with reference to the conditions of 'small and medium-sized states in Europe'. When Poland in the 1970s presented proposals for nuclear weapon-free zones in central Europe – with a specific central European argumentation – this was in principle a part of the Soviet scheme, but it was certainly done with a vehemence and a twist which originated in Warsaw, not Moscow. The exercise was partly repeated by Bulgaria in relation to a Balkan nuclear weapon-free zone in the 1980s (when the Bulgarians cultivated links with Greece via the 'politically correct' principle of anti-nuclearism). In eastern European societies, 'Europe' was mainly a term and idea employed by dissidents, signifying western, democratic, humanist or other similar orientations.

Western Europe in the American sphere

In the post-war situation, the United States played a crucial role in the recovery of western Europe. The USA not only helped western European countries to get on their feet again (with the Marshall Plan and Organization for European Economic Co-operation), but it also supported the principle of European union/integration. However, there were various American ideas about what forms European integration should or should not take, so the role of the USA must be seen also as a factor that set limits on integration. With hindsight, it is easy to see how all major steps in European integration have been dependent on American initiatives or support (Wallace, 1990; Rummel and Schmidt, 1990). The original EC project had strong American backing and the times when the project prospered, until recently, were always periods when the US administration was clearly positive towards integration.

The curious dialectic of Atlanticist and Europeanist was apparent in one key figure, Jean Monnet[2] . Charles de Gaulle and others suspected that he was only an American-influenced facilitator in Europe and certainly he worked to make sure that European integration took forms compatible with American policy. However, he also worked to inspire American policy. He was, in fact, a key actor in a strong transatlantic network, lobbying for co-operative structures within which western, Atlantic and European institutions could evolve in mutually supportive ways. (Grosser, 1978; 1980 edn, pp. 101–6).

In the post-war history of western Europe there has been a tension between Atlantic co-operation and specific western European co-operation, but in the security field in particular, the Atlantic (NATO) line has dominated. There have been only relatively weak moves towards clear western European co-operation in the

---

[2]   Jean Monnet (1888–1979), French statesman, distinguished economist and financial expert. He was president of the European Coal and Steel High Authority from 1952 to 1955, and in 1956 became president of the Action Committee for the United States of Europe.

security area. In other areas the manifestation of western European co-operation has been stronger. In the economic field there has been a relatively far-reaching integration especially concentrated on the development of the European Community.

Even in the economic field, however, the relationship with Atlantic/American structures remains complex. The immediate successes of west European growth and reconstruction, as well as the more long-term evolution of west European integration, happened inside US-sponsored global institutions of international finance and trade, such as the dollar regime and GATT (the General Agreement of Tariffs and Trade).

Generally, west European integration began within an American-sponsored western/global order. This meant that no direct blocks or prohibitions against Europeanization, as were being applied in eastern Europe, were imposed by the United States; but this benevolence had indirect effects on moulding and shaping the forms of European integration.

We have seen how, from the mid-1940s, the leading powers in the affairs of Europe were the USA and the USSR. Although they had incompatible ideological programmes the two superpowers could be represented as internationalist or at least having universalist programmes. Both of these 'nationalistic universalisms' (Morgenthau, 1948, pp. 248–63) were widely considered superior to traditional European 'realist' power politics. World peace, disarmament and national liberation were the 'idealist' programmes supported by the two superpowers (Jahn *et al.*, 1987, p. 24), though such programmes generated confrontation rather than co-operation. Likewise, on questions relating to the future destiny of Europe there was little agreement between the United States and the Soviet Union.

By 1945, the great European powers were either exhausted or had been destroyed. Europe symbolized war, nationalism and colonialism. So far, the European road seemed to have led to failure. As for the future, one possibility was to anchor politics outside Europe and let the two superpowers call the shots. The Cold War is a large theme for separate study. I am are not going to go beyond observing that the overlay of Europe by the superpower confrontation is marked by a duality. It can be seen as stemming from the differentials of power and a recognition of the superiority in power terms of the USA and the USSR. But perhaps it can also be seen as an unconscious abdication on the part of Europe – a feeling of relief that the superpowers were taking responsibility and control. At the same time, however, this mood of relinquishment was coupled with yearnings for the overcoming of superpower dominance. Such stirrings for reassertion, coupled with feelings of abdication, gave Europe a somewhat schizophrenic orientation in the immediate post-war period.

Another possibility for the future was to re-define Europe as a project, thereby overcoming the European past; it is to this process we now turn.

The EC – economic pragmatism or a new vision of Europe?

Looking back from a vantage point of the 1990s, it is tempting to see the movement towards political and economic integration in post-war Europe as a series of straightforward steps, with the occasional sideways move (see Table 1). In fact, such a bald catalogue masks some very different visions of Europe; it skates over different views of European integration and conceals the cut and thrust of European politics as governments wrestled with questions of national self-interest in the context of European economic and political integration.

In 1945 Winston Churchill, though out of office, was widely seen as a key figure for post-war Europe – and a federalist into the bargain. In 1940 he had proposed an Anglo-French Union just before the fall of France; 'there shall no longer be two nations, but one Franco-British union' (Urwin, 1991, pp. 9ff., 29–35). During the war he had argued for a Council of Europe. The British general election of 1945, however, brought about the replacement of Churchill with the anti-

Churchill, Roosevelt and Stalin at the Yalta Conference, February 1945 (photo: Hulton/Deutsch).

Table 1 Towards European integration

1947 plan for European Recovery Programme (Marshall Plan)

1948 signing of the Brussels Treaty

establishment of the Organization for European Economic Co-operation (OECC)

1949 formation of North Atlantic Treaty Organization (NATO)

formation of the Council of Europe

1951 establishment of European Coal and Steel Community (ECSC)

1952 signing of European Defence Community Treaty (EDC)

1954 rejection of European Defence Community by France

signing of Western European Union (WEU)

1955 Messina Conference on European integration

1957 signing of the Treaty of Rome

1958 commencement of the European Economic Community (EEC) – 'Europe of the Six'

establishment of European Atomic Energy Commission (Euratom)

1960 establishment of European Free Trade Association (EFTA)

Organization for European Economic Co-operation (OEEC) becomes Organization for Economic Co-operation and Development (OECD)

1963 signing of the Franco–West German Treaty of Friendship

1966 EEC agreement in a Common Agricultural Policy (CAP)

1967 formalization of the European Community (EC) through a merging of the institutions of ECSC, Eurotom and the EEC

1973 accession of United Kingdom, Ireland and Denmark to EC

opening of Conference on Security and Co-operation in Europe (CSCE)

1974 establishment of European Council, consisting of heads of national governments of EC member states

1975 conclusion of Conference on Security and Co-operation in Europe (CSCE) and signing of Helsinki Final Act

1979 establishment of European Monetary System (EMS)

1981 accession of Greece to EC

1983 signing of a Solemn Declaration on European Union by heads of state and government

1984 European Parliament approves draft treaty on European Union

revival of Western European Union (WEU) as a European defence forum

1985 European Council adopts the Single European Act (SEA) – agreement on an internal single market by the end of 1992

1986 accession of Spain and Portugal to the EC

1989 proposals for an EC charter of Fundamental Social Rights

1990 as a result of German unification, East Germany enters the EC

1992 signing of the Treaty of Maastricht – further steps towards economic and political union

integrationist (though not anti-European) Clement Attlee, who led a Labour government.

In 1946, Churchill argued in a major speech in Zurich (which had been discussed with Coudenhove-Kalergi beforehand) that it was imperative to establish a United States of Europe. Churchill's argument was, however, more a strong statement regarding the appropriate policies to be followed on the continent, rather than an espousal of a British European policy radically different from that of Attlee's. Churchill – in spite of his 1940 suggestion – did not now consider an Anglo-French union the core of European unity. Along with Monnet, Konrad Adenauer and many others, he now believed that Franco-German reconciliation had to be the starting point, and in the Zurich speech he said:

> The first step in the re-creation of the European family must be a partnership between France and Germany. In this way only can France recover the moral leadership of Europe. There can be no revival of Europe without a spiritually great France and a spiritually great Germany…Great Britain, the British Commonwealth of Nations, mighty America, and I trust Soviet Russia…must be the friends and sponsors of the new Europe and must champion its right to live and shine.
> *(Winston Churchill, 19 September 1946, Zurich University)*

Thus, the widespread hopes that Britain would lead European unification were to be thwarted, and the core moved elsewhere, while Britain concentrated on security matters and the partnership with the US. The British emphasis on its 'special relationship' with Washington was alarming to the French, making the UK a potential Trojan horse.

With the advent of the Cold War and the division of Europe and Germany, plans for an all-European unification became unrealistic and hopes for unification came to be centred on separate eastern and western arrangements. On the western side, from 1947, the US was actively engaged in strengthening western Europe. In 1948 Britain, France, Belgium, the Netherlands and Luxembourg, in the so-called Brussels Treaty, came to some common agreement in the area of security and defence, but this arrangement was quickly overtaken by the formation in 1949 of NATO.[3]

In western Europe a major objective for the adherents of European federalism was to construct a supra-national organization out of what became, in 1949, the Council of Europe. Opinion was split between federalist plans from France and Belgium and more minimalist plans, in particular from Britain. This split parallels the later difference between the EEC and the European Free Trade Association (EFTA) in their attitude towards political integration versus free trade. Because of these differences the Council of Europe was not shaped as a supra-national body and did not become a vehicle for integration.

---

[3] In 1954, the Brussels Treaty changed into the Western European Union (WEU), also including West Germany and Italy. But this move was only to pave the way for the inclusion of West Germany in NATO. The WEU remained marginal until the beginning of the 1980s, when it gained importance as a possible vehicle of the revived interest in European security co-operation.

Testifying to the symbolic qualities of the now relevant European union, it is worth mentioning that at the meeting in London (29 January 1949) where the Council of Europe was finally decided upon (after steadfast opposition from Britain), a final British victory consisted of defeating a proposal from France and Italy that the name of the new organization should be 'The European Union' (Urwin, 1991, p. 34).

The main theme of the late 1940s and early 1950s in the matter of European 'integration' was the competition between two lines: Britain – usually with support from Scandinavia and Ireland – wanted a restricted, inter-governmental kind of co-operation, whereas most of continental Europe (headed by France, Italy, Belgium, the Netherlands, Luxembourg and, when enlisted, West Germany) wanted a more

Konrad Adenauer (1876–1967), Mayor of Cologne, founder of the CDU (Christian Democratic Union) and West German Chancellor from 1949 to 1963. This picture shows him in the year of his retirement (photograph: Hulton/Deutsch).

far-reaching, supra-national integration operating in a federalist format. This involved setting up a European Parliament and on this basis re-casting the whole political organization of Europe and thereby transcending the prevailing nation-state mosaic.

The most important development towards western European integration, the process of forming the European Economic Community, subsequently the European Community, got under way in 1951 in Paris, when six countries (France, Belgium, the Netherlands, Luxembourg, Italy and West Germany) signed a treaty creating the European Coal and Steel Community (ECSC) – the first supra-national organization in Europe. Jean Monnet's original idea of a sectorial integration with supra-national powers was first of all directed at overcoming the old enmity between France and Germany, but it was also part of a gradualist and sector-specific approach towards general European unification, i.e. integration in specific areas with the hope that one issue would pull along the next towards general integration. The major motive was political: to guarantee a lasting peace between France and

Jean Monnet (1888–1979) a moving spirit in the cause of a 'United States of Europe' (photograph: European Community).

Charles de Gaulle (1890–1970), protagonist of France as a great power and president of the French Republic 1958–69 (photograph: Keystone/Hulton/Deutsch).

167

Germany. War between the two should be made not only 'unimaginable – but also materially impractical'. The plan also had an economic dimension – amongst other things the French steel industry needed safe supplies of coal.

The formal opening shot for the process had been a press conference in 1950 by the French Foreign Minister, Robert Schuman. His proposal was that coal and steel resources in western Europe should be pooled and co-administered by a supra-national authority. This should improve the market by reducing tariffs and other barriers, and specifically would handle the instability caused by the shortage of coal and oversupply of steel. As a first step towards more general political integration, a Franco-German *rapprochement* was seen as the essential relationship of the union. The plan actually stated:

> The French Government proposes that the entire French–German coal
> and steel production be placed under a joint High Authority within the
> framework of an organization which would also be open to the
> participation of the other countries of Europe.

(Grosser, 1980, p. 119)

The plan was drafted by Jean Monnet, who was then head of the French Planning Commission. In his conception the coal and steel union should be only the first step towards political integration.

The European Coal and Steel Community contained various institutional innovations of lasting importance: a supra-national authority (the High Authority) with considerable powers, direct income for the community in the form of taxation and thereby less dependence on the member countries, a Common Assembly which was 'the first international assembly in Europe with legally guaranteed powers' (Urwin, 1991, p. 50), and a Court of Justice with the task of ruling on the legality of any High Authority action – 'by rooting the whole ECSC structure in the last resort in the rule of law, the drafters of the treaty introduced a concept which was to be of tremendous importance for European integration as a whole' (Urwin, 1991, p. 51).

The trend towards economic integration continued. In 1958 an important step forward was marked with the formation of the EEC and Euratom. But those who drew up the Treaty of Rome (1957), thereby paving the way for the EEC, had a political as well as an economic agenda. In the words of Walter Hallstein, the first president of the EEC:

> We are not just integrating economies, we are integrating politics. We
> are not just sharing our furniture, we are building a new and bigger
> house.

(Quoted in Urwin, 1991, p. 76)

Political union was now seen as achievable as a consequence of economic integration.

The process of European integration witnessed numerous setbacks. A typical source of conflict was French suspicion that the Germans were too dependent on the United States. The major transatlantic controversies were played out with the US and France as the main combatants, and West Germany as the major variable

(Grosser, 1980). This led to conflicts over co-operative endeavours. The most conspicuous of these had been the aborted attempt to create a European Defence Community (EDC) in the period 1950–54. This revealed French ambiguity, in particular, since the French ended up opposing their own initiative because of its implications for French military sovereignty. Instead the process led, in 1955, to West Germany signing the Brussels Treaty and becoming a member of NATO.

Another of these conflicts was over the bilateral Franco-West German 1963 Elysée Treaty (a very general and in principle ambitious plan for close co-operation in culture, politics, economy and even security – the latter section not realized until the 1980s). To the agreement between de Gaulle and Adenauer, the Bundestag added a preamble, partly drafted by Jean Monnet, which offended de Gaulle because of its emphasis on transatlantic relations. (Grosser, 1980, pp. 140ff.) The treaty thus signified both the early and far-reaching attempts at Franco-German co-operation, and the political limits to it.

A major cause of disagreement in the 1960s between France and West Germany was over the different perceptions of the role of the USA in Europe. Though, as the debates between the Atlanticists and the Gaullists in the West German Christian Democrat party show, differences of opinion could be found within, as well as between, the two countries. (cf. Nolte, 1974).

A further complication arose over French attempts under de Gaulle to promote inter-governmental co-operation with West Germany, at the expense of EEC mechanisms. This was unacceptable to the smaller EEC countries so long as Britain could not operate as a balance against Franco-German domination. Without Britain, the small countries of the EEC were very much dependent on the thrust of supra-nationality.

Among the controversies of the 1960s should be mentioned French (de Gaulle's) opposition to British membership of the EEC, allegedly because this would be tantamount to giving the Americans a vote inside the community. (It was seen as part of Kennedy's 'grand design' for an Atlantic partnership). This 1963 refusal led at first to a strengthening of counter-integration in EFTA. The French line culminated from 1965 in clear crisis, with a French walk-out in 1966 ended by the so-called 'Luxembourg compromise', which institutionalized a national right to veto. Thus, the process of integration was stalled even though in 1967 the European Community had been formalized as a result of the merging of the institutions of the EEC, Euratom and the European Coal and Steel Community.

From 1969, Willy Brandt's social-liberal coalition government in West Germany was less supportive of the idea of a supra-national western European integration than its predecessors. Instead, the *all*-European orientation (i.e. including eastern Europe) and a *con*federal[4] view on the EC played a comparatively larger role in West German thinking. Brandt and his party 'stressed the role of the nation-state for the central European peace order' (Hacke, 1988, p. 169). This seemed to be derived from the emphasis on German policy and *Ostpolitik/détente.*

---

[4] 'Confederal' – a loose league of states such as the CIS, in contrast to 'federal' – a tighter construction of a new, joint state, such as the USA.

Willy Brandt (1913–1992), German Chancellor from 1969 to 1974 and winner of the 1971 Nobel Peace Prize. This picture was taken at the British Labour Party Conference in 1986 (photograph: Hulton/Deutsch).

The essential novelty of the Brandt government (at least in foreign policy) was the changed approach to the East and to the 'German Problem' (the division of Germany). Instead of a principled insistence on unification and very little contact with the East, as had been the policy of the preceding (Christian Democrat-led) governments, Brandt began a policy of movement, of reconciliation with Czechoslovakia, Poland, and the Soviet Union and ultimately a kind of half-way recognition of the GDR, which was not meant as renouncing the demand for unification but shifted the emphasis towards making sure the two halves actually stayed in contact and thus did not grow further apart. Furthermore, it was hoped that the influence following from increased contact might actually change the GDR. Thus Brandt in one way softened the policy of re-unification (in a legal and principled sense) but in another way he gave increasing emphasis to this by moving it from the realm of principles towards the world of processes. Although this new policy could be seen as a German response to an increasing pressure from other western states (USA and France) in the direction of a policy of *détente* in relation to Moscow – and thus completely along western lines – this new diplomatic activity from Germany did lead to widespread suspicions and concern about Germany finding its own way towards an agreement with the Soviets (cf. Henry

Kissinger's memoirs, *The White House Years,* 1979, pp. 405–12). The whole logic of Brandt's opening towards the East implied that he could no longer just concentrate on integration in the West and hope for this to exercise magnetism in the East; he had to start working for some kind of all-European framework (*Friedensordnung,* 'peace order') in which Germany might eventually reach unification, and in which the improved relations towards the East could be located as well.

In the 1970s, western Europe as a whole experienced great difficulty over economic development. The economic set-backs at the beginning of the 1970s, which were dramatically worsened in 1973 by the oil crisis, hit western Europe very hard. Economic problems persisted throughout the 1970s, furthered by the second oil crisis in 1978–79. Against this background, tensions developed between the EC countries and the USA, mainly because of the economic policy of the USA (leading to their budget deficit) and the fluctuations of the dollar. One consequence of this was that West Germany gave up supporting the dollar and together with France, at the end of the 1970s, initiated the European Monetary System (EMS). The relative economic stagnation in western Europe continued into the early 1980s. A major economic talking point during this period was 'Eurosclerosis', a condition that resulted in Europe lagging behind in the international economy. This, perhaps, was a factor in stimulating EC countries into renewed attempts at integration in the second half of the 1980s.

By this time, the EC had expanded its membership considerably, as well as its field of operation. The original six signatories to the Treaty of Rome were joined by the United Kingdom, the Republic of Ireland and Denmark in 1973, Greece in 1981, Spain and Portugal in 1986 and, in 1990, the former GDR was brought into the fold through unification with West Germany. The collapse of dictatorships in southern Europe in the 1970s did more than just promote the cause of the newly-established democracies in Spain and Portugal with the European Community. It meant, as far as western Europe was concerned, a return to a Europe that was politically and culturally acceptable in the wider world. With the admission of more of southern Europe, the EC could claim to include more of *historical* Europe than hitherto. It became entitled to parade as the *European* Community, when it included Greece, the cradle of democracy, and Spain, a major actor in European history and expansion. The image of western Europe thus became less problematic and this in turn served to promote European identity and strengthen the European idea.

Integration theory

The process of European integration managed to give birth to a theory – almost a discipline of its own – *integration theory.*[5] It seems appropriate to dwell on this,

---

[5]   The standard interpretation of integration theory is to present it in the form of three schools. In a simplified form it could be expressed as follows:

(i)   Functionalism is built around the idea that co-operation and politics in general should follow the logic of a theme and thereby settle at the appropriate level: i.e. ecological issues should follow the eco-region, disarmament is a global issue, culture is local, industrial planning is European, and so on. It is not really a *regional* (for instance,

since in many ways it can be seen as a formalized expression of the actual as-sumptions behind the practice of leading politicians and high-ranking civil servants. Neo-functionalism (the leading school of integration theory) stresses the (more-or-less automatic) self-propelling dynamics of integration, so-called 'spill over'. Integration on one issue carries with it integration in another (functional integration); in the course of the integration process political actors 'learn', i.e. re-direct their orientation and their practice towards (European) political bodies that become important. Eventually they might even switch their loyalties to new political structures ('political spill-over'). Finally an agency – in the EC primarily the Commission – is charged with the task of making integration proceed, and in negotiations it will try to handle political conflicts through 'upgrading the common interest' instead of always making compromises on the lowest common denominator (this third type is called 'cultivated spill-over') (Tranholm-Mikkelsen, 1991). The view presented is one of political élites, of incremental change, of 'learning' and redefining interests. In contrast to federalist integration plans, there is little talk of mobilizing the people, or of demanding things in the name of 'Europe'; nor is emphasis given to concentrated moments of choice or constitution-making. As with original functionalist theory, the basic idea is that by abstaining from the controversial 'high politics' decisions of security, prestige and power, one can gradually cultivate political change from below, from 'low politics'.

To some extent this could be presented as the reality of the 1950s and early 1960s, since a stable context was created by the superpowers, and inside this it was poss-ible to operate as if security and high politics did not exist. Because the basic con-flict was now between the USA and the USSR and these superpowers dominated

European) integration theory since it does not start out from a fixed regional set-up, but instead favours flexibility as to scale. The aim is to handle issues at the point where it is most rational for them to be addressed and hence the nation-state is not always the most suitable vehicle. Functionalism has a strong flavour of technocratic ideology: the main point is to prevent the handling of issues from being contaminated by politics. In an increasingly interdependent world it will be in the interest of everyone to allow issues to be organized according to their nature: form should follow function.

(ii)   Neo-functionalism is much more clearly a theory of regional integration (taking the aim of integration in a region like Europe as the starting point); actually neo-functionalism is the most important and influential theory of regional integration. It takes from functionalism the idea of avoiding too much politicization and trying to focus on concrete co-operation, but this strategy is linked to a theory which actually recognizes political processes and especially focuses on the role of élites and their capacity for gradual learning, i.e. how a process can become self-reinforcing by changing the way actors define their interests and interpretations. Thus, it avoids the idealist assumption about altruistic actors, but assumes that the process of integration can carry along the political (and other) élites in redefining their own rational self-interest in ways that increasingly make the supra-national institutions their referent instead of the nation-state.

(iii)   Federalism is (in this context) less of a theory and more of a strategy. In contrast to the élite-approach of neo-functionalism, it stresses the (occasional) mobilization of the masses. The élites are wedded to the existing (i.e. nation-state) structures but, since integration actually will be in the interest of all, the people would choose a European construction if they got the chance. Therefore, one should not (as the neo-functionalists want) avoid politicization, but mobilize people for the decisive move where power and authority can be transferred to a new constitution, a new supra-national unit.

Europe, the relationship between the medium to great powers in western Europe was not to the same extent influenced by security concerns about each other. Such concerns were located in a wider system that allowed for a strategy of downplaying high politics and working from low politics. Even in this situation, some elements of high politics continued to be a main source of non-integration. The different countries had different perceptions of the situation, different strategies for integration and still also mutual suspicions. Continued manoeuvring among the greater European powers remained an essential element of European politics (Hoffman, 1966; Hassner, 1968 a and 1968 b).

High politics also provided the Community with some important impulses. It could be argued that the 1956 Suez crisis, with its humiliation of the European 'great' powers (supplemented by the simultaneous Hungarian uprising, also testifying to superpower dominance), was a major consideration leading to the 1957 Treaty of Rome (Hyde Price, 1991, p. 32). The French colonial war in Algieria was an important factor behind the French policies in the EC of the1960s. And the controversies with peace movements and nuclear missiles in the early 1980s perhaps encouraged the signing of the Single European Act in 1985.

Integration: a European project

As Peter Bugge points out in the conclusion to his essay the Europe projects of the inter-war years were often handicapped by the confusion, on the one hand, of seeing Europe as one region among many; and, on the other, of seeing Europe as superior and thereby latently representing the universal rather than demanding regional thinking. When European values were assumed to be universal values, and European civilization was perceived as the same as world civilization, Europe was not a region in the world but the *centre* of the world. After 1945 this was different. Europe was politically and economically exhausted and the European system of nations, empires and the balance of power was shown to be discredited. Now the *regional* view was paramount, although (as we shall see) some implicit assumptions of superiority and inherent virtue keep reappearing. None the less, the fundamental question was: how could the disasters of the immediate past be avoided? The answer lay in the promotion of European unity and we have reviewed some of the historical aspects in the previous section. Here I want to pick out some of the characteristics of the project for European integration.

(i) The extent of Europe

With the onset of the Cold War, Europe, *de facto*, increasingly became perceived as western Europe and even the western Europe as represented by the six original signatories of the Treaty of Rome. (There is an intriguing approximation between the Europe of the Six in 1957 and the Empire of Charlemagne in 814 (Wallace, 1990, Map 3, p. 16), though claims for historical continuity with regard to the political core of Europe do not stand up to close scrutiny.)

If pressed on this apparent narrowing of Europe, leading integrationists replied that they were not defining borders, that borders were being created by others or, as Jean Monnet put it, 'the boundaries of the Six were not drawn up by the Six themselves, but by those who were not yet willing to join them' (cf. Wallace,

1990, p. 111). This is somewhat disingenuous because, as Britain found to its cost in 1963, a distinction needs to be made between those countries that declined membership and those that were refused membership. Nevertheless it is fair to say that the post-war politicians who, within the limits set by the superpowers, set out to re-build Europe, were 'less inclined to describe the outer boundaries of their imagined Europe than to organize the countries at its core' (Wallace, 1990, p. 20). For Monnet, a principal architect of European integration, Europe's core consisted of France, Britain and Germany.

This did not mean that visions of a wider Europe were totally obscured, but that the reality of the situation demanded that western Europe reorganize itself in the first instance. A way of prising eastern Europe out of the Soviet grip was to strengthen integration, peace and prosperity in the western part of the continent. Although the division between eastern and western Europe was regarded as artificial, none the less the practice of working within a west European frame of reference for decades produced a mental map wherein 'Europe' was often taken to mean either western Europe or even that part of Europe belonging to the European Community.

(ii)   Content

As to content, the EC project has focused on bread-and-butter political and economic issues and the promotion of peace and prosperity rather than on high-sounding abstraction and grandiose historical and cultural claims.

(iii)   Method

The method of integration has been a mix of neo-functionalism and occasional federalism. That is to say, technical (and not overly political) co-operation in some fields, leading to further co-operation and integration in others through the guidance of determined élites and in a process focused on élite politics (neo-functionalism). From time to time, the option of appealing directly to the people, asking them to transfer power to a European constitution and parliament in a grand federal gesture has been exercised (federalism). But in the mix of neo-functionalism and federalism, the former has dominated over the latter.

(iv)   Ideological/philosophical basis

It follows from the summary of content and method above that the ideological and philosophical aspects of the EC project do not reflect a very pronounced and strongly articulated presentation of Europeanism. Although there are times when the project has been couched in terms of great Europeans, shared values and long historical perspectives, it should be said that the proponents of integration have not drawn significantly on European history, or on historicist reification of 'a Europe with a destiny' in which its citizens are obliged to play a particular role. The logic, even the driving force of the EC project, has been mostly technical and to the extent that it engaged in agenda-setting this has been in terms of *a* future for Europe rather than *the* future for Europe.

(v)   Obstacles

Undoubtedly the continuing strength of nationalism – characterized by integrationists as short-sighted national egotism – has been a cause of strain. Additionally, in structural terms, the position of the USA has been a complicating factor – not so much in terms of the US being a negative, external power but more in the sense that European integration was, at the same time, a part of and a resistance to the American order.

(vi) *Perceptions and projects*

During the inter-war period, as Peter Bugge has shown, a useful distinction can be drawn between *perceptions* of Europe and *projects* for Europe. This essay is not built around such concepts. The reason for this is in itself an important point regarding the difference betwen the inter-war and post-war period. In the inter-war years, perception and project often meant a split between images of a desperate situation and grand designs for their solution. In the post-war period the fundamental difference is that there actually is a process of European integration and 'project' now means taking part in and influencing the process rather than issuing stirring calls for radical change. Perceptions and projects move closer and it makes sense to treat them together. Applying this terminology to the period 1950 to 1980 it could be said that the dominant perception of Europe is one of a regional group of peoples learning from their histories that they should follow either a co-operative way (Britain, Scandinavia) or a supra-national way (Continental, Europe of the Six) down a less nationalistic road. This is not the doomed nor driven Europe of the inter-war years; still less is it the nineteenth-century vision of Europe as the centre of civilization and world history. It is more the Europe of a group of peoples inhabiting a small continent trying to find a better way of organizing their regional affairs. The *project* of Europe is itself – not to launch itself on world history but to prevent another world war starting on European soil. Economic and political integration would provide peace and prosperity and may well lead to a stronger say in world politics but not a unique or dominant role. Furthermore, the project is in itself a process – a course of action which promotes European integration not by high-sounding rhetoric, but by practical, down-to-earth co-operation.

Europe as a common destiny?

During the course of the 1980s Europe began to emerge from the long shadows cast by the Second World War. The air of guilt stemming from colonialism, war and holocaust had largely evaporated and after four decades of superpower dominance it was the USA and the USSR rather than Europe that tended to attract criticism on the wider political stage.

Before the bar of world opinion, 'Europe' was accorded a positive rather than a negative cachet (Finkielkraut, 1986; Jahn *et al.*, 1987, p. 25). For example, in the mid-1980s the United Nations University launched a project on regional security with separate programmes for Asia, Latin America, Africa and Oceania; and, after six months of deliberation, Europe was included. The US and the USSR were presumably powerful and secure enough to manage without the attentions of the UN University, but not so Europe. Europe was grouped among the 'young' emergent continents but beyond this, within Europe itself, a more confident, assertive mood could be detected. At the level of culture, ideology and identity, Europe from the mid-1980s seemed to be regaining a sense of dynamism. Europe was once more emerging as a positive idea, something that Europeans should seek to realize, preserve and defend. It was against this backdrop that the process of integration within the European Community gained a new momentum.

By contrast the mood of the late 1970s and early 1980s had been much more tentative and uncertain. Perceptions of the EC were dominated by the controversial Common Agricultural Policy and concerns about the growing bureaucracy in Brussels. The EC could be compared with a cyclist. It had to sustain the momentum of integration or fall – in this case, not to the ground but at least to the baseline of a customs union (Kaiser *et al.*, 1983). In this respect we have already touched on the debate about 'Eurosclerosis', reflecting the fear that Europe would fall behind in the new technological revolution and lose its relative position in the world economy. These fears, coupled perhaps with concerns arising from superpower tension, were to be the main driving-force behind an attempt in the middle of the 1980s to give new impetus to the process of integration. The most important initiative was the series of meetings of the European Council in 1985 which agreed plans for institutional reform of the EC and the plan for an internal single market by 31 December 1992. In a masterpiece of symbolic politics a name and a deadline for the re-launch of old ideas was created. At a stroke, a political reality – 1992 – was conjured up and all actors in international as well as domestic politics were compelled to relate to it. Though it was assumed that the total programme would be implemented by 1992 the impetus of the project has had a self-reinforcing effect. In 1988–89, the project was expanded further with the so-called Delors plan for a monetary union (EMU). Thus it was not until the end of the 1980s that west European co-operation, latent in the European Monetary System since the end of the 1970s, was put into practice – though it should be said that it was only with some difficulty that agreement was reached on the first phase. Early in 1990 these plans were supplemented by a Franco-German proposal for a political union of the EC. Great difficulties, especially with the UK, were experienced in regard to these initiatives, but at the Maastricht summit in December 1991, despite a number of caveats and reservations, a course was set for economic and political union. Since then the Danish referendum of June 1992, rejecting the Maastricht Treaty, and the monetary crisis in October, which led to Italy and the UK leaving the Echange Rate Mechanism, have generated some uncertainty – but whatever the political fall-out arising from this, it can be said that, from the mid-1980s, the EC has undertaken significant new initiatives and created bold prospects for itself.

Although the 1970s have been characterized as a time when Europe seemed to be losing some of its dynamism, there was surprisingly some success in the foreign policy field. European Political Co-operation (EPC) had been set up through decisions taken in the early 1970s, and enjoyed a clear inter-governmental status. EPC worked well in the early rounds of the Conference on Security and Co-operation in Europe (CSCE), known as the Helsinki Process.[6]

[6]   The CSCE has something of a long history. It grew out of the various, mainly Soviet plans of the 1950s and 1960s for a European conference to sanctify the outcome of the

Besides the Helsinki process, the voice of EPC was heard on various issues of regional conflict – in the Middle East, in Central America and in Southern Africa. In these somewhat more symbolic areas, as well as in the community-based issues of external economic relations, the EC/EPC was increasingly seen by the outside world as one political actor. It can be claimed that this was important for the formation of European identity and for a renewed energy towards integration. The EC seemed to become a political reality for itself when it became so in the eyes of others.

In this regard, it is worth stressing that such a dynamic driven by foreign policy, runs contrary to the theory of neo-functionalism explored above and which has been utilized to explain the development of the EC. As we have seen, this theory foresaw a gradual expansion of integration from within – a 'spill-over' from 'technical' and 'economic' issues towards increasing co-operation in political and 'diplomatic' fields. Yet here we have an example of high politics exercising a stronger pull than low politics and, as such, demonstrating that the history of integration should not be seen entirely as a slow, internal process of learning the requirements of co-operation and discovering how to overcome national inertia. There is a dialectic between functionalism and the pressures on Europe from other actors, notably the USA, that serves to reinforce the process of integration.

American pressure for unity in western Europe helped in the formation of a core community in the economic field. Foreign and security policy was much more difficult to integrate since American dominance in this area was both direct and overt. Decisions on important questions, such as those relating to security and defence, were made at national level. These issues were played out in NATO, where the crucial point was how each of the European members related to the United States. Not until the first part of the 1980s did international developments produce the conditions for European integration, extending decisively into the security and foreign policy fields. A Europe in the early 1980s, under pressure from a re-intensification of the Cold War (Reagan, re-armament, intermediate nuclear weapons, peace movements) was followed in the late 1980s by a certain power vacuum (collapse of Soviet power and relative withdrawal of US involvement). Attempts to articulate a 'European voice' were the results of both situations (cf. Wæver 1989; Wæver *et al.,* forthcoming). On the face of it, one might expect either pressure and tension *or* vacuum and *détente* to encourage calls for Europeanization. Taken together, both processes fuelled such a demand. Particularly in Bonn and Paris the clamour for a European voice was heard across

Second World War. The CSCE was finally established in 1974 (in the form of a legal, non-binding, so-called 'final act') after various compromises, such as the inclusion of the USA and Canada, and a bargain to link a certain sanctity of borders with an obligation to respect human rights as well as a principled option for peaceful change. The East interpreted the outcome as a document for stability, for the respect of borders and for non-interference in the internal affairs of states. The West emphasized human rights and change. The dynamic tensions of the document and what became a 'process' – a number of follow-up conferences – were important for European developments in the 1980s. The CSCE was seen as a symbolic all-European forum, pointing to the existence of ties across a divided Europe, and its inclusion of human rights as an item on the agenda was of significance for various groups in the East. As such, it reflected an all-European image which began to capture the attention of people in Europe.

the political spectrum, though the resulting song had various tunes. Increasingly, co-operation among the EC countries proved to be somewhat difficult since the project called not merely for a correction of the policies of the two 'Euro-managers' in Washington and Moscow, but for the taking of actual responsibility.

One, two, many 'Europes': the re-emergence of central Europe

Notwithstanding the importance of EC developments, it is necessary to take a wider perspective on transformations in the perceptions *of* and projects *for* Europe. A straw in the wind was the crop of essays and books on Europe that started to appear from the mid-1980s, particularly in France, and sometimes linked to central European communities in exile. After all, Milan Kundera's influential essay, 'The tragedy of central Europe', was written in Paris for a Swedish journal and gained wide currency when it was re-published in the *New York Review of Books* in 1984.

A common theme to emerge from this new self-reflection in Europe was the stress on Europe's *essence* being in its diversity, its complexity, its lack of a single centre and its absence of uniformity. For instance, Edgar Morin in his *Penser L'Europe* (1987), argues that Europe can be defined by its contradictory and complex nature, by its 'critical rationality' and its 'self-criticism'. In one sense, this is not a bad description of one strand of European history. What is more problematic, though, is to distil from these characteristics a European essence, which may be presented in political debate as the genuine meaning of Europe, the hallmark of Europe's true nature.

Another influential, indeed, symptomatic book was Hans Magnus Enzensberger's *Ach Europa* (1987). In many ways, this is the least missionary of the genre. It treats the peripheries rather than the central locations of Europe, and it allows the characters that Enzensberger meets on his travels to speak for themselves. In some ways, Enzensberger reflects the diversity of Europe more fully than Morin. And yet in Enzensberger's text there is a hidden agenda. In various parts of Europe he shows how society has never been as thoroughly organized as the powers-that-be have wished. There is always an indefinable force that remains with the people – not necessarily a power to act, but a power to resist development, to resist being planned. Europe is thus projected as a collection of localized societies, a plurality of forms ranged across diverse theories and models. National traditions are re-lived in new ways. At heart, the heroes of Enzensberger's Europe are the people that everywhere tacitly resist order – even in Sweden!

All this relates to an idea of *civil society* that was influential in the 1980s. Networks established by people operating outside the sphere of the state, it was assumed, could exist in parallel with or even in opposition to formal state structures. In some interpretations of developments in eastern Europe this was seen to be the decisive factor behind the revolutions. Left-wing groups in the West also took up this idea in the hope that they could cast themselves in the same heroic role as their comrades in the East. As with Enzensberger, the idea involves some vague mix of the silent, unruly masses and movements led by intellectuals articulating what the people really want. One effect of this was to promote an image of a transnational, European civil society, existing as an alternative to the established national states. In projecting Europe as such a single, transnational, multi-faceted local society the concept acquires an anti-establishment hue. Thus Europe is lined up in social movements that are against state, politics and political parties.

For much of the post-war period, the political/security debate over Europe was couched in East–West terms. From the early 1980s, this situation began to change, as instanced by Gorbachev's notions of a 'common European home' and the wave of literature coming from France about Europe. Europe was frequently on the tongue of Russian, French and German commentators and with different voices singing in the name of Europe perhaps we should ask ourselves: did this represent a sudden and surprising chorus of agreement? The answer is no. If we scratch the surface we can see that the commentators were not all referring to the same Europe. These 'Europes' had different boundaries from the West as well as the East – different organizing principles, and different 'European' values. (Jahn *et al.*, 1987; Wæver, 1989; Wæver, 1990). To some, Europe stretched from the Atlantic to the Urals, i.e. a codeword for excluding the Americans, while others hypothesized how Europe could blossom as soon as the Russians were excluded. To some, the European project was dependent on the creation of a strong centre (Brussels), while others claimed that the essence of Europe was its very lack of a centre.

The tendency to see security and politics as questions of *Europe* became much more obvious after the conclusion of the INF treaty in 1987 (dismantling the highly symbolic intermediate range nuclear missiles in Europe), the new *détente* and the changes in the East. It was widely assumed that these processes would somehow lead to a 'Europeanization' of Europe. 'Europeanization' signified not a specific development, but an empty space to be filled. The old order with its limitations had been removed, and several projects were now competing to fill the vacated space. These discourses necessarily moved away from previously held reference points. Since the point was to install a new order as legitimate, a new pattern as 'natural', there was a tendency towards 'deeper' references, a search for new principles. The result in the 1980s has been a much closer link between the fields of security on the one hand and culture, history and geography on the other. The arguments have pointed inwards (to cultural identity), backwards (to history), downwards (to geography), all purporting to project something seemingly solid and almost pre-political – but in fact reinforcing the argument *for* politics (cf. den Boer's essay and the nineteenth-century tendency to mobilize the past as argument).

The first 'Europe' debate of the 1980s was a discussion on the theme of central Europe among exiled and opposition 'east Europeans'. This debate broke new ground in developing an interest in Europe as a cultural and political problem, and for addressing politics as a question of culture. The previously mentioned article by Milan Kundera on central Europe was above all an appeal to the West not to ignore its own Europeanness by forgetting Prague (Kundera 1984). It contained, however, a very clear political programme, and one that posited a specific relationship between culture and politics – culture as the reference guide for politics. Kundera's argument was basically as follows: in speaking about culture there is a clear border between Europe, on the one hand, and non-Europe, equalling Russia/Soviet Union, on the other. Unfortunately, after the Second World War the

Mikhail Gorbachev (1931–) General Secretary of the Communist Party of the Soviet Union 1985–1991; President of the USSR 1988–1991. The author of glasnost *(openness) and* perestroika *(restructuring) (photograph: Hulton/Deutsch: Richard Maw).*

political frontier had been wrongly placed between western Europe and central Europe, which territory came to be seen as 'eastern Europe'. The solution, of course, would be to redress this mistake, and move the political border to its correct location, between Russia and Europe.

Furthermore, the original central Europe discourse had a peculiarly indeterminate nature. Central Europe is neither geography, nor history, neither a place, nor a programme – but 'a way of thinking' (Milosz); 'a culturally connected area' (Leszek Kolakowski); 'a culture idea – or fate' (Kundera); it 'only exists as a state of mind' (Stefan Kaszynski). In a field where no political action seemed realistic, and no alternative was allowed, intellectual and cultural exchange was the only means of opening political space. (Later, when 'ordinary' politics had re-emerged in these countries, this specific mixture of culture, history and geography with all its ambivalences was no longer seen to be a prerequisite for articulating a voice in the region.) More important then was the notion of a 'return to Europe' – taking central Europe to Europe, or even to the West – an idea that had been implicit in the central Europe discourse all along.

'European values' as the continuation of war by different means

Central Europeans did not monopolize the debate over Europe. Other, more powerful voices – particularly French, German and Russian – took up the 'Europe theme'. This section will focus on these *competing* Europes. Close reading of these different 'Europes' is a privileged way of gaining access to the political struggles and developments of the 1980s and early 1990s. In this period the concept of Europe became a keyword and a central conceptual battleground. The fact that other struggles were mirrored in this competition for defining (or conquering) the meaning of Europe, explains why a stress on *competing* Europes, rather than on general, shared trends, is to be the focus at this point in the story. 'Europe' has indeed become a focal point for grand politics. (For more elaborate presentations and documentation of the different Europes, see Wæver 1989, 1990 and Wæver *et al.*, forthcoming.)

For the sake of argument, this presentation is made as if one could talk of *the* French or *the* Russian way of thinking about Europe. This is obviously not the case; a more comprehensive study would show how each national discourse is, in reality, a layered structure, where different groups disagree wildly on certain issues, but may then share a more basic code and set of concepts. This in turn might be contested by some marginal groups; and with these the majority would then share a yet more abstract, more basic conception of state, nation and Europe (for methodology, see Wæver *et al.*, forthcoming, Chapter 1). These Europes do not refer to public opinion nor to the average citizen, but to *political discourse*, to the logic of political argumentation which is shared among opponents in the setting of a national, political culture.

That there *are* such national differences as to what is generally emphasized in a culture, and thereby what is meant by Europe, can be seen from the set of four books comprising this course. Who is writing what? The French write about institutions, the Germans about grass roots and society, the British about relations with the outside world, and the critical task of deconstructing the concept of Europe is given to the small nations, the Dutch and the Danes!

German 'Europe'

In Germany, the central Europe debate was transformed into a debate about *Mitteleuropa*. One reason for this is that Germans tend, quite naturally, to speak in German. The change of word was, however, more than a matter of translation. Whereas for Milan Kundera 'central Europe' was the area *between* Germany and Russia – an area eternally weak and shaped by resistance to its powerful neighbours – the *Mitteleuropa* discussed in Germany was one that (surprise, surprise!) contained Germany. The *Mitteleuropa* concept thus referred to a real area with a decisive political weight, rather than being a question of purely cultural identity. Inevitably, *Mitteleuropa* has connotations of 'Germany and its surroundings', the German area. (On the difference between central Europe and *Mitteleuropa*, see Wæver, 1980, pp. 49–51; Garton Ash, 1990; Rupnick, 1990. The social democratic journal *Die neue Gesellschaft* in 1986 even reprinted a selection from Naumann's book *Mitteleuropa).*

In the first decades of the century, as we have seen in Peter Bugge's essay, there were plans for a *Mitteleuropa*. These were schemes for a federation, or a confederation, a *Reich*, or a tight alliance; i.e. a project in state terms, of creating a stronger state, or aligning states. This has been largely absent from the *Mitteleuropa* writings of the 1980s. Now, *Mitteleuropa* is thought of as circumventing the nation-state. It is neither a coalition of nation-states, nor a European hyper-state. Rather, it is a space cutting across and around borders and is different from the state structures that these borders contain.

The most interesting of the writings on *Mitteleuropa* were probably neither the openly neutralist on the left nor the blatantly nationalist on the right. The views of some leading social democratic intellectuals (for example, Peter Bender, Peter Glotz) seem more typical for the *Zeitgeist* ('spirit of the times') in Germany. *Mitteleuropa* was seen not as a concrete political programme (which was thought unrealistic), but as an impulse for more enlightened behaviour across the East–West divide in central Europe. It leads, according to Bender (1987), not to a policy different from the *détente* in the rest of Europe, but just to more of it. Glotz (1986) is explicit in denouncing the nation-state as a 'disastrous idea' – and he has often been criticized for exhibiting a new '*Reich Romantik*' ('romanticism for the Empire').

In fact, much of the German debate on Europe did not refer specifically to *Mitteleuropa* as such, but it reflected a basic mode of thinking about politics and security in Europe which is encompassed by the concept. A favourite slogan across all German parties has been that they should not change borders, but 'change what borders mean'. This is quite logical. Before the events of 1989, this seemed to many the only way to proceed with the German question and has a pedigree going back to Willy Brandt's *Ostpolitik* initiatives. State unity was seen as impossible, but its 'content' could be attained without tampering with the formalities of states, borders and social systems. The Social Democratic Party (SPD) especially, in its new thinking on German policy, went so far down this road that (without this being stated explicitly) the old objects of state unity seemed no longer to be valid. And thus it became increasingly important to stress how unity could be obtained at the level of culture, in common policies of *détente* and reform, and to some extent in economic terms as well. Germany, paradoxical as it may sound, could be united *in* two states. After all, what do states mean – the colour of uniforms, a flag, a national anthem? More important is the *content* – if people can meet, cultures and economy can grow together (Bredow and Brocke 1986).

And though German–German developments refused in 1989 to follow this social democratic scheme, this logic is still relevant, because it applies to relations in other areas of central Europe. (Even those locations that no longer contain German populations still have a link to German culture and latently, to the German economy.) For these relationships to develop, the method in our age is to downgrade the importance of borders. Half a century ago, another German 'internal pressure' led to attempts to move borders. In the Europe of the 1990s, this is no longer a viable option and, to some extent, similar pressures (a German state smaller than the German nation, and an economy able to expand its geographical coverage) are given a different outlet. For German national policies (in relation to minorities; Poland) and in economic policies (Czechoslovakia, Baltic republics, Hungary) it makes sense to underplay the significance of borders.

In CDU circles this logic has surfaced as a means of resolving the problem of the German–Polish border (the Oder–Neisse line). There are several statements by CDU spokesmen in the *Bundestag* (for instance July 1989, November 1989, March 1990) concerning the Oder–Neisse border, where it is argued that the problem can only be solved by arriving at a Europe where borders have lost their meaning. Thus, the argument runs, Germany would grow together across the border. The CDU argument on Silesia takes exactly the same form as the SPD pre-1989 argument on German–German relations. Jan Kroll, spokesman for the Silesians, the main German minority in Poland, has as his motto: 'I want to live in a Europe without borders'. That is understandable. Then his German communities can grow together (with the rest of 'Germany'), without having to question the border.

Support for minority rights is clearly on the German agenda. And so is a strengthening of regionalization, of the *Länder* (the German states, sixteen since unification) acting across the borders, building networks and avoiding action by 'Germany'. Federal Germany remains passive and a German *Mitteleuropa* is constructed by firms, *Länder* and individuals linking up in a tight pattern of interaction.

After German unification, it is said, some people in the neighbouring countries listened for the sound of marching boots. They would have been better advised to listen for the sound of tiptoeing. They should be grateful, too. As there *is* a German 'over-pressure' as regards the economy as well as differences in size between present and past Germany, this form of expansion is clearly to be preferred to any other available. In the post-war period Germany has kept a low profile in power politics. And, as in the case of Japan, this has paid off. Keeping a low profile leaves more space for economic activity. A Germany with a low-profile *state* can tie eastern and northern Europe into its networks without provoking anti-German alliances in Europe.

The notion of competing Europes is closely related to the different concepts of the state. The West German post-war concept of the state has been a direct reaction against the earlier, idealist tradition of the 'power state' which previously had been seen as typically German (q.v. Fichte, Hegel and the historians of the '*Machtschule*' or 'power school'). In the Federal Republic of Germany the state has been treated at the level of a practical problem – a system to be kept neither too strong nor too weak. Political thinking has remained linked to the concept of the state – not to the idea of the state as the embodiment of power and will but to the notion of the state and power as a practical issue that requires handling or may even be seen as a potential threat to be curtailed (Wæver *et al.*, forthcoming).

Thus, naturally, the concept of Europe has been related to processes where formal state structures and state action begin to lose their importance. The less the nation-states signify in a future Europe, the better for Germany (cf. Stürmer 1990). In German thinking, projects for nation and Europe can thus be fulfilled where political structures are weak or absent.

French 'Europe'

For the French, this kind of approach is not politics. It cannot be. For them, political thinking has to be about the state, about an actor, about coherence and about will. In most variants of French thinking the state is centralized, demarcated by clear borders and endowed with a certain mission. If Europe is to become a political reality, it will have to take on these qualities.

In the time of de Gaulle, the slogan (though not actually his expression) was *L'Europe des patries*, respecting the full sovereignty of the *état-nation* ('state-nation'). This seemed logical in relation to the pedigree of the state-nation – the state-nation was the only foundation on which the new Europe could be built. In 1983–4 there came a dramatic shift in French European policy. France started to press for the European Community to exercise a state-like role in as many areas as possible – to operate as a political actor with a defence identity and a cultural mission. It seemed as if France had experienced a volte-face. On the contrary, the political thinking was the same – just one level up. Now Europe had to be what France had always wanted to be. France had become too small, and its mission must be taken over by 'Europe' (Schubert 1988). Thus the French concept of the state is repeated at the level of Europe, and the apparent turn-round of 1983–4 in reality is based on continuity at the level of political thinking. Europe must now be what France should have been and could somehow remain. It must include a political and defence identity, its own values and recognition by external actors.

This seems incomprehensible to the Danes and probably to the British, who think more in zero-sum terms: what is given to Brussels is lost to Copenhagen or London – what is won back to the nation is taken away from a federalizing Europe. Not in France, where a Mitterand can say: 'The more Europe there will be, the more France'. The explanation lies in French thinking about the nation, which implies that the nation has a mission and that it has to act and be recognized by others, first on the European and then on the international scene. This is not to suggest that the French regard themselves as a chosen people with a mission. The French idea of France is not that the French people are superior in principle; but the values France represents are *universal* values: human rights, political rights, and the idea of the state-nation (cf. den Boer's section on the eighteenth century). The French have, through the French Revolution, a particularly intimate relationship with these values. It is this logic that made it possible for de Gaulle to state in his New Year's speech 1967:

> Our action is directed toward goals which are connected and which, because they are French, reflect the desire of all men.
>
> *(Grosser, 1978; 1980 edn, p. 184)*

In this way an inner link is forged between France and Europe. The Europe created must necessarily have a heart that beats in French. To be political, Europe must have a pulse that only France is capable of supplying (Moïsi 1989). This secures for France, when transferring its ambitions to Europe, a knowledge that the European project is worthwhile; that it is sufficiently French. We are not talking of control by France, nor French influence in the narrow sense, but about Europe being constituted and acting in a way that is French.

This reveals the logic of French Europe, but *where* precisely is it? The German one was located at the centre of the continent, within a complex network, and de Gaulle's was 'Atlantic to the Urals'. But the new French Europe, of necessity, has been *western* Europe. This follows from the tasks Europe is called upon to fulfil. Only western Europe, or more precisely the EC, can attain state-like qualities and become coherent enough to act decisively. Thus it is unacceptable to the French to have a Europe with an unclear border or uncertain membership. (In the 1980s the Germans were often suspected of wanting a Europe that just 'faded out' somewhere to the east, a Europe including neutral and even eastern states; in other words, a very un-statelike Europe, unable to act in unity.)

The contrast between German and French approaches is of special importance because in many instances these states have co-operated on European integration. It has often been said that European integration only moves forward when France and Germany are in agreement. So it is of special interest to understand the very dissimilar sources of their policies. Germany is interested in the inward side of Europe, whereas France is interested in its outward side. For German thinkers, the big issue on Europe is whether relationships in the region can be changed so that Germany will be able to unfold as nation, culture and economy with less hindrance from the East–West division and from other borders. For France the main issue is whether the sense of France and its mission (and its economy) can be regained through the constitution of a Europe that is able to act and earn respect from others.

This is illustrated by means of Figure 1. Germany's Europe takes the form of diffuse networks, France's is (a child's drawing of) a sun. It has to shine on the surrounding world – and one is well advised not to look too closely into its centre because, until the espousal of federalism in 1988, what for France, was institutionally at the heart of Europe was somewhat unclear.

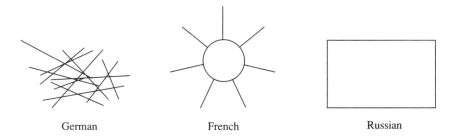

German   French   Russian

Figure 1   Three Europes

Russian 'Europe'

The Russian illustration is a box. Let me explain. In the Soviet discourse on Europe of the 1980s, the slogan was Gorbachev's 'common European house' (or 'home'). The Soviet Union had launched many post-war European projects but the West had always been suspicious of the line that *we* Europeans should stand together in peace, but *we* are being thwarted by the intrusive presence of the Americans in Europe. So when Gorbachev started singing the praises of a 'common European house', the West initially heard the same old song. However, two novel features soon emerged. First, in Gorbachev's version, the emphasis was much more clearly placed on cultural and historical arguments. We Europeans, it is argued, belong together because of a shared culture and history. This is a way of establishing a fundamental basis for a specific political arrangement, but it also cuts the other way so as to establish certain values and traditions as binding on the Soviet Union. The will to take this on board relates to the use of the 'European home' argument in Soviet/Russian politics (probably no less important than its external use). It was a slogan of the European line – or the Westernisers – in the Soviet Union.

Secondly, after some toing and froing, the standard version of the 'common house' became one where the United States' right to participation was acknowledged (and the CSCE was presented as the institutional framework for the construction of the house).

If it (the box) is not to keep the Americans out, what then is the purpose? It is, of course, to keep the Russians in! With the general decline (and eventual disappearance) of a Soviet power and position, Soviet/Russian Europe has slithered in recent years from being offensive to defensive. The original version could be characterized as offensive in that it was aimed at winning the hearts of west Europeans, and the West Germans in particular (Malcolm 1989a and 1989b). But with the events of 1989 it became clear that the Soviet/Russian struggle was not intended to increase influence in western Europe, but to minimize the *loss* of influence in eastern as well as western Europe. As one Sovietologist has put it:

> There will in any case be some sort of European Home, and a home in which the European part of the USSR will have a place is the only alternative to one from which it is shut out.
>
> *(Shenfield, 1989, pp. 7ff.)*

The 'common European House' gradually became part of a policy whose main aim was to prevent the Soviet Union – and later Russia – from being excluded from Europe.

Moscow used to have a solid presence in Europe – with tanks and troops. Without this, a presence has to be created in the political sphere, through participation in European institutions and, first and foremost, the CSCE Helsinki process. (Despite all the dramatic changes of 1991 – including the disappearance of the Soviet Union – it is likely that this logic will be one of the few constants in the foreign policy of Moscow.)

The 'box logic' about the borders of Europe – who is in, who is out – is at the centre of Moscow's thinking about Europe. The Russian project cannot gain a decisive victory – hence the aim is to make sure that whatever kind of Europeanization emerges there will be a place for Russia in the new order.

The competition between these Europes is not one that is likely to end with one of them as victor. It would probably not be very acceptable to live in a Europe fully organized along German, French or Russian lines, nor in any other self-articulated version. Nor would this be politically possible, since the Europeanization process has the character of bargaining and mutual stabilization which precludes *either/or* outcomes. Europeanization is therefore most likely to come about as the parallel birth of all three Europes. Since 'Europe' is about something different for each power, all three Europes are gradually becoming more real at a time when the old East–West order is receding. This pattern of events is borne out, at least, in reaction to developments in Germany in the autumn and winter of 1989–90 and it is to this aspect that we now turn.

Europeanizations

The three Europes of the 1980s were depicted above in a somewhat static manner. In the interplay of events immediately following the collapse of the Berlin Wall we will see them behaving in a more dynamic fashion. Let's begin with France.

French reaction to events in Germany in 1989–90 has been somewhat confused. This is understandable. Such developments brought the basic dilemmas of French foreign policy into the open. The changes in eastern Europe had to be welcomed since they represented French Revolutionary democratic values (Mitterand pointed out that these events were continuations of the impulse from the French Revolution). Freedom, democracy and a nation which has become whole could not be opposed while one was loyal to France. But the unification of Germany was not exactly a French idea. After various shifts, French policy attained a certain organizing principle (not always consistently followed) by which France, through a kind of west European *Ostpolitik*, would try to maintain its own position in a Europe where the two Germanies were coming together. Western Europeanization and all-Europeanization were thus fused into a specific combination that created a workable French policy line.

The clearest expression of this changing emphasis in French European policy was – in all its brilliant ambiguity – President Mitterand's New Year speech at the end of 1989, in which he presented a vision of an 'all Europe' confederation (excluding the Soviet Union, at least in the first phase). How could this be? We have just explained that France was decidedly focused on the EC, and now Mitterand is talking about 'the whole of Europe'! The political élite in Paris (and the French press) reacted with disbelief – what was Mitterand doing, was he selling out on EC integration? He was not. This was not to be seen as a retreat from the EC project, but as an attempt to give the EC a different purpose, a larger meaning. Confederation, he argues, is an aim, a vision, but it will take a long time before a confederal Europe is capable of operating as an effective political unit. For the foreseeable future the EC will remain *the* political actor. In previous French think-

Berliners celebrate the dismantling of the Wall at the Brandenburg Gate, November 1989 (photo: Deutsche Press-Agentur).

ing on 'Project Europe' the EC was the end as well as the means. Now that the aim is widened to include all of Europe in a confederation, there is an increased need for an EC capable of bringing this about. In order to be a force in wider Europe, the EC must exercise greater political clout – only through political means can the EC create a Europe larger than itself. This – the strengthening of the EC as a political project – is Mitterand's *grand dessin.*

The French stress on the Community's *Ostpolitik* is very logical, because this is the only way to counterbalance German economic dominance in eastern Europe. German firms act without a covering policy – their economic calculations lead them to make specific investments. German economic expansion therefore grows from *laissez-faire,* i.e. non-state processes. French companies, on the other hand, have neither the strength nor the motive for comparable investment. Thus, the less political 'help' is extended to eastern Europe, the more German economic dominance will take hold. The place for France to be, therefore, is at the head of the EC's policy towards the East. Eastern Europe should not be left to chance (for chance, read Germany), but helped/managed/controlled by joint *political* action. Eastern Europe becomes politicized and multilateralized. Proposals for big EC joint projects for eastern Europe – such as the Bank of Reconstruction and

Students from the John F. Kennedy School in Berlin carry off souvenirs that had 'fallen off' the Wall, November 1989 (photo: Deutsche Press-Agentur).

Development – emanate from Paris (while Germany is *doing* a lot more bilaterally in assisting former Soviet republics and eastern European countries that were previously controlled by the Soviet Union). For an understanding of the French position, it is important to notice the way in which eastern Europe is now being included in the Europe project. Eastern Europe is perceived not as a part of Europe in action, but as the *mission*, the *task* for western Europe.

In Germany the initial federal government response to the breaching of the wall was guided by fear of provoking reactions from the four Allied powers, Britain,

France, the United States and the Soviet Union. It was feared that German time would run ahead of European time, and so Kohl actually tried in November and December 1989 to slow down developments so as to stave off four-power intervention. In this first stage, the Kohl government tried to keep the speed of German development down so that Europe could catch up. The Bonn government could not opt directly for its real aim, state unity. In November 1989 an overt policy of unification could well have triggered four-power meetings against Germany. (A hint of this came with a meeting of the Four in December called by the Soviet Union in the old 'control council' building in Berlin). At this stage a four-power meeting would probably have resulted in a confirmation of the divided *status quo*. Symbolically, a reversion to four-power responsibility for Germany would have been a dramatic setback to German sovereignty; it would have actually erased thirty-five years of patient foreign policy designed to build up sovereignty, thus returning Germany to the immediate post-war situation of Allied supervision.

While speculation ran wild in London, Paris and Washington, and redrawn maps of Europe with a united Germany appeared in the newspapers, the political establishment in West Germany tried to define the situation in terms of stabilization and democratization in the GDR (see, for example, Stürmer 1989). Reading contemporary newspapers, one often got the impression that the German press was two weeks behind the others, especially in their terminology (which avoided terms such as 'unification' and especially 'reunification').

From February 1990, however, it became clear that West Germany could not control developments. The East Germans decided – partly with their feet, partly by clear signals given by the election – to join with the West Germans. But this 'loss of control' for Bonn was actually a diplomatic *victory*. In this way all potential four-power vetoes were circumvented. How do you veto a collapse? East Germany seemed to cave in and stream under the door to the Federal Republic. This was not *Bonn*'s policy of reunification. Bonn, seemingly, could not be blamed, for it did what Paris and Moscow asked for. Or, rather, Bonn did very little. It did not stabilize the GDR – this was more than could be expected. Nor did it clearly destabilize it. It did nothing.

That unification would come, and rather sooner than expected, became clear with the Kohl/Genscher visit to Moscow in early February 1990, when Soviet endorsement of unification was attained. From now on German policy became much more focused on European developments. The dilemma of German and European time remained, but German developments could not be slowed down. European developments had to take on German speed. *This did not mean a Europe on German terms; quite the contrary, it meant German speed and Franco-Russian form.* Germany started to approach the EC much more along French lines, and it was the German foreign ministry that came up with the bulk of the ideas for all-European security structures. The Soviets were in fact rather slow to formulate those demands that should logically have been theirs, and the plans were worked out in the foreign ministry – in Bonn! (see *Der Spiegel,* 12 February 1990, p. 23). These plans were not especially in the German interest, but they made a lot of sense in the Soviet Union. It was the Soviet Union (later Russia) that had to fear dropping out of Europe. The Russians needed reassurance as to their future links to Europe.

Some even hoped for the channelling of resources and support from the West. In other words, in the terminology of the three competing Europes, *from February 1990 German diplomacy became very active in building the French and the Russian Europe.* Why? Because the Germans were getting their own Europe – one with room for national unity and economic expansion in central Europe, though the high cost of German unification had yet to be realized. But in order to keep the overall process stable it is necessary to keep a balance between all three major Europes.

France and Russia have been accommodated largely because they could most easily impede the German process of unification. This is not because they hold the strongest cards, but on the contrary because they hold the weakest. They are the two powers that have been most deeply hurt by these developments. German unity affects them directly, and their status has in fact been defined in relation to, or by contrast with Germany. French identity in the post-war world rested largely on its *difference* from Germany, France being fully sovereign and independent, one of the four occupying powers, and possessing nuclear weapons. Now that Germany is becoming a 'normal' state – a triumph for Bonn's post-war foreign policy – France is thereby reduced in stature. Furthermore, nuclear weapons seem of decreasing symbolic value, while the economic imbalance works in the opposite direction. As Dominique Moïsi has put it: 'the balance between the Mark and the Bomb is sliding to the advantage of the former' (*Die Zeit,* 9 December 1988). Furthermore, the French mission involved in 'transcending Yalta' is lost when Yalta is actually overcome.

For many Russians, the occupation and possession of eastern Germany was the ultimate symbol of victory in the Second World War and the guarantee against its repetition. Letting go the main prize of victory was seen by many as an offence to millions of dead Russians. In the words of Alexander Prokhanov, writing in the January 1990 issue of *Literaturnaya Rossiva*:

> As the colours and contours of Europe's political map are changing, the bones of Russian infantrymen stir in their unknown graves.

West German foreign minister Hans-Dietrich Genscher offered a revealing insight into the question in an interview in May 1990:

> We do not want to push the Soviet Union to the edge of Europe. She should rather continue to be incorporated in Europe as a whole, and that includes the political dimension of Europe…We do not want anyone to feel themselves the loser because of German unification…The CSCE provides a guarantee for the Soviet Union that it can play a full role in Europe. The Soviet Union has opened its doors and in such a situation we must go through the door, not let someone slam it shut from this side.
>
> *(The European, 11–13 May 1990, p. 9)*

Why, you might ask, is the United Kingdom not on a par with France and Russia? First, because the UK is not affected to the same degree by developments in Germany. There is no identity crisis over German unification. Secondly, Britain has not really joined in the competition for the formation of the image of Europe.

British reticence over Europe has meant that she is not part of that game. Only when one talks of defence and security in narrow terms does Britain enter the stage, since she claims a mediating role between the USA and Europe.

The United States, with more justice, could be included. US policy has played an active and constructive role in the German–European unification process (the US being the most pro-unification of the four), and has furthermore succeeded in securing in the new Europe a surprisingly strong position for NATO, and an acceptable shape for the CSCE as a fall-back option, should NATO later be marginalized. NATO and the CSCE in some ways are moving in parallel as truly inter-governmental, all-European, consensus-based 'safety nets' with a special role for the 'quasi-European' Russians and Americans. Thus, paradoxically, the USA can be included in the analysis by replacing references on the previous pages to 'Russia' with 'Russia – and to some extent the US' and 'the CSCE' with 'NATO and the CSCE'.

The logic of this is captured when we recognize that we are now actually making something akin to a peace settlement. Its stability depends on not putting the loser in too degraded a position. At this point, more than forty-five years after the war, the losers of the war, Germany and Japan, have won the peace. The problem for the peace settlement will be whether it is acceptable to the losers of the post-war peace, France and Russia, who will see a relatively high and privileged position decrease unless they can find new channels for what they deem meaningful to their nation, state, politics and security. As Henry Kissinger pointed out, in his 1954 dissertation on Europe after the Napoleonic wars, a state may not be treated only from the outside as a factor in the balance – an arrangement is only stable if all major powers can perceive the new order as compatible with its own vision:

> No power will submit to a settlement, however well-balanced and however 'secure', which seems totally to deny its vision of itself.
>
> *(Kissinger, 1957, p. 146)*

In Europe, therefore, we see the following pattern emerging: a parallel strengthening of the EC and the CSCE, and the growth of informal German networks in *Mitteleuropa*. The EC and the CSCE are not tied together in any unified, European construction. They each work on their own wavelength. They are driven by a common dynamic – by being interlinked as a matter of *Realpolitik* – but they are not parts of a single machine. They are perceived in different ways by different powers, but the political logic of the situation makes them mutually dependent. The EC and CSCE stand as different European projects and, in a turbulent period, have served to promote the complex process of Europeanization.

Searching for the idea of Europe in the 1980s has inevitably forced us into a world of politics, security issues and power-manoeuvring. Europe is a far less logical construction than any junior security expert or political scientist could draw up. A neater European architecture is easy to imagine. But politics is different. A constellation of interacting projects, each containing their 'Europe' is actually the illogical Europe in which we are living.

These dynamics move at three different levels:

- super-state creation in EC (France);
- classical state-to-state relations in CSCE and NATO (USSR/Russia and USA);
- sub-state and non-state politics (around Germany).

We are not so much witnessing a concentration of power in Europe – nor a struggle over 'Brussellization' versus national diversity – but rather a dispersal of power and authority across various levels.

A neo-medieval Europe?

On the matter of the dispersal of power and authority there are some striking parallels between the emerging Europe and the Europe of the Middle Ages. The medieval system consisted of a complex patchwork of overlapping authorities. Authority was personal (with the ruler), not residing in institutions; property rights were not absolute but contingent in that they entailed obligations; and there were some universal principles that were supposed to supply legitimacy to all rulers (Ruggie 1983). The rights of government were territorial but they did not entail mutual exclusion (i.e. where one state has exclusive competence to legislate, levy taxes, etc., another is excluded) and therefore the result was the famous patchwork of overlapping rights of government that were superimposed on each other such that each was incomplete, i.e. not 'sovereign' rule (Ruggie, 1992/93). In looking at Europe today there are some strong reminders of the criss-crossing authority relations that typified medieval social and political organization. In some respects the EC is moving towards a super-state, yet the CSCE process is strengthening traditional inter-state co-operation. At the same time, sub-state processes are of increasing importance (especially around Germany): some are non-territorial (business); others are sub-state actors (*Länder*) promoting a more independent foreign policy.

Issues in Europe, even quite important ones, are decided at different levels. From 1993, money, tariffs, border controls, move to the increasingly European (EC) level; but the nuclear button remains in Paris, London, Washington and (hopefully) Moscow; while law-making is spread across the EC, national and *Länder* levels. Since there have been democratically elected, legitimate and authoritative competences long in existence at regional, national and international levels, this in itself is not new. But what is new is the fact that there is no longer one level that is *primary*. The principle of sovereignty, exclusivity and territoriality is giving way to a pattern of overlapping authorities reminiscent of the medieval system. Authority and power are not generally moving towards a bigger sovereign unit. The EC is not simply becoming a territorial super-state. Power and authority, especially post-Maastricht and the Danish referendum, are being disseminated via the principle of *subsidiarity*. Some matters remain at the level of the nation-state and some at the inter-state level, particularly those relating to the CSCE and NATO initiative. Some are undergoing Brussellization and some are moving down towards a Europe of the regions – networks, local authorities, business and other initiatives emerging across state borders.

There are different ways of looking at present-day trends in Europe. Is the EC the real sovereign state while the member states are actually becoming increasingly like county (regional) authorities? Or have the member states still retained their sovereignty, in which case the EC is just an international organization? Or is this simply a false dichotomy in that none of them is sovereign? If it is a false dichotomy (and I am inclined to think this is the case) it must be because change is happening at the level of sovereignty, of the territorial state. It is important to get this clear because slight conceptual inaccuracy can lead us astray. The focus should be on the *end of the territorial state* (and thereby the neo-medieval theme, since the territorial state has defined the modern epoch in contrast to the medieval), but most debate phrases possible change in terms of the likely *end of the nation-state,* which is a different debate. The national idea arrived on the scene in the late-eighteenth century and was fused with the already existing principle of the territorial state (which had so far been based not on national but dynastic legitimacy). For the last two hundred years or so the territorial state has therefore been combined with the national idea (making up the nation-state), but if we focus on the nation-state we end up in a discussion of nationalism, and the national idea persists. However, change *is* taking place, but at an even deeper level: that is to say at the level of sovereignty and the territorial state. Thus nations continue but the states that they relate to are not what they used to be, since the *state* is changing, with authority being dispersed across several levels in our 'new middle ages'. Hence present west-European developments entail decisive changes between the unit of identification (the nation) and the unit of political organization/authority (the state – and increasingly the EC).

In the emerging European order, nations are still very real and it is interesting to speculate on what will happen if the underlying structure (sovereign territorial states) fades, while the modifying one (nations) remains. In such a situation, security issues will take the form of *societal* security – the security problems of a community with only weak political institutions. This projection would apply more to the EC nations than to those of eastern Europe, where it could be argued that nations are simply seeking to move from multi-nation-state organization to nation-state political structures.

In this Europe, societal security will be high on the agenda. Because of the changing relationship between state and society there will be more and more security problems, demanding *security policies* of a new kind. What can a nation/society do when it feels threatened as a nation/society and when it is less able to use the instruments of the state to contain people, ideas and technological developments that are felt to be undermining the sense of national cohesion? It will be compelled to act *itself*: i.e. threats to a culture have to be met *in the arena of culture itself*. Nations will have to defend their national identity through cultural means, through reflecting on and intensifying their cultural expression, rather than calling upon the state to block off such challenges. As *cultures* feel more threatened and at the same time less able to use state measures as a means of defence, cultures will need culture. A cultural community, it is assumed, will in most cases first of all defend itself by activating and intensifying its forms of cultural expression.

State and society potentially move away from each other and societies become security *actors* in their own right. This is where the parallel to the Middle Ages comes in. In the medieval system – in contrast to the modern state system – one had no fixed idea of 'international relations' or 'foreign policy', as an activity limited to a specific kind of unit (state) and only to be conducted among these and on the basis of equality. Of course, to the casual observer relations between emperors, popes, kings, archbishops, barons, cities, universities, guilds and knights might resemble international relations. All, for example, negotiated and signed formal agreements, sent diplomatic missions, settled their disputes by arbitration and war and regulated at least part of their behaviour in accordance with commonly accepted laws and customs. However, it would be wrong to suppose that these relations were

> international, in the modern sense of the term, for they occurred not between sovereign territorial states, but between individuals and corporate groups. A clear distinction between 'international' and 'domestic' relations was thus impossible to draw in medieval Europe.
>
> *(Holzgrefe, 1989, pp. 11ff.)*

Comparisons between our times and the Middle Ages are of course problematic, since there are numerous differences, but the various parallels are first of all manifestations of a common difference from the modern state system. The purpose of using the medieval metaphor is primarily to free our minds from the confines of the modern state system. Our concepts and thinking about politics are so deeply prejudiced by concepts from the modern system of states, territoriality and sovereignty, that new developments are almost invisible. With the present-day fluidity, we need to treat these concepts again as questions.

Beyond the nation, beyond the state: concepts of a Europe of regions

In the literature and debate on regionalization and a 'Europe of Regions', 'region' is used at various levels:

(i)   One can talk of a 'region' as the unit smaller than the existing state (as for instance in the Swedish sense of '*regionalpolitik*' – politics dealing with the regions, especially the weaker ones).

(ii)   One can talk of 'regions' in the form of state-to-state co-operation, such as, for instance, arrangements within the 'pentagonal', now 'hexagonal' (Austria, Czechoslovakia, Hungary, Italy, Yugoslavia as long as it existed, and Poland since 1991) or central European co-operative structures involving Poland, Hungary and Czechoslovakia.

(iii)   One can combine the two, arriving at the concept of *trans-border regions*, consisting of regions in the first sense linking across borders to   regions, towns, small states, thereby forming political, cultural and economic networks.

The latter is the main focus of this section, partly because it is a truly new phenomenon, and partly because it is this kind of region which is likely to take on a specific role in the emerging division of labour between Europe, nation and region.

There has been in recent years an increasing awareness of new patterns of co-operation such as the areas along the Danube; the constellation of Catalonia, southern France and northern Italy; the eastern Alps (Alpe Adriatic); the western Alps (Arge Alp) and the Baltic Sea Region. In some places we see old patterns being reactivated as co-operation among *countries* – for instance the 'hexagonal'/'pentagonal' co-operation between the old countries of the Habsburg Empire. Such a co-operation is 'regional' in the sense that it is part-Europe and it does not follow external definitions of economic groupings or power-blocs but reactivates a pattern 'from below'. But it has nothing to do with regions *in* the states. In other places we see *parts of states* co-operating with other part-states (for instance German *Länder*) across national boundaries. 'Alpe Adriatic' in the eastern Alps consists of Friaul, Trentino-Southern Tyrol, Venezia, Croatia, Slovenia, Kärnten, Upper Austria and Steiermark, with Bavaria and Salzburg as observers. Here we are talking about regionalization in the dual sense as (i) a 'region in Europe', and (ii) as independent politics by the regions in their respective countries.

In the case of Baltic co-operation (on which we will concentrate at the end of this section) there has been talk of 'a new Hansa' (referring to a network of trading towns in northern Europe in the fourteenth and fifteenth centuries). The 'Hansa' metaphor denotes a co-operative arrangement between towns, ports, communities – not states. Although we might be witnessing a growing co-operation among *states* around the Baltic, Baltic co-operation is likely to be expressed, primarily, by a number of non-state actors such as business firms, theatre groups and municipal authorities, i.e. in the interplay of regionalization *in* the states.

In regionalist circles there is a tendency to present the regions as more 'true' than other communities. This kind of regionalism often looks like 'romantic nationalism' one level down. The regionalists love to point out that the nation-states are artificial constructs where identity and culture were *constructed* as part of a political project. It is, however, exactly the same with the regions: they are not given by nature, just lying there waiting to be discovered. There are no 'natural' regions. We have similarities and commonalities along various dimensions in a complex, criss-crossing network. This does not make the project of a region less valuable or real. After all, the nations have proved to be emphatically real.

Recognizing this political character of regionalization makes conflict-management easier, in the sense that one is more likely to see contrasting views as legitimate. There is no reason why the relationship among the emerging regions should be harmonious. J. G. Herder and the other early thinkers on nationalism believed that nationalism was peace-making, because if all people were allowed national self-determination and limited themselves to their own land, there would be harmony. As we know, it was slightly more complicated than that! First, there were problems of drawing the correct borders between one land and another. Secondly, there were problems of finding out who should be seen as having a legitimate right to constitute themselves as a state: 'Basques', 'Catalans', 'Corsicans', and 'Bretons' – or 'Spaniards' and 'French'? Exactly the same problems will emerge if the grip of the nation-state is loosened and we allow the 'natural' regions to unfold. Where is the eastern border of Transylvania, the border between Macedonians and

Bulgarians or the southern border of the 'northern Cape'? Again, as with the nations, besides the problem of borders we have the problem of descending levels; i.e. the problem of *who* should be seen as belonging to 'regions'. As Ernest Gellner has written:

> The vogue of ethnic revival could of course go on forever, like a recurring decimal. If Byelorussians are distinct from Russians, then Byelorussians in turn have a distinct dialectical minority in the south of their country, the Polishchuks. Presumably there also exists a variant dialect within Polischuk.
>
> *(Gellner, 1990, p. 293)*

In practice, we are not in a situation where the regions are on course to take over as the sole legitimate political units. They are emerging in the context of the continued existence of nation-states, of inter-state co-operation and supra-national integration. The form regionalization is going to take is therefore not exclusively a regional concern and it needs to be seen in the context of a configuration of change at many levels in Europe. This raises the question of whether a 'Europe of Regions' really takes us beyond the nation, or is merely replicating it in smaller sizes and thereby multiplying it! Regionalization has been speeded up in the 1980s with East–West German unification, the ending of the Cold War, and with accelerating European integration.

Regionalization in Europe involves a specific German factor. As argued above, especially in the wake of German unification, it is important for German policy to dispel reactions of fear and to discourage counter-coalition against Germany. Such a policy requires German energy to be channelled into non-threatening forms, playing down the divisive nature of borders. Regional networks and the downgrading of frontiers fit German Europe much better than the Europe of France or Russia.

Many of the trans-regional formations were submerged by the Cold War overlay, which aspired to arrange all relations to correspond with the overarching bipolar order. Thus as Europe reappears, several smaller patterns emerge with it. They are not security regions or alliances, in fact they often have very little to do with security. But they are made possible by the removal of a security overlay. The new European order is likely to make all the smaller European sub-regional identities easier to (re)develop (Buzan *et al.*, 1990, pp. 219–23).

There is, however, a security dimension. It is worth noting, especially in eastern Europe, that the trans-border regions have a potentially stabilizing function (Buzan *et al.*, 1990, especially pp. 220–23 and pp. 558–66; von Plate 1991, especially pp. 560–62 and 565). Bernard von Plate argues that cultivating trans-border arrangements is the best way of ensuring that 'the reawakening of the ethnic groups leads neither to a nationalistic *Kleinstaaterei* [fiddling with small states], nor to the violent change of interstate borders'.

The end of the East–West conflict and the deepening of the west European construction of a Community are elements in the more general multiplication of identities that has taken place in Europe in the 1980s. Political/social identities are seen as less fixed, less capable of being reduced to a single dimension, or one set of loyalty relationships. Thus, the creation of a 'Baltic' (as well as a 'European') identity should be understood in its intricate relationship to processes of identity-formation (and identity-differentiation) on various levels. Several trans-, sub- and supra-national communities can interact in ways that create new political options. Linking up these emerging patterns of sub-regional and sub-state political identity to territorial politics could be crucial to the future of eastern Europe. The revival of independence and 'nationality' in post-eastern bloc Europe could easily take the classical track of building up overly strong national identities, which would make it difficult for eastern Europe to maximize the benefit from the changes in western Europe. A possible alternative could be a strengthening of multiple identities, local, regional and national. This would make it easier for eastern Europe to link up to EC developments, and would give eastern Europe a chance to escape the perennial dilemmas of national conflicts and insecurities within and between states. Trans-regionalism might play a decisive role in this respect. Bernard von Plate spells out in detail the role such regions might play in relation to the recognition of new states, and therefore could have played in the case, for example, of the recognition of Slovenia and Croatia. Such questions could be addressed by 'linking recognition to a catalogue of principles, elevating the sub-regional units and equipping them with greater autonomy' (von Plate, p. 560), thereby permitting the regions to relate to each other across borders within the trans-region and allowing people classified as minorities to maintain links with their compatriots in the main country and with other ethnic groups in the state where they are citizens. This could prevent (make superfluous) both irredentism towards minorities in neighbouring areas as well as concern by neighbours about 'their' minorities within the respective countries.

Regionalism also makes it possible for ethnic minorities to have more intense contacts with their fellows in neighbouring countries without raising the issue of border revisions. Although the security factor has been decisive as an opening move, as a change which makes regionalization *possible* – the driving forces behind regionalization are, paradoxically, to be found in those processes relating to European integration.

Current debates might give the impression that an EC-Europe would be strongly centralized, with all processes following a pattern of transmission from the core to outer concentric circles – and with either Germany or a strong Brussels at the hub of the circle. But there are reasons to suggest that integration in Europe will allow other patterns to emerge alongside this new centralization. In an EC union, the sub-regional level is likely to gain increasing importance alongside the state level and the all-union level. The 1980s have already witnessed a growing interest in a number of sub-regional communities in Europe.

The main reason for this interest is probably the loosening of the state framework in Europe as a result of the steady opening up of a European political space. This European space has partly been created by the transfer of authority to the EC, and partly (especially in eastern Europe) it accompanied the surge of independence following the withdrawal of Soviet control. The EC may in some fields be a proto-state, but it is much less threatening for minority identities than a nation-state.

There is no single EC language, and no attempt to create a unified educational system. The homogenizing enthusiasm of the nation-state is not likely to be repeated at the European level. Europeanization therefore tends to go hand-in-hand with a strengthening of political and cultural sub-state projects. European unification spells differentiation. The various 'control mechanisms' and ways of 'disciplining' regions have become less effective. Or more generally, as Giandomenico Majone puts it,

> the same process that pushes towards economic and political integration
> also produces regional consciousness and a growing desire for
> identification and also membership in a community more distinct and
> culturally homogeneous than national society. This process is not
> peculiar to Europe, but it may find here its most advanced expression.
> *(Majone, 1990, p. 68)*

In the first instance, the regions produced by this kind of process are the mini-ones: regions as smaller communities within states (but seldom across borders). The mechanism is one of increased functional differentiation according to scale, leading to large-scale administration of complex economic and technological systems, and more localized anchorage of culture and community. Only as a derived effect can this 'regionalization' lead also to regionalization in the sense of 'trans-border-regions' (such as the Baltic Sea Region). When the regions (in the micro-sense) become more autonomous and more powerful, they display a tendency to search for foreign relations, and strengthen their own position by relating to other regions. Linking up across borders is a source of special strength and would appear to be the lesson derived from studying federated states in international relations, especially the example of Germany (Michelmann and Soldatos 1990).

Under this heading, it should be noted that the relationship between 'regions' in the micro or *Länder* sense and the European Community is now becoming more complex and controversial. In the 1970s there was a tendency to move away from the nation-state towards a simultaneous strengthening of sub- and supra-national or global processes. At that time, however, the movements below the level of existing states were all more or less ethnic projects aimed at strengthening smaller nations such as Scotland, Wales, Brittany, Corsica, the Basque country and the Lapp people. These were classical movements of secession, though sometimes reduced to the level of claims for increased autonomy for a specific people. During the 1980s, the struggle became less intense, probably due to the idea that with the developments in EC integration, secession would not be necessary. The micro-nation(alist)s turned European and gambled on Brussels mastering the nation-states. At the end of the 1980s and in the early 1990s, the picture began to change. Again, on the one hand, there was the rise (and partial success) of the 'micro-nations' in eastern Europe (Balts, Slovenians, Slovaks, etc.) and, on the other hand, the increasing awareness of the difficulty of formulating the 'constitution' of the emerging European Union in a way that was satisfactory to the regions. At the point of setting up something like a federal union, it became clear that it would make a difference whether a unit was a sovereign (nation) state, or a *Land,* or a partly autonomous region. Thus the arguments of the 1980s – that nation-states were losing sovereignty to the EC and hence the gap between nation-state and regions/minorities was closing – ceased to hold and the regions/micro-nations began to press for a fully fledged partnership in the emergent 'European Union'. The nation-states might have been weakened, but they were still in a different class from the regions/*Länder* – so why not join them? Why should Slovenians and Slovaks, Estonians and Icelanders, be able to contemplate joining the Community as 'member states', whereas Catalans and Corsicans, Scots and Lombards will forever remain bound to 'regions'?

Thus the ploy of 'regionalization as EC integration' is not as compelling as it might once have appeared. But the issue is real and not to be cast aside as irrelevant or bizarre in relation to the 'real' integration of the nation-states. No panacea has been found. Even trans-border-regionalization, like Baltic Sea co-operation, will be stimulated by ongoing EC integration, although the relationship will be complex and perhaps conflictual.

The lesson seems to be that a 'Europe of Regions' when it means a Europe built of hundreds of small communities ('the Switzerification of Europe'), is probably not as realistic or as workable as its advocates portray. Furthermore, democracy, citizenship and other important gains of modern society have been cultivated in the nation-state framework and this inheritance should not be dismissed too easily. In the event, the regions are perhaps not as viable a proposition as the trans-regions.

The Baltic Sea Region

We can illustrate further the logic and dynamics of the *new* regionalization by trying, somewhat provocatively, to develop the following thesis: *Northern Europe will find its place in a 'Europe of the Regions', but the region will be the Baltic Sea Region.*

Why Baltic? Is this region more 'real' than Scandinavia (Norden[7])? No, on the contrary, Swedes and Lithuanians have very little in common. But existence of identities is not static. Nations were discovered/invented by intellectuals, historians and politicians – they did not have a prior existence; but after the projects of nation-building had taken their course, they became very real indeed. The Baltic Sea region could take on such a reality. There are three reasons why the Baltic project has an impetus at present. (For further elaboration, see Wæver 1991.)

The first reason is that it is *new*. The Nordic (Scandinavia) belongs to the old Europe, the Baltic to the new. Or, to put it differently, after 1989 we are supposedly living in a 'new Europe', but what in practice does it mean to you and me? We need a concrete, local 'new Europe' in which to participate and that is why most of the new regions in Europe have come into existence along and across the

[7] *Norden* is Scandinavian terminology for 'Scandinavia' – specifically, it means the members of the Nordic Council: Iceland, Norway, Sweden, Finland and Denmark, plus the semi-independent areas Greenland, Færoe Islands and Aaland Islands. (In Scandinavian – and geological – terms, Scandinavia normally excludes Finland, Iceland and sometimes Denmark.)

old East–West border. Not because there are many tangible gains to be made, but because this co-operation used to be impossible, and therefore it is now interesting.

The second reason is that it takes the appropriate *form* for a European region: it is *non-state based*. If it was to contain such enormous units as 'Russia' or 'the Federal Republic of Germany', it would not be attractive to the small Nordic countries. But a region including St Petersburg, Estonia and Schleswig-Holstein is a different proposition. And most of it will be organized in a decentralized way with business, cultural initiatives, academic links and so on. This corresponds, in particular, with the networks clustering around Germany in the new Europe. Germany in the emerging Europe channels its energies into non-state forms in order to avoid negative reactions among the other states. This comfortably matches Baltic co-operation. Nordic co-operation, by comparison, is a classical state-to-state co-operation.

Thirdly there is in northern Europe at present a widespread feeling – in business and also in some political circles – that this is a critical moment with regard to the place of northern Europe in the new European *economic* architecture. Will it be peripheral or a growth region? Traditionally, this has been a low-growth area, unlike the 'booming banana' (i.e. growth corridor) stretching from southern England along the Franco-German border to northern Italy, southern France and north-eastern Spain. There is an initiative – or rather a number of initiatives – to create a dynamic growth region centred on Copenhagen, Kiel, Gothenburg and possibly stretching out to Oslo, Gdansk and Stockholm. Only time will tell whether or not this 'Baltic' project will develop into a 'blue banana'.

Thus there are two converging tendencies affecting the fortunes of the region. First, the glimmerings of a 'Baltic identity' with the new Baltic Republics at the centre of such aspirations. Secondly, the economic 'don't-miss-the-boat' argument (i.e. join the European mainstream now or forever remain an economic low-growth area) of Copenhagen standing up to Hamburg and Berlin, of Kiel and Gothenburg making a last-minute move into Europe. The first steps in converting these tendencies into a structural network have been taken by intellectuals who, in conferences, scientific journals and think-tank reports have begun to give the notion of a 'Baltic Region' some legitimacy. This has created the context for the wider discussion of a Baltic region as a non-state network for co-operation. The more the news media promote the image of Baltic identity, the more the region is seen as natural and important – a vehicle for all kinds of business, and political and cultural contacts. As it becomes the 'natural' framework for seeking partners, so it begins to take on the reality of a network. The two areas in which the Baltic region has begun to make an impact are culture and infrastructure. Culture because of the relation to identity-formation, and infrastructure because this is seen as an economic pre-condition for development.

A combination of present tendencies and future projections points to the viability of the Baltic Sea region as a trans-border region in the emerging Europe. If you think this is simply indulging in an imaginative exercise, then beware! The supposed rationale for regionalization in western Europe is the declining fortunes of the nation-state. As the pull of sovereignty weakens, regionalization acquires more scope. History and cultural geography are being revised to take account of the dual processes of Europeanization and regionalization, which are altering the general structure of European political space. As part of this process there is sometimes a tendency to present the regions as 'natural'. This applies to some extent to trans-border regions, but much more to sub-national units such as the German *Länder*. They are presented as offering strong local identifications for their populations. Of course, this is a mistake. Not every Bavarian knows all others, nor are they identical. All political communities of this size are imagined – like the nations, and Europe!

The idea of Europe

Limits to Europe

In current debate on Europe there is no clear sense of the geographical boundaries of Europe. This does not indicate a lack of conceptual clarity; rather, it mirrors the actual political form that Europe is taking. It is logical in relation to the political forces and developments at the end of the 1980s and the beginning of the 1990s – the revolutions in eastern Europe, the break-up of the Soviet Union, the ending of the Cold War and the strengthening of the process of integration in the EC. Europe is a magnetic field. Russia is not external, North Africa is not external – they are just outer peripheries.

European politics, after the end of the Cold War, can be presented in the form of 'concentric circles'. The image of 'concentric circles' describes a widening sphere of influence: the EC, EFTA, eastern Europe, Russia. This differentiation makes it possible for Europe (*de facto* materialized in the EC) to *act* and most of the impulses for *all of Europe* emanate from Brussels, although only a part of Europe belongs to the EC. Even if all the European states sat around one (CSCE) table they could not reach the same amount of 'agreement' as is now produced by the slightly unbalanced procedure of 'concentric circles'. The capacity for action by the EC results in a hierarchic Europe. The asymmetrical relationship includes EC–EFTA relations. In the words of Helen Wallace and Wolfgang Wessels, 'most of the pressure has come from the EFTA side; most of the terms have been set by the EC, its agenda and working methods' (Wallace and Wessels 1990). Whether it is industrial standards, trade policy or security – most decisions travel from West to East. The EC makes decisions that only bind its members but the EFTA countries have no real alternative but to adapt. When they have made the necessary adjustments the former eastern bloc countries will also have to follow suit if they want to stay in the game; and then the ex-Soviet republics will have to deal with this reality.

The eastern border is therefore not a line (Ukraine in, Russia out; or Moldavia in, Ukraine out; or the Balts in, and so on) – it is more like an impulse that just 'runs out' somewhere on the eastern plains. There is no eastern border – just a gradual *thinning out*. This statement is not meant as a timeless interpretation of the geographical situation but as a description of the political and economic realities in post-Cold War Europe.

Definitions of Europe

With Europe very much in the ascendant it is timely to reflect on what Europe means – does it stand for something, does it exemplify certain principles or values, does it have a particular identity?

Europe considered negatively

In an article on national identity and the idea of European unity, Anthony D. Smith argued that:

> Identities are forged out of shared experiences, memories and myths, in relation to those of other collective identities. They are in fact often forged through opposition to the identities of significant others, as the history of paired conflict so often demonstrates. Who or what, then, are Europe's significant others?
>
> *(Smith, 1992, p. 75; footnote added)*

In a sense this posits a negative definition of identity, of defining Europe in relation to opposites. So, to echo Smith's question, who are Europe's significant others? The realities stemming from the ending of the Cold War and the collapse of the Soviet Union suggest that Europe can scarcely look to the East for differences in systems and values against which to define itself. A more realistic possibility perhaps is the Middle East. It is a candidacy with a certain frightening logic to it. Geographically and culturally there is a mix of distance (providing a sense of mystery and difference) and closeness (with a Moslem presence in western European societies introducing images of a fifth column and threats to the individual and the community). Yet despite the acknowledged cultural and historical differences it is difficult to regard the Middle East as a real threat to Europe in political or economic terms. Paradoxically the main challenge to Europe – the feared economic powers whom the EC programme of 1992 was designed to combat – comes from the 'friendly', co-capitalist states of the USA and Japan and not the so-called 'alien' Middle East.

Looking ahead, probably the most important question for Europeans is how well the European economy will perform by comparison with the economies of the USA and Japan. In the future will there be two main centres of technology, innovation and capital – or two-and-a-half, or even three? During the 1980s it dawned on many that the USA and Japan were outstripping Europe and that even the 'two-and-a-half' interpretation might seem somewhat optimistic. With the 1992 initiative the image that Europe could be a third economic superpower was (re)created – but whether this image becomes real or proves to be an illusion will be one of the key issues of the 1990s.

This then is the main 'struggle' in which Europe is engaged. Europe has two 'enemies' but only in the economic and technological fields and this kind of competition is not very serviceable in generating identity. The USA and Japan are hardly appropriate counter images for Europe – nor is the Third World. A disintegrating Third World might become an object for European politics but is scarcely suitable for identity formation – a prospect rendered even more unlikely by the existence of ex-colonial ties.

The attempt to define Europe in terms of its opposites has not produced any clearcut solutions. Perhaps the current absence of a significant external threat to Europe has softened the force of this kind of identity construction. It therefore seems appropriate to adopt a more positive approach, looking at Europe *per se* and considering whether it can be defined by virtue of internal characteristics and inherent principles.

Europe considered positively

During the 1980s and the early 1990s, Europe's political stock has risen considerably. The dual movements of EC integration on the one hand and the collapse of the Soviet Empire on the other are widely seen as a kind of victory for the idea of Europe. The states in the western part appear to be willing to hand over sovereignty to a supranational political construction and the states in the eastern part are 'returning to Europe' now that Soviet control has been lifted. In this context arguments that use 'Europe' as a baseline have a certain political force and encourage speculation about the meaning of Europe, the question of European identity and the existence of distinctive European values and principles.

The contemporary quest for the meaning of Europe and an understanding of the European idea need to be set into an historical context. We have seen in Pim den Boer's essay how notions of what constituted Europe changed according to historical circumstances and how, after the French Revolution, they became linked to a self-conscious historical perspective. Peter Bugge showed how, in an age of nationalism, the idea of Europe was expressed in visionary projects. And casting our minds back to 1945, we have seen in this essay how the process of integration was regarded as a means of avoiding the disaster of further European civil war. So we need to be aware that the European idea is not a fixed entity and that it can encompass some wide variations – both democracy and Fascism have flourished on European soil. At a time when Europe is being praised for its plurality and its cultural diversity, it should be remembered that Europe has often served the interest of particular states, persons or groups and at times it has been suppressive of differences and variations.

In attempting to define Europe from a positive standpoint it could be claimed that European identity is characterized by certain political principles – democracy, freedom of opinion, constitutionalism. It is true that such principles can be found operating in contemporary Europe but they can also be found in the USA, Australia, Japan and elsewhere and cannot be said to define Europe in any exclusive sense.

Similarly even more abstract notions such as self-criticism, doubt and scepticism are advanced as being distinctively or typically European (see the references to Morin, Enzensberger and Kundera in the section entitled 'One, two, many Europes' above). There is some basis for pointing to these philosophical approaches as being rooted in Europe. According to Morin, European energy and dynamism consisted in a specific mix of ideas, philosophy and technology which has generated constant reflection and self-reflection (Morin 1987). The terms modernization (i.e. economic and technological dynamism) and modernity (i.e. constant reflection and self-reflection on the process) have been applied to these developments, but Sverker Sörlin reminds us that there is a distinction.

> Modernity is European. It is from it that the Europeans have approached the world. Modernization has today spread far beyond Europe. But outside the West, which also includes that 'neo-Europe' that was created in America, Australia and New Zealand and in the European enclaves on the other continents, modernity is still only vaguely and undecidedly received. In many places it has not broken through, or it is resisted by strong forces...Thinking in differences is probably, ultimately, a part of that which is human – but saying yes to it belongs to modernity.
>
> *(Sörlin, 1990, pp. 19–20)*

But again, since Europe is being equated with the West, a distinct European cachet cannot be strictly applied.

If we resort to historical and cultural explanations of European identity then not only do we have to contend with the divergencies already referred to but we also see the residual strengths of the *states* of Europe and not *Europe per se*. This point has been elegantly been made by Anthony D. Smith:

> ...there is the deeper question of popular myths and symbols, and historical memories and traditions. Here we are placed firmly back in the pre-modern part of each national state [from where it draws its energy and images and where Europe has no similar well]. There is no European analogue to Bastille or Armistice Day, no European ceremony for the fallen in battle, no European shrine of kings or saints. When it comes to the ritual and ceremony of collective identification there is no European equivalent of national or religious community. Any research into the question of forging, or even discovering, a possible European identity cannot afford to overlook these central issues.
>
> *(Smith, 1992, p. 73)*

The search for a European identity has led us across some difficult terrain. Whether we attempt to define Europe from a positive or a negative standpoint we are left with uncertainties. The idea of Europe is elusive, susceptible to change and strongly conditioned by historical contingency. Indeed, interrogation of the meaning of Europe along historical or cultural lines leads us to query whether a European nation-state is a feasible proposition at all.

A European nation-state?

The nineteenth century nation-state created the image of the nation as an eternal community dating back to time immemorial. Will the European project be based on similar projections? It has been argued by the German philosopher Jürgen Habermas and others that a European nation-state is an illusion and a self-defeating enterprise. Taking this line, if attempts are made to carry forward the European project in the form of the nineteenth-century nation-state then these are bound to fail:

> ...our task is less to reassure ourselves of our common origins in the European Middle Ages than to develop a new political self-confidence commensurate with the role of Europe in the world of the twenty-first century.
>
> *(Habermas, 1991)*

How, then, is the European project to be advanced? Habermas' suggestion is to focus on a 'European constitutional patriotism'. National identity in contemporary 'post-national' Europe is formed by allegiance to the political principles of democracy and the constitutional state, which has, however, to be reflected through the prism of the specific national culture and historical memory. This is the form *national* identity can/should take, it was argued by Habermas and with him many centre-left Germans in the 1980s. And actually it is also the way to be *European* today, he now says, because these principles are to a large extent shared by all the member countries of the EC.

Therefore, it is dangerous and self-defeating to think of a link between European history and culture on the one hand and European politics on the other in terms of the former necessitating the latter. European integration is not coming forth because it is 'natural' and 'necessary', not because we 'are' European and therefore 'have to' create a political expression for this our true identity, but because it is a project in which sufficient political energy is invested (cf. Wind, 1992). There may well be good reasons for integration but these are different from the image of necessity being created by the appeal to history. This *was* the way nation-building succeeded and one might therefore legitimately ask, is it not necessary in the European case too? The European idea might not be 'true', but no narration of the past is 'true' without any specific perspective, and perhaps politics has always involved an ability to remember selectively (Nietzsche, 1888); or in the words of Ernest Renan:

> Yet, the essence of a nation is that all individuals have many things in common, and also that they have forgotten many things.
>
> *(Renan, 1882)*

Probably, some element of this rewriting of history is involved in any major political project. On the other hand, it is very likely that the European project is different from the nineteenth century nation-building project, in that it is not about constructing the same kind of exclusivity. In spite of the various meanings and focuses of the concept of nation – from French civic to German ethnic – it is hard to disagree with Anthony D. Smith (1991), who states that the concept and politics of the nation have worked according to both sets of connotations, and thereby also inevitably with the link to the ethnic, romantic, 'German' conception of a people existing in itself as a pre-political reality: a reality which is given an ultimate value is not only above the individual but in the last instance is the source of identity and meaning for the individual (Berlin, 1978; 1982 edn). This logic is to a very limited extent at play in the European project. It is difficult to tell *very heroic* stories about 'Europe' as a subject, as a soul wandering through history. *Still* difficult – or inherently impossible? Yet to come, or out of reach?

It is possible that the nature of European political identity is more in tune with post-modern patterns of identification, i.e. it functions in a matrix of 'multiple identities', where each of us may be many, many things – baker, railway enthusiast, mother, conservative, from Hamburg, etc. Of course, people always were many things, but in the epoch of nationalism, one identity was the trump card. Probably always – at least metaphorically related to the option of *war* — the national identity was the *primary* one in cases of conflict between loyalty to the different identities. This might now be changing, dissolving into a true multiplicity of identities – among these the national and the European (Knudsen, 1989; Buzan *et al.*, 1990, pp. 56ff.).

If we take as an assumption that the European Community continues its process of integration towards economic and monetary as well as political union, and probably takes on increasing numbers of European countries, a key question will be: what kind of identity does this new construct generate/demand – and how will it relate to national identities? Will the EC then have a European identity taking the form of the nation-state – a national, European identity – and thereby crush the old, national identities? Or is it not a question of identity at all?

The dilemma of Europe and nation can be seen as being generated most fundamentally by the tension between, on the one hand, an economy becoming more and more global and, on the other hand, cultural communities becoming, if not generally entrenched, then at least not able to extend infinitely. Nathan Gardels has referred to a tension between a civilization of the soil and civilization of the satellite (1991, p. 21). To this there are basically two different responses:[8]

(a) Go for a compromise at an in-between level, i.e. a Europe that is big enough to be the basis for economy and small enough to be a community and have cultural identity;

(b) Rely on the general 'post-modern' multiplication of identities described above, and be confident that, in the future, we can be national on some issues, European on others, global cosmopolitans on yet further issues; sometimes city-loyal, other times more concerned about our professional identity or that stemming from hobbies, sexual orientation or what have you. In this perspective the doubling in Europe and nation will just be a part of a general multiplication.

Neither response is ultimately convincing. The economy cannot be contained at the European level, and cultural identity definitely can not be lifted to the European level. The total disintegration of personal identity into identity atoms might not be psychologically manageable – it might be yet another example of enlightenment belief in rational human orientations, again producing an emotional reaction towards meaning and belonging. Is this the dynamic behind the re-emergence of neo-Nazis in Germany, the country where people have most

---

[8]   This argument I owe to Pierre Hassmer.

consistently been asked to avoid centralized identity and rationally delegate it to the appropriate place, be it 'the West', the *Land* or the EC?

Possibly a more realistic approach than the infinite multiplication of identities can be outlined in the following way (although the stability of even this can be questioned):

- At the European level, a political state identity along 'French' lines is generated. Foreign and security policy becomes the focus of a 'republican' construction of a state-subject, a 'nation' (in French). To this belong 'citizens', peoples who choose at the level of politics to identify with the values of this state-subject, who are patriotic in terms of politics – but do not necessarily feel that they are in any organic sense one big family. It can be rather hollow, as long as the shell is hard.

- The national level (together with, in some places, the regional one) remains the focus for cultural identity, for community. The 'German' type nation remains at the national level – but in its original Herderian form, where the nation is so important that expression in a state becomes unnecessary (Wæver *et al.*, forthcoming).

This pattern can be discerned in recent trends and it has the advantage of not demanding from people numerous political identities, but *two* clearly defined positions, each attaining a considerable weight in the area where it counts.

Anthony D. Smith has rightly argued that, in practice, the 'French' and 'German' concepts are not separate, but actually both at play when people, commonsensically talk of nations (that is why we can actually get along using this single word for two phenomena, that seem to be almost unrelated: state/territory and a linguistically united *Volk*). But the two can possibly move again in separate directions, which we can only talk clearly about by disentangling the two meanings of nations, calling them, for instance, *civic state-nation* (France) and *organic people-nation* (Germany). Then our future could possibly consist of a dualism, with Europe as the civic state-nation and our old nation-states as organic people-nations. Identity and politics are delinked and refocused. If this process is really under way, it means that one major *idea of Europe* in the 1990s will embrace Europe as a non-ethnic, non-organic, political, civic 'nation' or 'republic'.

The contemporary relevance of 'the European idea'

So, what is the role of European 'identity', and of images of a common past? Are they politically significant, and of what do they actually consist? Is it a feeling of being one? Or of just not being total strangers? Or is this not the question at all? Is the decisive dynamic the one whereby 'Europe' is constituted (defined) in contrast to something non-European? Or, rather, is the construction of Europe geared to a set of inherent values and principles? Where does this finally leave us as to 'perceptions' and 'projects' of Europe? What are the evolving ideas of Europe – and what happens to the idea of a 'European idea', and to the idea of a 'history of the European idea'?

First, it can be underlined that, as indicated in the sections on the post-war period and especially the one on the 1980s, perceptions and projects have merged to an unprecedented degree. They have probably always been related, but previously – especially in the inter-war years – often in an inverse relationship: when a desperate and desolate perception of (the state of) Europe was used as an argument for far-reaching projects, and measured against the task, the then state of affairs could only be found wanting. During the post-war period, the two notions became increasingly linked as companions in real – and successful – attempts at influencing the shape of politics in Europe. Therefore, they also became even more closely linked to the main political constellations (concepts of Europe became high politics, powerful instruments), and one could discern during the 1980s a considerable logic to the 'French Europe', the 'German Europe' and the 'Russian Europe'. Politics of course continued within these countries, but such ideas of Europe were closely linked to their specific traditions of political thought as well as to their actual political problems and concerns.

Secondly, it can be noted that there is (as in the different national projects) a competition between, on the one hand, more 'romantic', organic concepts of a European 'identity', projecting pictures of European continuity, coherence and inherent values and using these as arguments for a European policy; and, on the other hand, more 'rationalistic' and political concepts of a European *political construct* being set up either technocratically for certain purposes, or based on certain civic, political values that are shared and to which the citizens of a European republic could pledge their loyalty.

Anthony D. Smith has argued that in the second tradition it is easier to manage the relationship between national identity and European identity: the two do not run into frontal conflict (1992, p. 56). In the last section ('A European nation-state'), it was suggested that possibly a combination (and to some extent a separation, a division of labour) of the two traditions fits more closely to what is happening, and what is actually more manageable. The civic tradition goes European, while the cultural tradition becomes even more national (or regional) to an extent where it de-couples itself from questions of politics and becomes more a matter of culture-politics. State and society become less closely linked, and we become Euro-state citizens while still belonging to our older culture-nations. Such loyalties might very well conflict from time to time, but not necessarily frontally, since they move partly on different wavelengths.

Thirdly, there is a tension between attempts to construct Europe on the basis of inherent values and attempts to construct Europe by contrast to some external 'other' – most powerfully a 'threat'. Avoiding both approaches is hardly an option and it is most likely that a mixture of the two will evolve. A very strong differentiation against an external other might not materialize but we can hardly expect not to see a certain increase in comparisons between Europe and, for instance, the Middle East, together with more talk about 'European' interests and 'European' defence. We might not get any clear idea or definition of European values(s), but probably more and more people will slowly take for granted that somehow there is such a thing as a specific European tradition. And, at the same time, intellectuals who are constantly pointing out that there *is* no European essence, and who are too clever and enlightened for any of this argumentation, will try to keep their thinking free of such Euro-metaphysics as displayed in this book of essays, while half-consciously going along with the notion of a general strengthening of the European self-image and the self-evidence of there being a 'Europe', a 'European idea' and a 'history of the European idea'.

References

BENDER, P. (1987)'Mitteleuropa: Mode, Modell oder Motiv?', in *Die neue Gesellschaft,* **4**, pp. 297–304.

BERLIN, I. (1959; 1991 edn) 'European union and its vicissitudes' (address read on 21 November 1959 at the Third Congress of the Fondation Européene de la Culture in Vienna; published 1959 by the FEC in Amsterdam), reprinted in BERLIN, I. (1991) *The Crooked Timber of Humanity: chapters in the history of ideas,* ed. by Henry Hardy, New York, Knopf.

BERLIN, I. (1978; 1982 edn) 'Nationalism: past neglect and present power', *Partisan Review* 1978; reprinted in BERLIN, I. (1982) *Against the Current: essays in the history of ideas,* Harmondsworth, Penguin.

BREDOW, W. VON and BROCKE, R. H. (1986) *Das deutschlandspolitische Konzpet der SPD,* Erlanger Beiträge zur Deutschlandpolitik.

BUZAN, B., KELSTRUP, M., LEMAITRE, P., TROMER, E. and WÆVER, O. (1990) *The European Security Order Recast: scenarios for the post-Cold War era,* London, Pinter.

ENZENSBERGER, H-M. (1987) *Ach Europa: Wahrnehmungen aus sieben Ländern. Mit einem Epilog aus dem Jahre 2006,* Frankfurt, Suhrkamp; English trans. (1989) *Europe, Europe: forays into a continent.*

FINKIELKRAUT, A (1986) *La défaite de la pensée,* Paris, Editions Gallimard.

GARDELS, N. (1991) 'Two concepts of nationalism: an interview with Isaiah Berlin' in *The New York Times Review of Books,* 21 November 1991, pp. 19–23.

GARTON ASH, T. (1990) 'Mitteleuropa?' in *DÆDALUS: Journal of the American Academy of Arts and Sciences,* **119** (1), Winter 1990, pp. 1–22.

GARTON ASH, T. (1991) *We the People,* London, Granta.

GELLNER, E. (1990) 'Ethnicity and faith in eastern Europe' in *DÆDALUS: Journal of the American Academy of Arts and Sciences,* **119** (1), Winter 1990, pp. 279–94.

GLOTZ, P. (1986) 'Deutsch-böhmische Kleinigkeiten, oder: Abgerissene Gedanken über Mitteleuropa', in *Die neue Gesellschaft,* **7**, pp. 584–5.

GOLLWITZER, H. (1951) *Europabild und Europagedanke: Beiträge zur deutschen Geistesgeschichte des 18. und 19. Jahrhunderts,* Munich, Beck.

GROSSER, A. (1978; 1980 edn) *The Western Alliance: European–American relations since 1945,* London, Macmillan (1st published in French in 1978).

HABERMAS, J. (1992) 'Citizenship and national identity: some reflections on the future of Europe', in *Praxis International,* **12** (1), pp. 1–19; paper originally presented at the symposium 'Identité et différences dans l'Europe democratique: approches théoretiques et pratiques institutionelles', Brussells, 23–25 May 1991.

HACKE, C. (1988) *Weltmacht wider Willen: die Aussenpolitik der Bundesrepublik Deutschland,* Stuttgart, Klett-Cotta.

HASSNER, P. (1968a) 'Change and security in Europe. Part I: The background', *Adelphi Papers,* No. 45, February.

HASSNER, P. (1968b) 'Change and security in Europe. Part II: In search of a system', *Adelphi Papers,* No. 49, July.

HOFFMAN, S. (1966) 'Obstinate or obsolete'? The fate of the nation-state and the case of Western Europe', in *DÆDALUS: Journal of the American Academy of Arts and Sciences,* **95** (3), Summer 1966, pp. 862–915.

HOLZGREFE, J. L. (1989) 'The origins of modern international relations theory' in *Review of International Studies,* **15** (1), January, pp. 11–26.

HYDE-PRICE, A. (1991) *European Security beyond the Cold War: four scenarios for the year 2010,* London, Royal Institute of International Affairs/Sage.

JAHN, E., LEMAITRE, P. and WÆVER, O. (1987) *European Security: problems of research on non-military aspects,* (Copenhagen Papers No. 1), Copenhagen, Centre for Peace and Conflict Research.

JOENNIEMI, P. and WÆVER, O. (1992) *Regionalization around the Baltic Rim – background report to the 2nd parliamentary conference on co-operation in the Baltic Sea Area,* Oslo 22–24 April 1992; Nordic Seminar and Working-group Reports No. 1992:521, Stockholm, The Nordic Council.

KAISER, K. *et al.* (1983) *Die EG vor der Entsheidigung: Fortschritt oder Verfall,* Bonn, Union Verlag.

KISSINGER, H. (1957) *A World Restored,* Boston, Houghton Mifflin.

KISSINGER, H. (1979) *The White House Years,* Boston/London, Houghton Mifflin.

KNUDSEN, A. (1991) 'Mikronationalismens dannelseshistorie'. in LINDE-LAURSEN, and NILSSON, (eds) *Nationella identiteter i Norden – et fullbordat projekt?,* Stockholm, Nordisk Råd.

KUNDERA, M. (1984) 'The tragedy of central Europe' in *New York Review of Books,* 26 April 1984.

KUSY, M. (1989) 'Wir, die mitteleuropäischen Osteuropäer' in HERTERICH, F. and SEMLER, C. (eds) (1989) *Dazwischen Ostmitteleuropäische Reflexionen,* Frankfurt am Main, Suhrkamp.

LEMAITRE, P. (1989) 'Crisis and revolution of Soviet-type systems', *Working Paper 16,* Copenhagen, Centre for Peace and Conflict Research.

MAJONE, G. (1990) 'Preservation of cultural diversity in a federal system: the role of the regions' in TUSHNET, M. (ed.) (1990) *Comparative Constitutional Federalism: Europe and America,* New York/Westport/London, Greenwood Press.

MALCOLM, N. (1989a) *Soviet Policy Perspectives on Western Europe,* London, The Royal Institute of International Affairs, Routledge.

MALCOLM, N. (1989b) 'The "common European home" and Soviet European policy', *International Affairs,* **65** (4), Autumn 1989, pp. 659–76.

MICHELMANN, H. J. and SOLDATOS, P. (eds) (1990) *Federalism and International Relations: the role of subnational units,* Oxford, Clarendon.

MOÏSI, D (1989) 'French policy toward central and eastern Europe' in GRIFFITH, W. E. (ed.) *Central and eastern Europe: the opening curtain,* Boulder, Westview Press.

MORIN, E. (1987) *Penser l'Europe,* Paris; translated (1991) *Concepts of Europe,* Holmes and Meier.

MORGENTHAU, H. J. (1948; 1978 rev. edn) *Politics among Nations: the struggle for power and peace,* New York, Knopf.

NIETZSCHE, F. (1888; 1969 edn) 'Vom Nutzen und Nachteil der Historie für das Leben' in *Werke*, Volume 1, Karl Schlechta, Hanser Verlag/Ullstein Materialen.

NOLTE, E. (1974) *Deutschland und der kalte Krieg,* Munich/Zurich, R. Piper.

RENAN, E. (1882) 'What is a nation?' in BHABHA, H. K.(1990) *Nation and Narration*, London/New York, Routledge.

RUGGIE, J. G. (1983) 'Continuity and transformation in the world polity: toward a neo-realist synthesis' in *World Politics,* **35** (2), pp. 261–85.

RUGGIE, J. G. (1992/1993) 'Territoriality and beyond: problematizing modernity in international relations', forthcoming in *International Organization,* Winter 1992/1993.

RUMMELL, R. and SCHMIDT, P. (1990) 'The changing security framework' in WALLACE, W. (ed.) (1990) *The Dynamics of European Integration,* London, Royal Institute of International Affairs/Pinter Publishers.

RUPNIK, J. (1990) 'Central Europe or Mitteleuropa' in *DÆDALUS: Journal of the American Academy of Arts and Sciences,* **119** (1), Winter 1990, pp. 249–78.

RUTH, A. (1984) 'The second new nation: the mythology of modern Sweden', *DÆDALUS: Journal of the American Academy of Arts and Sciences,* **113** (2), pp. 53–96; a postscript (in Swedish) by Ruth is found in *UNDR* (1988) no. 52, p. 54.

SHENFIELD, S. (1989) 'Between Moscow and Brussels: the future of eastern Europe' in *Détente,* **15**, pp. 7–8.

SCHUBERT, K. (1988) '"Abschied" vom Nationalstaat – "Flucht" nach Europa? Anmerkungen zum neuen französischen Europa–Diskurs' in *Dokumente* 1988, **5**, pp. 341–50.

SMITH, A. D. (1991) *National Identity,* Harmondsworth, Penguin.

SMITH, A. D. (1992) 'National identity and the idea of European unity' in *International Affairs,* **68** (1), pp. 55–76.

SÖRLIN, S. (1990) 'Signalement av Europa – en identitet i dialog med sig själv', *Nordrevy,* 1990 (4) and 1991 (1), pp. 19–35.

STÜRMER, M. (1989a) 'For a different East Germany in a stable co-operative Europe', *International Herald Tribune*, 13 November 1989.

STÜRMER, M. (1989b) 'Die Deutschen in Europa: auf dem Weg zu einer zwischen-staatlichen Innenpolitik', *Europa Archiv,* **24**, pp. 721–32.

STÜRMER, M. (1990) *Europa Archiv.*

THOMPSON, E. P. (1982) *Beyond the Cold War,* London, Merlin Press/European Nuclear Disarmament.

KELSEN, J. (1991) 'Neo-functionalism: obstinate or obsolete? A reappraisal in the light of the new dynamism of the EC', in *Millennium,* 20 (1), Spring 1991, pp. 1–22.

URWIN, D. W. (1991) *The Community of Europe: a history of European integration since 1945,* London, Longman.

VAJDA, M. (1989) 'Ostmitteleuropas "Enteuropäisierung"' in HERTERICH, F. and SEMLER, C. (eds) 1989) Dazwischen Ostmitteleuropäische Reflexionen, Frankfurt am Main, Suhrkamp.

WÆVER, O. (1989) *Hele Europa: Projekter – kontraster,* Copenhagen, SNU.

WÆVER, O. (1990) 'Three compcting Europes: German, French, Russian' in *International Affairs,* **66** (3), pp. 477–94.

WÆVER, O. (1991) 'Culture and identity in the Baltic Sea Region' in JOENNIEMI, P. (ed.) (1991) *Cooperation in the Baltic Sea Region: needs and prospects,* Tampere, TAPRI report No. 42, pp. 79–111 (new edn forthcoming, New York, Taylor and Francis, 1992).

WÆVER, O. (1992) 'Nordic nostalgia: northern Europe after the Cold War' in *International Affairs,* **68** (1), pp. 77–102.

WÆVER, O. (forthcoming) 'Territory, authority and identity: the late 20th century emergence of neo-medieval political structures in Europe', Paper for the first general conference of the European Peace Research Organization, November 8–10 in Florence, workshop on European identity, in BALASZ, J. and WIBERG, H. (forthcoming) EUPRA Conference proceedings.

WÆVER, O., HOLM, U. and LARSEN, H. (forthcoming) *The Struggle for Europe: French and German concepts of state, nation and European union.*

VON PLATE, B. (1991) 'Subregionalismus: eine Zwischenbene in einer gesamteuropäischen Ordnung', in *Europa-Archiv,* **46** (19), 10 October 1991.

WALLACE, W. (1990) *The Transformation of Western Europe* (Chatham House Papers), London, The Royal Institute of International Affairs/Pinter Publishers.

WALLACE, W. (1990) (ed.) *The Dynamics of European Integration,* London, Royal Institute of International Affairs/Pinter Publishers.

WALLACE, W. and WESSELS, W. (1991) 'Introduction' in WALLACE, H. (1991) *The Wider Western Europe: reshaping the EC/EFTA relationship,* London, Royal Institute of International Affairs/Pinter Publishers.

WIND, M. (1992) – 'Eksisterer Europa? Reflektioner over forsvar, identitet og borgerdyd i et nyt Europa' in SØRENSEN, C. (ed.) *Europa – Nation, Union: Efter Minsk og Maastricht,* Copenhagen, Fremad.

Acknowledgements

Ezra Pound, 'Hugh Selwyn Mauberley' (Section IV, Part I) from *Collected Shorter Poems*, reprinted by permission of Faber & Faber and New Directions Publishing Corp. Inc.

Notes on contributors

Pim den Boer

Pim den Boer (b. 1950) studied history in Leiden and Paris. He obtained his doctorate in 1987 in Leiden with a thesis entitled *History as a Profession: the professionalization of historians in France 1880–1940* (English translation forthcoming: Princeton University Press). From 1978 to 1988 he was a lecturer in history at the Institute of History, University of Utrecht. In 1988 he was appointed Professor of the History of European Culture at the University of Amsterdam.

Peter Bugge

Peter Bugge (b. 1960) is a Senior Research Fellow at the Slavisk Institut at Aarhus University. He graduated in 1989 as Cand. Mag. in social and political science and Czechoslovak studies. He has published extensively in academic and other journals on Czechoslovak politics and history, and on Czech and central European culture. He has translated most of Vaclav Havel's essays into Danish.

Ole Wæver

Ole Wæver (b. 1960) is a Senior Research Fellow at the Centre for Peace and Conflict Research, Copenhagen. He has taught international relations at Aarhus University (1987–1989), Copenhagen University (1990–) and the European University Institute in Florence (1991). He is the author of a number of articles on European security, Scandinavia, Germany, international relations theory, foreign policy theory, European and national identity and the concept of security. He has written and co-authored several books, including *Hele Europa: Projekter – Kontraster* ('All Europe – projects – contrasts'; SNU, 1989); *Introduktion til Studiet af International Politik* ('Introduction to the Study of International Relations'; Copenhagen, Politiske Studier, 1992); *The European Security Order Recast: scenarios for the post-Cold War era* (with Barry Buzan *et al.*, London, Pinter, 1990) and *Identity, Migration and the New Security Agenda in Europe* (with Barry Buzan *et al.*, London, Pinter, 1993).